Cancún and the Riviera Maya

Caroline Vien
Alain Théroux
Alain Legault

ULYSSES
TRAVEL PUBLICATIONS
Travel better... enjoy more

Authors	**Artistic Director**	**Cartography**
Caroline Vien	Patrick Farei (Atoll)	Patrick Thivierge
Alain Théroux		Yanik Landreville
Alain Legault	**Translation**	
	Tara Salman	**Computer Graphics**
Editors	Tracy Kendrick	Stéphanie Routhier
Daniel Desjardins	Danielle Gauthier	
Stéphane G.	Emmy Pahmer	**Illustrations**
Marceau		Lorette Pierson
	Page Layout	Myriam Gagné
Project Director	*Typesetting*	
André Duchesne	Tara Salman	**Photography**
	Jacqueline Grekin	*Cover Page*
English Editing		Grant V. Faint
Tara Salman	*Visuals*	Image Bank
Jacqueline Grekin	Anne Joyce	

Distributors

AUSTRALIA: Little Hills Press, 11/37-43 Alexander St., Crows Nest NSW 2065,
☎ (612) 437-6995, Fax: (612) 438-5762

BELGIUM AND LUXEMBOURG: Vander, Vrijwilligerlaan 321, B-1150 Brussel,
☎ (02) 762 98 04, Fax: (02) 762 06 62

CANADA: Ulysses Books & Maps, 4176 Saint-Denis, Montréal, Québec, H2W 2M5,
☎ (514) 843-9882, ext.2232, 800-748-9171, Fax: 514-843-9448, www.ulysses.ca

GERMANY AND AUSTRIA: Brettschneider, Fernreisebedarf, Feldfirchner Strasse 2,
D-85551 Heimstetten, München, ☎ 89-99 02 03 30, Fax: 89-99 02 03 31,
cf@brettschneider.de

GREAT BRITAIN AND IRELAND: World Leisure Marketing, Unit 11, Newmarket Court,
Newmartket Drive, Derby DE24 8NW, ☎ 1 332 57 37 37, Fax: 1 332 57 33 99

ITALY: Centro Cartografico del Riccio, Via di Soffiano 164/A, 50143 Firenze,
☎ (055) 71 33 33, Fax: (055) 71 63 50

NETHERLANDS: Nilsson & Lamm, Pampuslaan 212-214, 1380 AD Weesp (NL),
☎ 0294-494949, Fax: 0294-494455, E-mail: nilam@euronet.nl

PORTUGAL: Dinapress, Lg. Dr. Antonio de Sousa de Macedo, 2, Lisboa 1200,
☎ (1) 395 52 70, Fax: (1) 395 03 90

SCANDINAVIA: Scanvik, Esplanaden 8B, 1263 Copenhagen K, DK,
☎ (45) 33.12.77.66, Fax: (45) 33.91.28.82

SPAIN: Altaïr, Balmes 69, E-08007 Barcelona,
☎ 454 29 66, Fax: 451 25 59, altair@globalcom.es

SWITZERLAND: OLF, P.O. Box 1061, CH-1701 Fribourg,
☎ (026) 467.51.11, Fax: (026) 467.54.66

U.S.A.: The Globe Pequot Press, 6 Business Park Road, P.O. Box 833, Old Saybrook, CT
06475, ☎ 1-800-243-0495, Fax: 800-820-2329, sales@globe-pequot.com

Other countries, contact Ulysses Books & Maps (Montréal), Fax: (514) 843-9448

"At four o'clock we left Pisté, and very soon we saw rising high above the plain, the Castillo of Chichén. In half an hour we were among the ruins of this ancient city, with all of the great buildings in full view, casting prodigious shadows over the plain, and presenting a spectacle which, even after all we had seen, once more excited in us emotions of wonder."

John Lloyd Stephens
Incidents of Travel in Yucatán

Table of Contents

List of Maps

Map Symbols

❶	Tourist Information	℗	Parking
◎	Beach	⟩	Golf
✈	Airport	(	Telephone
🚢	Passenger Ferry	✉	Post Office
🚗	Car Ferry	▲	Ruins
🚌	Bus Station	Ⓗ	Hospital

	Ulysses' favourite
☎	Telephone number
⊞	Fax number
≡	Air conditioning
⊗	Ceiling fan
≈	Pool
ℜ	Restaurant
⊛	Whirlpool
ℝ	Refrigerator
K	Kitchenette
△	Sauna
⊘	Exercise room
hw	Hot water
pb	Private bathroom
sb	Shared bathroom
ps	Private shower
bkfst	Breakfast included

ATTRACTION CLASSIFICATION

★	Interesting
★★	Worth a visit
★★★	Not to be missed

HOTEL CLASSIFICATION

$	$50 or less
$$	$50 to $80 US
$$$	$80 to $130 US
$$$$	$130 to $180 US
$$$$$	$180 or more

The prices in this guide are for one room,
double occupancy in high season,
not including taxes and service charges.

RESTAURANT CLASSIFICATION

$	$10 or less
$$	$10 to $20 US
$$$	$20 to $30 US
$$$$	$30 and more

The prices in the guide are for a meal for one
person, not including taxes, drinks and tip.

All prices in this guide are in American dollars.

Write to Us

The information contained in this guide was correct at press time. However, mistakes can slip in, omissions are always possible, places can disappear, etc. The authors and publisher hereby disclaim any liability for loss or damage resulting from omissions or errors.

We value your comments, corrections and suggestions, as they allow us to keep each guide up to date. The best contributions will be rewarded with a free book from Ulysses Travel Publications. All you have to do is write us at the following address and indicate which title you would be interested in receiving (see the list at the end of guide).

Ulysses Travel Publications
4176 Rue Saint-Denis
Montréal, Québec
Canada H2W 2M5
www.ulysses.ca
E-mail: guiduly@ulysse.ca

Canadian Cataloguing in Publication Data

Vien, Caroline, 1964-

> *Cancún, Riviera Maya*

> *2nd ed.*
> *(Ulysses due south)*
> *Translation of: Cancún et la Riviera Maya*
> *Previously published as: Cancun, Cozumel, 1997*
> *Includes index*

> *ISBN 2-89464-214-8*

1. Cancún (Mexico) - Guidebooks. 2. Riviera Maya Region (Mexico) - Guidebooks. I. Théroux, Alain, 1968- . II. Legault, Alain, 1967 June 12- .III. Title. IV. Title: Cancun, Cozumel. V. Series

F1333.T4313 1999   917.26'704836   C99-940865-8

"We acknowledge the financial support of the Government of Canada through the Book Publishing Industry Development Program (BPIDP) for our publishing activities."
We would also like to thank SODEC for their financial support.

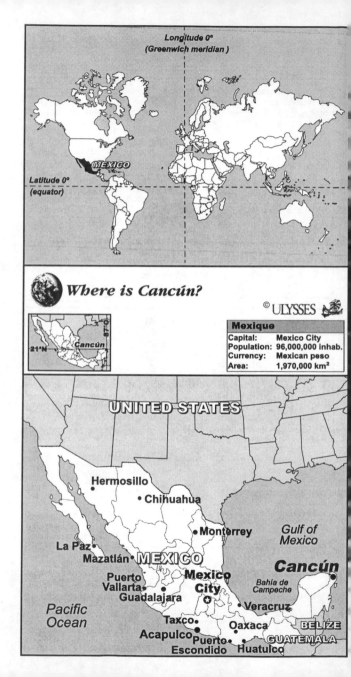

Longitude 0°
(Greenwich meridian)

MEXICO

Latitude 0°
(equator)

Where is Cancún?

© ULYSSES

Mexique
Capital: Mexico City
Population: 96,000,000 inhab.
Currency: Mexican peso
Area: 1,970,000 km²

87°O
21°N
Cancún

UNITED STATES

Hermosillo
• Chihuahua
• Monterrey
La Paz •
Mazatlán • MEXICO
Puerto
Vallarta •
Guadalajara •
Mexico
City
Taxco •
Acapulco • Puerto
Escondido • Huatulco
Oaxaca

Gulf of
Mexico

Cancún
Bahía de
Campeche

Veracruz

BELIZE
GUATEMALA

Pacific
Ocean

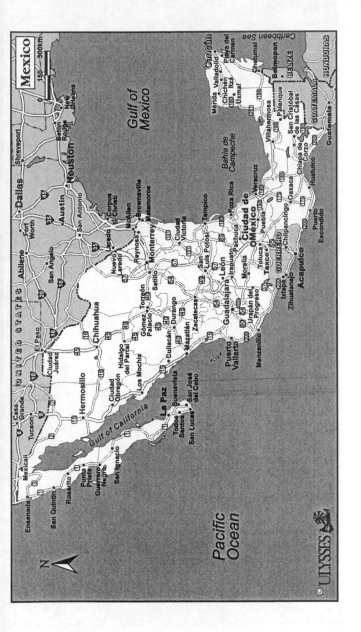

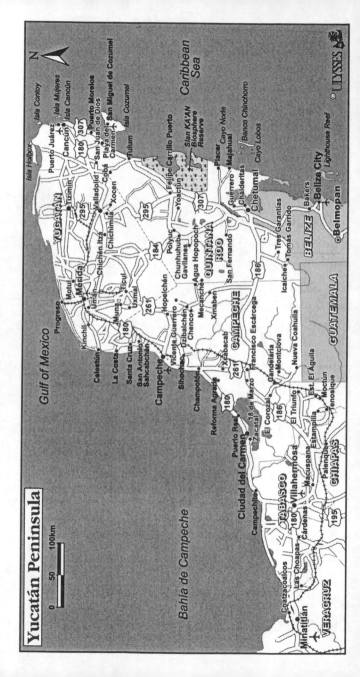

Portrait

Cancún and Cozumel
are the two major gateways into the
State of Quintana Roo, a region that is bordered by the Riviera
Maya and welcomes
droves of tourists.

Here, you can discover
the heart and soul of
the Yucatán Peninsula, its
people and treasures, both
past and present, including
archeological sites such as
Chichén Itzá, remains of the
great Mayan empire.

Tree-studded plains full
of thousand-year-old
archaeological sites; outstanding beaches; tropical
fish; lagoons and coral reefs
like the one off Palancar on
Cozumel... these are a few
of the treasures to be found
in this unique region, making it one of the most popular tourist destinations in
the northern hemisphere.
The Yucatán was clearly
blessed by the gods (Mayan
or Catholic – take your
pick!).

This region is easy to
explore. The Yucatán
Peninsula is covered with
flat, well-laid out roads
lined with interesting villages. Archaeological sites,
some in progress, others
swallowed by the jungle;
swimming with dolphins;
scuba diving... these are

just some of the region's many attractions, all located close enough to each other that you can enjoy them all, on your own or with a guide, even during a short stay in the region.

The Chichén Itzá ruins and Isla Mujeres are easy to reach from Cancún. Visitors can also take the Cancún-Tulúm Corridor and go down the Riviera Maya until the vast Sian Ka'an biosphere reserve. The Cobá ruins are easy to reach from Tulúm. It is also easy to travel from Cancún to Cozumel or vice versa by boat or by plane.

Cancún is a highly developed seaside resort tailor-made for night owls and people who like lots of action. But lovers of the great outdoors – and especially of aquatic activities – will find lots to do on the Riviera Maya. And the ocean, with its long golden-sand beaches bathed with beautiful, foaming, turquoise waters, is mystifying.

If there is one attraction that is not to be over-looked, though, it's the people. The Yucatán Peninsula was the cradle of the Mayan civilization, and the modern Maya are hard-working, patient and humble people with a slow and studied way of life. Their shy, courteous manner conceals a serene empathy and a genuine kindness, a smile all their own.

Geography

A peninsula in southeast Mexico, the Yucatán, land of corn (maize) and hene-quen, is divided into three parts: the State of Campeche, to the west, remains untouched by mass tourism; the State of Quintana Roo, a long, narrow stretch of land along the eastern shore, is home to Cancún, Tulúm, Cozumel and Isla Mujeres; to the north, forming the tip of the peninsula, the State of Yucatán stretches out into the Gulf of Mexico and boasts the region's most important archaeological site, Chichén Itzá, as well as the colonial town of Mérida.

A large part of the peninsula is composed of lime-stone rocks perforated by sinkholes known as *cenotes*, some of which used to be the scene of grisly Mayan sacrifices. Some cenotes have become very popular with scuba divers. Among the Yucatán's most fascinating attractions, the cenotes are the only visible bodies of water on the peninsula, whose few rivers and lakes are underground.

Cenotes

The reason there are so many *cenotes*, or sinkholes, in the Yucatán is that the peninsula is composed of limestone. The entire region is scattered with caves, some empty, others full of cool, crystal-clear water, a phenomenon found nowhere else in Mexico. The ancient Maya marvelled at these natural wells, and, after settling in the area, made them into sacred places. They built their villages near the cenotes, the only source of potable water in the region. They also believed that these natural wells, which they referred to as *dzonot* (a term that became "*cenotes*" in Spanish), were the refuge of the rain gods.

The caves riddling the peninsula are washed by underground rivers, which, repeatedly swollen by rainwater then shrunken by droughts, erode the limestone subsoil, causing the earth's crust to collapse.

Eventually exposed, these amazing fissures, which vary in size from the northern to the southern part of the peninsula, are almost perfectly round, their sides marked by erosion.

Today, dog-paddling children and experienced divers alike are regular visitors to the Yucatán's cenotes, some of which have become major attractions, while others remain untouched by the tourist frenzy.

Most cenotes are good places to go swimming, but scuba diving in them requires more caution, as there is a risk of getting lost in the maze-like underwater caverns or suddenly feeling claustrophobic. Exploring the nooks and crannies of a cenote is a thrilling experience, but one best left to experienced cave-divers.

The following are a few of the most popular cenotes:

Cenote Sagrado (sacred cenote): Located on the Chichén Itzá archaeological site, 201km from Cancún via Route 180, this cenote is popular because of the amazing finds that archaeologists have made here (about 50 skulls, hundreds of jade and gold vessels, etc.). As indicated by its name, this place was an important Mayan religious site, where sacrifices were carried out. Sixty metres in diametre and 40m deep, it is unusable today, due to its stagnant waters.

Sin Nombre (nameless): This cenote lies about 100km south of Cancún on Route 307, not far from Puerto Aventuras. To get there, follow the signs.

Xel-Há: This charming cenote is located near some Postclassic Mayan ruins, in front of the Xel-Há national park, on the other side of Highway 307. Most tour operators don't show tourists this cenote, so you will have to get there on your own. No swimming.

Tan-Kah: This cenote is located 137km south of Cancún (Route 307), near the Tulúm ruins, beside a restaurant called La Casa del Cenote. Access is gained by a small road marked on the highway by a wooden sign. Swimming permitted.

Sasil: Located near Valladolid, this little cenote is a typical little lake with steep shores. On Sundays, this spot is popular with local residents, who come here for a bite to eat at the nearby restaurant. Swimming permitted.

Zaci: On Route 180, which runs through Valladolid, there is a sign on the way into town showing the road to this cenote, where you will find a small store that sells refreshments. Swimming permitted.

Dzitnup (Xkekén): This lovely cenote, also on Route 180, 7km from Valladolid, has been frequently photographed for the big geographical magazines. It is a cavern whose high ceiling, adorned with colourful stalactites, lets in delicate sunbeams, which plunge into pure, shallow, turquoise waters that beckon visitors to come in for a dip. Access is gained by a small road.

Fauna

Thanks to its special geographical position, lagoons, cenotes and brackish creeks, and because it is a peninsula, the Yucatán makes an ideal habitat for a wide variety of animals.

Concerned about the unbridled destruction of the forest and other vegetation brought about by the region's tourist development, Mexican authorities are taking steps to preserve and showcase certain areas that lend themselves perfectly to ecotourism. The two most important projects involve the coralline island of Contoy, located north of Isla Mujeres and home to nearly 80 species of birds, and the fascinating Sian Ka'an ecological park, designated a UNESCO biosphere reserve in 1986 and located a few kilometres south of Tulúm.

Jaguar

The reserve is home to a variety of wild animals, including pumas, jaguars, manatees and crocodiles.

Even the most unadventurous tourists – those who never even set foot out of Cancún's hotel zone – will come across countless lizards, those placid little spies that blend into the landscape, only drawing attention to themselves when they scamper off.

The iguana, easily recognizable by its dark skin, is one of the most commonly found reptiles on the island, but geckoes, as tiny as insects, and black iguanas also roam the peninsula, and can be spotted atop a

Maya temple, watching a guide get bogged down in his own explanations, or on the table of a seaside restaurant.

Pelicans, which often travel in pairs, soar over the beach with a single flap of their wings, watching the tourists soaking up the sun. The gleaming, black frigatebird also flies about near swimming areas, spreading its long, narrow wings and practising its hovering skills, opening its forked tail periodically to maintain its delicate balance.

Terns, for their part, often make a racket near restaurants, fixing a menacing eye on those customers who don't immediately toss them a piece of bread.

Tourists who venture inland might spot a toucan, the symbol of many southern countries. In the northernmost part of the peninsula, near Río Lagartos, there is a colony of flamingoes with an estimated population of nearly 30,000.

Flamingo

Other animal species, such as jaguars, snakes and ant-eaters, can be observed on short expeditions outside the populated areas.

Marine Life

The underwater world off the shores of the State of Quintana Roo is a para-dise of multi-coloured coral and countless varieties of fish in all different shapes and sizes.

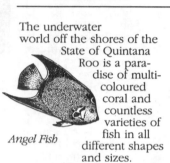

Angel Fish

Scuba diving and snorkel-ling – the best way to ob-serve the underwater world – are so popular that they account for 35% of the tour-ist activity on the island of Cozumel, renowned for its coral reefs, which stretch many metres and attract divers from all over the world.

Sea Turtle

The limpid water, as mentioned above, makes it possible to observe a vast number of aquatic plants and animals in the sea and in various parks and re-serves. Fans of sport fishing have a ball here as well, as Cancún and Cozumel orga-nize annual competitions

during which many record catches are made.

The number of creatures inhabiting the region's wa-ters is so vast that we could-n't possibly provide an ex-haustive list here. Below, however, we have men-tioned a few of the species you are likely to encounter on even the briefest excur-sion.

Cancún

Grouper, red snapper, bar-racuda and bluefin tuna are among the species that can be spotted during underwa-ter excursions in the hotel zone.

Isla Mujeres

On the south side of the island, Parque Nacional El Garrafón is home to a wide variety of animals, and there are tortoises everywhere you look. The park is a refuge for many species of fish, including angelfish, recog-nizable by their bright white and yellow stripes, and *sar*, usually found around staghorn and black coral, where they like to hide. The damselfish zeal-ously protects its territory and won't hesitate to attack foolhardy swimmers who venture onto its turf, lured by the beauty of the sea anemones strewn across the ocean floor. Other, more imposing species, many sought-after by fishermen, patrol the same waters – *ludjan*, grouper, red snapper, barracuda and tuna, among others.

Coral

Cozumel

A ferocious fish with a terrifying set of teeth, the great barracuda haunts the waters around the reef that bears its name, and can also be found near the San Juan reef. It is not always necessary to comb the ocean floor in scuba gear to see the wonders of the sea: by simply boarding the boat that plies the waters between Playa del Carmen and Cozumel, you're sure

Dolphins

to see some flying fish or magnificent dolphins leaping joyfully out of the water.

Noteworthy species found in the Cozumel region include the wahoo, the blue shark or shortfin mako, the mahi-mahi, the tuna, the sailfish and large numbers of swordfish, as well as the blue marlin, the star of Ernest Hemingway's novel *The Old Man and the Sea*.

Near the "little sea" (*Chakanaab* in Maya), tropical fish and coral are legion. You will spot a parrotfish through the branches of staghorn coral here; an angelfish, easy to overlook at just 2cm long, near some "diploria" coral there; and in the distance, but clearly visible in this limpid water, a 2kg marlin From May to September, visitors have a chance to observe giant turtles laying their eggs in the area.

Flora

The Yucatán jungle is nothing like the Amazon forest. The landscape is characterized by a dense, low forest made up of coconut trees, banana trees and sapodillas, whose latex, called *chicle*, was once used to make chewing gum.

Chicle

In the late 19th century, American pharmacies started carrying a new product called "Adams New York Gum", a box containing little balls of a gummy substance known as *chicle*, which was to be chewed but not swallowed.

A kind of latex extracted from the sapodilla, a large tree that is very common in Central America and the Yucatán, this gum was imported and marketed in the United States by American inventor Thomas Adams around 1880. Although new to Americans, *chicle* already existed as "chewing gum"; in fact, the Maya and Aztecs had since recognized its hygienic and digestive values, and knew how to collect it.

Chicle is obtained by cutting several large, deep X's into the bark of the sapodilla. The liquid then flows out and is collected by *chicleros*, after which it is boiled, cut into cubes and exported.

At the beginning of the century, Chicago businessman William Wrigley added mint and fruit flavours to the gum and dubbed his creation the Chiclet. The product was so successful that the tremendous demand for raw material from the Yucatán prompted a migration to the peninsula, especially in 1920. In the 1950s, however, a less expensive substitute for *chicle*, polyester, replaced the natural substance.

Though the industrial-scale collection of *chicle* is now a thing of the past, many sapodillas in the Yucatán still bear large scars. Tour buses sometimes stop to show tourists some roadside specimens. This happens, notably, during trips to Chichén Itza and around the Xcaret site. In the cities, the trees are scraggly; they are most common in Valladolid and at Playa del Carmen.

Fruits found in this region include avocados, oranges, limes, grapefruits and papayas. Corn (maize) and beans are widely cultivated in this part of the country. Henequen-growing (for sisal hemp; sisal is a type of agave) is carried out mainly in the northeastern part of the peninsula, and is on the decline.

All along the roads, around the archaeological sites and in the parks, lovely silk-cotton trees display their pretty reddish-orange flowers to passersby.

It is also worth noting the contribution made by landscape gardeners, who have put some natural colour back into Cancún, especially in the hotel zone, where concrete often predominates. Alongside the roads, on medians and in the parks, kilometres of imaginatively sculpted shrubs form a motionless, green menagerie of big birds and other animals.

Climate

The rainy season lasts from May to September, a period characterized by high temperatures and humidity, especially in June. During the rest of the year, the weather is mild and dry.

Like on Caribbean islands, the tourist area of Cancún and the Riviera Maya faces the most formidable of enemies, namely the hurricanes that make their annual rounds from September to November, sometimes leaving desolate landscapes in their wake.

Hurricanes Gilbert (1988) and Roxanne (1995) hit the State of Quintana Roo hard, teaching inexperienced entrepreneurs who had built hotels and restaurants too close to the shore a brutal lesson.

History

Prehistory

Many scientists now believe that the disappearance of the dinosaurs was caused by a gigantic meteor hitting the earth 65 million years ago, a theory supported by a research expedition carried out in January of 1997. For months after the collision, a thick cloud of dust hung in the sky, the temperature soared and floods swept the land, wiping out 70% of all species. In 1989, what is believed to be the point of impact was discovered in the Yucatán: an immense, circular crater known as the Chicxulub crater (named after a small village several kilometres

The Vanishing Coconut Tree

Over the past few years, a worrisome epidemic has struck coconut trees (*Cocos nucifera*) in tropical regions. This disease, known as LY, for Lethal Yellowing, first started attacking trees in Florida in the mid-1970s, then spread to the Mexican state of Quintana Roo, Haiti, Jamaica and most recently Belize.

Caused by a primitive bacterium transported by insects that inject it into the leaves of the coconut tree they are feeding on, the disease invades and obstructs the tree's vascular system. After turning yellow, the tree loses its leaves and branches until nothing is left but its bare trunk. A major project to reforest those areas already affected or at risk with a more resistant species is presently underway.

north of Mérida), which measures between 180 and 300km; the diametre of the meteor that supposedly created it is estimated at 10 to 20km. The famous cenotes, the round sink-holes common in this region, are believed to be another result of these up-heavals.

In the Quaternary period, during the glacial epoch, the level of the sea dropped for a brief period, enabling the inhabitants of the Asian continent to cross the Bering Strait to Alaska. For thousands of years, these nomadic peoples gradually occupied the continent from north to south, all the way to Tierra del Fuego. The oldest traces of human life found in Mexico to date are rudimentary stone tools dating back some 31,000 years; the oldest anthropological discovery is Tepexpan man (12,000 years old). Gradually giving up hunting and gathering, the tribes started settling and taking up farming and fishing around the year 7,000 BC. The first villages were thus built along the shore.

The Archaic Period

Corn was first cultivated here around the year 5,000 BC, at which time the civilizations started to become more sophisticated. Clay figurines dating back 5,000 years indicate a certain development in religion around this period. The Olmec civilization reached its apogee in 1,200 BC. The Olmecs had their own hieroglyphic writing, a complex calendar and a system of numeration, and greatly influenced later civilizations (the Maya, Zapotecs, Mixtecs, Toltecs and Aztecs) through their art and social organization. Vestiges of their society include a number of colossal basalt heads up to three metres high and three large ceremonial sites. In 1986, however, a stele covered with a different and earlier kind of hieroglyphic writing from the Olmecs' was discovered in Veracruz, providing evidence that another civilization flourished in this area several hundred years before the Olmecs.

Another important stage in Mexican history was the era of the dazzling city of Teotihuacán, a religious centre. This metropolis, located near Mexico City, was built around 200 BC. It is the largest pre-Columbian city discovered in the Americas to date. Though it is not known who founded Teotihuacán, there is no doubt that the city's political, cultural and religious power extended tens of kilometres. It appears to

have reached its peak between AD 300 and AD 650.

By AD 200, Mexican civilizations were already highly developed from an architectural, artistic and scientific point of view. Astronomy and mathematics, in particular, seem to have been central to their concerns.

The Mayan Civilization

The greatest constructions of the Mayan civilization were built around AD 200 and were inscribed with the codex (manuscripts made up of ideograms drawn on bark that relate historical events).

Mayan civilization reached its peak between AD 200 and AD 900. There are three temples dating from that era on the Yucatán Peninsula: Chichén Itzá (5th century), Uxmal (6th century) and Cobá (7th century).

Later, the Maya gradually abandoned their towns, apparently because of droughts and the arrival of various warlike peoples. By the year 900, the martial and commercial influence of the Toltec civilization had superseded that of the pacific Mayan priests. Nevertheless, the Toltec and Mayan civilizations coex-

Portrait

isted and intermingled. The Chichén Itzá archaeological site, among others, features ornamentation typical of both civilizations.

The decline of the Toltecs was swift, however, and the Aztecs stepped to the fore around the year 1300.

Mayan Art

Through their technical and commercial achievements, they succeeded in dominating their rivals and borrowing their good ideas.

The Aztecs founded Tenochtitlán (now Mexico City). Their power stretched great distances, but their reign was brief, only about 150 years long, for they were defeated by the Spanish during the conquistadors' first invasion of Mexico.

The Spanish Conquest

The tale of the Spaniards' encounter with the Aztecs has given rise to all sorts of speculation, but one thing is certain: it was one of the most important and troubling moments in the history of the world. The first contact between the Mexicans and the Spanish took

place in 1512, when the priest Jerónimo de Aguilar and the navigator Gonzalo Guerrero were taken prisoner by the Maya on the shores of the Yucatán. Guerrero won the respect of his captors, learned their language and married Princess Zacil. The couple had three sons, who were the first mestizos. In 1519, the zealous conquistador Hernán Cortés set out from Cuba without authorization, leading a fleet of about 10 boats and 500 men. He freed Aguilar, who was still being held captive on the island of Cozumel, and made him his interpreter. Cortés then headed into the centre of the future Mexico. Near present-day Veracruz, he met with the emissaries of Aztec chief Montezuma. The chief believed Cortés and his companions to be messengers of the god Quetzalcóatl; the Aztec religion predicted the arrival of a god, who would come from the east, around 1519. The red carpet was thus rolled out for the Spanish in the great city of Tenochtitlán, which was at least as big as if not bigger than the largest European cities at the time. They stayed there undisturbed for several months.

Nevertheless, the Europeans felt themselves to be

prisoners, and perhaps they really were. A number of Aztec leaders were supposedly plotting an attack, and Cortés, deciding to take the initiative, captured Montezuma and held him hostage. The chief, still thinking that Cortés might be a god, tried to make his people believe he was still free in order to prevent an attack on the Spanish. The Spaniards, meanwhile, began their program of destruction, starting with the Aztec idols.

During this period, the Spanish Crown sent an expedition to stop Cortés. Upon getting wind of this, Cortés hastened to Veracruz with some of his men. He defeated the army sent to stop him and returned to Tenochtitlán, where fighting had broken out. He was permitted to enter the city, but only to make it easier to surround him. Montezuma, still alive, tried to defuse the situation. He died on the battlefield; some claim he was killed by the Spanish, others by his own people.

On June 30, 1520, the so-called *Noche Triste* (Sad Night), the Spanish were defeated and left the city. They did not give up the fight, however. Since arriving in Mexico, they had managed to ally themselves with the various tribes hos-

tile to the Aztecs. With this invaluable support, they patiently constructed pieces of boats, which they then transported beyond the mountains, assembled and put in the lake surrounding the capital. On August 13, 1521, after three months of bitter fighting, the Spaniards and their native allies seized Tenochtitlán, which had already been destroyed in the battle.

In 1522, Cortés had the city rebuilt. It was thenceforth named Mexico City (Ciudad de México) and became the capital of the country.

Portrait

Missionaries

The first Franciscan missionaries arrived in 1523 and quickly started building monasteries, soon to be followed by the Augustinians and the Jesuits. The law required owners of *encomiendas* – vast stretches of land granted to deserving soldiers – to protect those natives living on their property and convert them to Christianity. Hospitals and irrigation systems were built, and the natives were introduced to European methods of farming and craftsmanship. In 10 years, during which millions of natives were converted, scores of pre-Columbian monuments were demolished, numerous natives were reduced to a state of slavery and there was widespread plundering of their wealth and resources.

In his book *Relaciones de las cosas de Yucatán*, Bishop Diego de Landa recorded numerous observations about Mayan society, while at the same time expressing his disgust for their custom of carrying out human sacrifices. He then destroyed many codices full of symbols, which contained the history of the Mayas. Historians believe that he is largely to blame for our inability to solve the mystery of the Mayas, since their knowledge and beliefs were no longer passed on to their descendants.

 Though the indigenous peoples adopted the Catholic religion imposed upon them, adapting it to their own beliefs, they were harshly oppressed by the Spanish, who mistreated them and threw them in prison. By creating haciendas, which resembled small-scale feudal domains, the Spaniards decisively tipped the scales in their own favour. They stripped the natives of their land and forced them to work on the haciendas. The meagre salary they were allotted could only be spent in the *tiendas de raya* (hacienda stores), where everything was very expensive. They had no choice but to accumulate debt, entering a vicious cycle that kept not only them, but also their children, who inherited their father's debts, prisoners of the system. Their plight did not end when Mexico became independent, after 11 years of war (1810-1821), as the land simply changed hands. Finally, the flames of revolt, fanned for too long, started to flare up.

The Caste War

After suffering such harsh mistreatment, the natives, bereft of hope, lashed out violently against what later came to be known as the "Caste War". This bloody revolt surprised the Spanish, as the natives had theretofore been completely submissive. In Valladolid, they massacred all the whites. The conflict spread to most of the towns in the Yucatán. Mérida, in spite of repeated calls for help to France, the United States and Spain, was about to fall when it came time for the Mayas to return to their corn fields; in their culture, growing corn was a sacred task, and they felt that they could not put off their duty any longer. The Spanish colonists took merciless revenge. Men, women and children were indiscriminately slaughtered, imprisoned or sold as slaves. The Mayan population, already decimated by epidemics and poor living conditions, dropped from 500,000 to 300,000 between 1846 and 1850. Some natives succeeded in taking refuge in the mountains and putting up a fierce resistance. The Cruzobs, an autonomous people based near the port of Bacalar (a few kilometres north of Chetumal), controlled the entrance to the Yucatán for over 40 years, taking many whites prisoner.

The Resistance

It was difficult for the government to control the peninsula, isolated as it was from the rest of the country. In 1877, the Mexican government, under President Porfirio Díaz, began to take a serious interest in the Yucatán problem. It wasn't until 1901, however, during a battle led by General Ignacio Bravo, that the federal army succeeded in seizing a village and building a fort there. This fort was continually attacked by the natives for a year before reinforcements arrived. The natives continued to wage a guerilla war until 1915, in spite of increasingly violent attacks by Díaz's soldiers. In 1920, hundreds of thousands of natives were struck down by epidemics of smallpox and influenza. The great demand for chicle led to a native migration from the State of Quintana Roo to the State of Yucatán. Finally, in 1935, the Cruzobs agreed to sign a peace treaty with the federal army.

Trade-wise, the northern part of the peninsula, a major producer of chicle, agave and henequen (for sisal hemp), became more and more important. Mérida, the capital of the Yucatán, was inhabited by wealthy hacienda owners, who exploited the natives and *mestizos* in their fields while leading a life of leisure and luxury. In 1915, President Venustiano Carranza, under the protection of General Alvarado and 7,000 armed men, appropriated all this wealth by imposing enormous taxes on hacienda owners. He used this money to drive back the revolutionary forces led by Pancho Villa and Emiliano Zapata.

Plunging the owners into even deeper depths of despair, the governor of Mérida, Felipe Carrillo Puerto, elected in 1922, helped the natives create a trade union, an education centre, a road to Chichén Itzá and a sort of political group known as the "leagues of resistance". The abandoned haciendas were parcelled out to them. After making all sorts of enemies, Puerto, along with his brothers, was finally assassinated by rebels in 1923.

The Revolution

The Revolution, which lasted 10 years and claimed the lives of a million Mexicans, broke out in 1910 as a result of Porfirio Díaz's fraudulent re-election. It was launched by Francisco de Madero and led by various revolutionary leaders. Madero, an ally of Pancho Villa's, succeeded Díaz in 1911, but was overthrown during an uprising led by General Huerta, then assassinated in 1913. This event triggered a popular revolt, led for 10 years by Villa, Obregón, Carranza and Zapata. These four leaders had numerous disputes, resulting in wars between the various revolutionary factions, at the expense of the farmers and workers. Nonetheless, the Revolution put an end to the landowners' blatant unfairness and brought about a redistribution of wealth.

The Revolution also spawned a new constitu-

tion, parts of which are still in effect today. Schooling was provided for all children and the possessions of the Church and major landowners were redistributed. On the down side, it also caused chaos in the government and massive inflation. The various community groups could not agree on a plan of action, and changes were slow in the making.

Relations with the United States

Mexico's relations with the United States also suffered as a result of the Revolution. President Woodrow Wilson waited a long time before officially recognizing Venustiano Carranza as the new Mexican president and offering him assistance. Carranza was finally recognized by the United States as President of Mexico in 1916.

Carranza was recognized by the United States as President of Mexico in 1916. Nevertheless, the revolution continued. Zapata fought on relentlessly until his assassination in 1919. Pancho Villa, for his part, was killed in 1923. In 1917, a new constitution abolished the hacienda system and limited the presidential mandate to four years. Schools were built and rural properties were confiscated and distributed to peasants. Conflicts with the Church intensified.

It wasn't until Lázaro Cárdenas became president (1934-1940), however, that the inhabitants of the peninsula began benefitting from these reforms. It was he who declared Chetumal capital of the State of Quintana Roo.

Modern Mexico

From 1940 to 1970, the Yucatán was finally linked to the rest of Mexico by rail. Despite major economic problems, Mexico made progress during this period. An irrigation system was built, enabling the farming industry to develop. More and more roads were laid out. However, corruption infiltrated the government, and economic disparity was on the increase. Mexico's reduced ability to compete on the world markets led to tough economic times, and the country experienced a rise in terrorism.

In 1980, large petroleum deposits were discovered in Mexico, making it the world's fourth-ranking oil-producing nation. At the same time, however, due to high inflation, corruption and economic mismanagement, the country found itself saddled with a budget deficit that led to a massive flight of capital. In 1982, President López Portillo hosted the North-South Conference in Cancún in an effort to liberate Mexico from the vicious circle of debt.

A project conceived in the 1960s, the seaside resort of Cancún came to life in 1974, following the construction of an extensive infrastructure. The region has been developing at a faster pace since 1982; in fact, tourism is now the second most important sector of the economy on the Yucatán Peninsula.

Politics

Yucatán and Quintana Roo are two of the 31 states in the federal republic of Mexico, which also has a Federal District encompassing Mexico City.

Though the constitution allows for a multi-party

Portrait

system, Mexico was up until very recently a "single-party democracy". Political pluralism became a reality in the 1980s, with the emergence of the National Action Party (PAN) and the Democratic Revolution Party (PRD), the two major opposition parties. These parties compete for government seats, alongside the Institutional Revolutionary Party (PRI), whose power remained uncontested for a long time.

In 1929, a constitutional revision changed the presidential term from six years to four years and allowed non-consecutive re-eligibility. The same year the Party of the Mexican Revolution was founded; it has been called the Institutional Revolutionary Party, or PRI, since 1945. Since its inception, the party has furnished the country with every single one of its presidents, including Ernesto Zedillo, chief executive and head of state since December 1, 1994. His term ends on November 30, 2000.

The U.S. is now Mexico's principal trading partner, accounting for over 65% of the country's exports. However, numerous agreements have been signed in an effort to increase the number of its trading partners (President Salinas de Gortari signed a free-trade agreement, NAFTA, with Canada and the U.S. in 1992), since all is not rosy between the two neighbours. Points of friction include the presence of illegal Mexican workers in the U.S. and the Americans' refusal to recognize Spanish as a second language, despite how widely spoken it is within their borders.

The winds of change were blowing during the elections of July 1997. For the first time in the 68 years that it has lead the government, the Institutional Revolutionary Party (PRI) has been weakened. Ernesto Zedillo, head of the party, is still the president, but the PRI has lost its majority. The opposition parties, the PAN and PRD, both obtained good results, with close to 30% of the votes each. The PRI also lost ground in Mexico City's mayoral office where the leader of the Democratic Revolution Party (PRD), Cuauhtémoc Cárdenas, was elected mayor during the same elections. Mexicans can thus look forward to a democratization of their institutions.

The Economy

Mexico has a fairly diversified economy. Mining, manufacturing, the petroleum industry (60 billion barrels of reserves), electronics, textiles and tourism are all highly developed sectors.

With 21.7 million visitors in 1996, Mexico ranks seventh in the world as a tourist destination. Tourism plays a large role in the Mexican economy, especially in the State of Quintana Roo. For years, in fact, it was the country's main source of revenue. The cities of Acapulco, Puerto Vallarta and Cancún alone welcome millions of visitors each year. Since the beginning of the debt crisis, in 1982, exchange rates have been highly advantageous for foreign tourists.

From 1976 to 1982, Mexico, the fourth-ranking oil-producing nation in the world, experienced massive inflation, which slowed its development to a halt. Nevertheless, the tourist industry in Quintana Roo continued to flourish, since investors were confident that tourism could pull the region out of its predicament.

In October 1982, President José López Portillo organized a conference in Cancún to come up with ways of stopping the flight of capital. He nevertheless left his successor, Miguel de la Madrid Hurtado (elected in 1982), a nation suffering from massive inflation. The country's accession to the General Agreement on Tariffs and Trade (GATT) in 1986, a new debt conversion agreement signed in 1987, and a decrease in protectionism forced the Mexican people to cope with stringent economic measures and high unemployment.

In 1994, a new flight of capital led to a 60% drop in the value of the peso, and the country's economy still hasn't bounced back, despite drastic austerity measures and the aid obtained by President Ernesto Zedillo from the International Monetary Fund (IMF). The rate of inflation, which reached a record high of 160% in 1987, dropped below 10% in 1996, however.

The People

Mexico, land of mixed ancestry. The Mexican people, as a whole, form a *mestizo* society that has managed to integrate the legacies of the past into its day to day life.

For tourists, this fact becomes evident during a guided visit to a Mayan site, during which the guide, who has all the physical attributes of his Iberian descendants, will automatically and rather unaccountably identify himself with his supposed Maya ancestors, readily qualifying the Spanish conquest as barbarous.

For its part, the "pure" Mayan society still in existence has to struggle to assert its rights and shout its demands from the rooftops, especially in regards to the progressive exploitation of Mayan culture as a tourist attraction, which often results in buses making deliberate detours to picturesque little villages whose isolated inhabitants live in step with the past.

Mayan Society

Though little is known about the origins of the Maya, it is believed that a fairly large Mayan community was founded in Cuello (Belize) in 2000 BC. The first Maya to inhabit the Yucatán Peninsula seem to have settled in Dzibilchaltún (in the northern part of the Yucatán), where stone temples were erected in the 5th century A.D.

Scattered settlements started grouping together, leading to the development of great Mayan cities, where scientific discoveries and remarkable inventions were made. The towns and ceremonial centres reached a considerable size during the Classic Period, from 200 BC to about AD 900. Urban centres abounded, with their symmetrical plans, large avenues, aqueducts and sewer systems, gigantic pyramids and palaces, and their pelota courts the size of soccer fields.

The scientific and social achievements of the Maya were equalled only by their artistic accomplishments.

The gigantic statues, rock sculptures, paintings and abstract decorations of the Mayan temples still make this civilization stand out from the other cultures of the world.

All these achievements are that much more amazing when you consider that the Maya never used the wheel (except for children's toys) or draught animals. These pre-Columbian civilizations, whose economy was comparable to that of Europe during the Stone Age, succeeded in constructing temples that would be hard to build today.

Mayan cities were very precisely laid out according to units of time. Each ornament and each step of a temple represented a unit of time. The Mayan calendar is a combination of two calendars, making it possible to identify a specific day millions of years in the past or the future. Each day, laden with good or ill portents, was analyzed by the rulers, who made their decisions accordingly.

Chichén Itzá's heyday ended around the year 1200, when Mayapán reached its apogee. Mayan civilization entered its decline around 1450, when this last great metropolis was abandoned.

Today, many descendants of the Maya live inland on the Yucatán Peninsula. They are easily recognizable by their small stature, dark complexion and flat profile. The women wear *huipils*, a sort of light dress, made with a square piece of white cotton, embroidered at the neck and on the sleeves.

Arts and Culture

Music

Music occupies an important place in Mexicans' day to day life. In Cancún, musicians compete for space in front of restaurant terraces, singing ballads about a lost or unrequited love, some sorrow or another, or a quarrel. These ballads are inspired by 19th-century Spanish songs that were "Mexicanized".

Mariachi music is definitely the style best-known abroad. Groups of musicians decked out in traditional *ranchero* gear, mariachis have a proud, erect bearing. Each band has a guitarist, a violinist, a trumpet-player and a singer, and their songs, of Spanish origin, are enriched by the cultures of France and central Europe.

The traditional instruments are the trumpet, the guitar, the marimba and the harp. Some pre-Columbian instruments are still in use, although they have been slightly modified.

On Isla Mujeres, where a "Musician's House" was recently established, popular local music is omnipresent during festivities and social events. Considered the father of the music of Isla Mujeres, troubadour Virgilio Fernández, who died in 1962 at the age of 60, sang about his island in songs with evocative names like *Mujer Isleña*, *Mi son pa Contoy*, *Bahía Isleña*, etc. Today, there are numerous bands on the island, two of the most noteworthy being Trova Isleña and Isolda y Marilü Martínez. The band

Portrait

Bahía, made up of four musicians with a penchant for romantic tunes, and Vocas y Cuerdas, a group of singers and guitarists who play songs by Fernández, among others, are two of the region's most popular acts.

The Yucatán also has an ambassador on the electronic pop music scene. Aleks Syntek, a native of Mérida, displays a great deal of talent and originality. His albums, whose sales pass the million mark, are computer-assisted musical productions. His music is sweeping the nightclubs.

Since 1990, Cancún has been hosting an annual jazz festival in May, featuring such greats as Etta James, Ray Charles, Carlos Santana and Tito Puente. The concerts are held on an outdoor stage at Ballenas beach.

Finally, several Mexican composers have made a name for themselves in the world of classical music. They include Manuel Ponce (1886-1948), Julian Carillo (1875-1965), Carlos Chávez (1899-1978) and Silvestre Revueltas (1899-1940).

Dance

Many of the dances found in Mexico date back to pre-Columbian times. Pagan dances, forbidden by the conquistadors, were advocated by Franciscan and Dominican missionaries, who no doubt viewed them as a means of integrating the Catholic religion into the native culture.

Dance plays a prominent role in Mexican festivities. The list of dances includes the stag dance, the feather dance, the Quetzal dance, the old folks' dance, the *Sonajero*, the *Conchero* and the *Jarana*. The last-mentioned is native to the Yucatán. One of the principal Mexican dances, which can be seen on numerous occasions, is the *Venado* (stag dance) of the Yaquis, Mayos and Tarahumaras of northern Mexico.

During your stay in Cancún, you can get a good overview of all these dances by going to see the Ballet Folklórico de Cancún, which performs every Saturday night at the Centro de Convenciones. The show, which includes dinner, recaps the major movements and various trends in in traditional Mexican music, according to time and region.

A Few Actors and Actresses

María Félix
Cantinflas and Tin Tan (two popular comics)
Pedro Infante
Dolores del Río

Films Shot on Location in the Yucatán

Against All Odds (USA, 1985), by Taylor Hackford, with Rachel Ward and Jeff Bridges

Zorro Rides Again (USA, 1937), by John English, with John Carroll

Rastro de Muerte (Mexico, 1981), political thriller by Arturo Ripstein, with Pedro Armen Dariz, Jr.

La Momia Azteca (Mexico, 1957), followed by *Attack of the Mayan Mummy* and *Face of the Screaming Werewolf* (USA, 1964), by Rafael López Portillo

Marie Galante (USA, 1934), by Henry King, with Spencer Tracy

Film

The Beginnings

Like most Latin American countries, Mexico discovered film at the beginning of the century, in the middle of Porfirio Díaz's dictatorship. Film-makers, busy following the dictator's official activities, didn't see the Revolution coming. All Mexican cinematic productions aimed at showing a cultivated, civilized, progressive country, in keeping with the upper classes' wishes.

The Revolution, however, led to the birth of the political documentary, the first in the world, according to some critics, to tackle contemporary problems. The film *Memorias de un Mexicano* (1959), by Carmen Toscano, is a compilation of films made by Salvador Toscano, a pioneer of Mexican cinema, during the final years of the Díaz dictatorship.

At the same time, fictional foreign films were exerting a strong influence on the public's tastes. From 1916 to 1930, fictional Mexican films imitated foreign models, and had melodramatic plots. Perhaps the only exception is *La Banda del automóvil gris* (a silent film about a gang of criminals from Mexico City, 1919). From that point on, melodrama played a predominant role in Mexican cinema.

The year 1930 marked the advent of the "talkie". Antonio Moreno's *Santa* is the prototype of the prostitute melodrama with a naive narrative, a genre that would subsequently become very popular. The year 1938 saw the birth of the *ranchera* comedy, films with simplistic scenarios centred around a certain kind of hero, the *Charro*, a Mexican cowboy riding about in search of adventure.

The Golden Age

In the 1940s, when the United States suspended its Hispanic production in order to concentrate on anti-Nazi propaganda, Mexico became the world's leading producer of Spanish-language films. This was the "golden age" of Mexican cinema, marked by an impressive number of productions and the apogee of melodrama, nationalism and religious sentiment.

Mexican film echoed the official line regarding national unity, re-claiming the pre-Hispanic past and redefining the role of the Amerindian in society. *Cabaretera* (harlot) movies, derived from the prostitute-as-heroine tradition, led to a revival of the moral melodrama and dominated the screen. This trend endured until the early 1960s.

Hollywood know-how got the better of these modest productions, and the Mexican film industry collapsed in the early 1960s. Only a few directors, no doubt influenced by Italian neorealism, shot films about the "real" Mexico.

Contemporary Mexican Cinema

In 1964, the Centro Universitario de Estudias Cinematograficas de México, the Mexican university centre for studies in film, was founded, followed by the Instituto Nacional de

A Few Directors

Roberto Sneider
Dos crimenes, 1995

Alfonso Arau
Como Agua para chocolate, 1992 (*Like Water for Chocolate*, from the novel by Laura Esquivel)

Jaime Humberto Hermosillo
El Compleaños del Perro, 1974
The Passion According to Berenice, 1976
Shipwreck, 1977
María de mi Corazón (Mary my Dearest), 1979
Doña Herlinda and Her Son, 1984
Intimacy in a Bathroom, 1989
La Tarea (Homework), 1990

Felipe Cazals
Aunt Elizabeth's Garden, 1971
Canoa, 1975
Apando (The Isolation Cell), 1975
Las Poquianchis, 1976

Arturo Ripstein
Time to Die, 1965

The Castle of Purity, 1972
El Lugar sín Límites, 1977
La Viuda Negra, 1977
Trace of Death, 1981

Paul Leduc
Frida Kahlo, 1984
John Reed, 1971

Emilio Fernández
Janitzio, 1938

Luis Buñuel
Buñuel, who was born in Spain in 1900 and died in Mexico in 1983, liked to say that he had learned his trade in Mexico. Upon arriving here in 1946, he returned to his career as a film-maker, which he had abandoned in 1932. He shot 21 films in Mexico between 1946 and 1965, including:

The Forgotten Ones, 1951
Nazarín, 1959
The Young One, 1960
Viridiana (Spanish-Mexican co-production), 1961
The Exterminating Angel, 1962
Saint Simeon of the Desert, 1964

Portrait

Cinematografia, in 1970, in order to help out the film studios. Thanks to these two institutions, many quality films were put out in the early 1970s. However, the privatization of production companies led to the closing of hundreds of movie theatres. To make matters worse, thousands of films were destroyed in a fire at the Cinemateca Nacional, the national film archives, in 1982. Since the early 1980s, furthermore, many Mexicans have given up going to the movies, preferring to watch *tele-novelas*. These television soap operas, whipped together at lightning speed, are extremely popular throughout Latin America.

Literature

Bishop Diego de Landa destroyed almost all the Mayan codices. Afterward, he redeemed himself slightly by recording his observations of the Mayan people in his *Relaciónes de las Cosas de Yucatán*. However, a number of Aztec documents have survived to this day thanks to other missionaries, however. Four collections of writings in Náhuatl (the language of the Aztecs and certain ethnic groups) were safeguarded by a Spanish monk named Bernardino de Sahagún (1500-1590). These works, heroic poems for the most part, have a strong lyrical quality. Other extant Náhuatl writings, translated into Spanish, were the work of poet-king Netzahualcóyotl (1402-1472), King Huegotzingo and Aztec Prince Temilotzin. The Náhuatl literature was translated by Eduard Georg Seler (1849-1922), among others. In his *Collected Works in Mesoamerican Linguistics and Archaeology* he paints a relatively complete portrait of pre-Columbian literature.

Mayan literature, for its part, is represented by *Rabianl-Achi*, a play explaining the customs and lifestyle of the Maya. One of the few remaining copies of the *Popol Vuh* (see p 244), translated by Fray Francisco Ximénez in the early 18th century, is a source of information on the customs and traditions of certain Mayan ethnic groups. Mexican literature written in Spanish originated, of course, with the Spanish conquest, whose leading chroniclers were Bernal Díaz de Castilo (1492-1580), a companion of Hernán Cortés; Bartolomé de las Casas (1474-1566); Jerónimo de Mendieta (1525-1604) and Antonio de Solis (1610-1686).

The colonial era was dominated by the omnipresent Spanish influence, preventing the evolution of a uniquely Mexican literature. Certain writers nonetheless succeeded in creating original works: Juan Ruiz de Alarcón y Mendoza (1581-1639) and Iñes de la Cruz (1648-1695), a nun considered to be one of the greatest poets of the Spanish language of the 17th century. Carlos de Sigüenza Y Góngora is a worthy representative of the new Spanish baroque. In the days of José Manuel Martínez de Navarrete (1768-1809), who drew his inspiration from French neo-classicism, Mexico was in search of a national identity.

When nationalist uprisings started raging in Mexico in 1810, almost all the country's literature converged around the topic of independence, forming one huge polemic. The realistic novel came next, focusing largely on politics. Toward the end of the 19th century, many Mexican writers were influenced by Spanish and French romanticism. A counter-current emerged immediately afterward, led by Manuel Gutiérrez Najera (1859-1895), considered the father of modern Mexican literature.

In Mexico, the Revolution marked the advent of con-

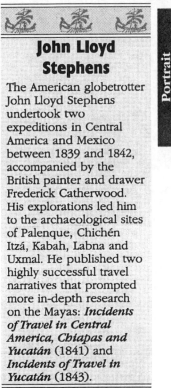

John Lloyd Stephens

The American globetrotter John Lloyd Stephens undertook two expeditions in Central America and Mexico between 1839 and 1842, accompanied by the British painter and drawer Frederick Catherwood. His explorations led him to the archaeological sites of Palenque, Chichén Itzá, Kabah, Labna and Uxmal. He published two highly successful travel narratives that prompted more in-depth research on the Mayas: *Incidents of Travel in Central America, Chiapas and Yucatán* (1841) and *Incidents of Travel in Yucatán* (1843).

temporary literature inspired by nationalist sentiments. Mariano Azuela (1873-1952) is the principal representative of this movement. One of his more noteworthy works is *The Underdogs* (published in Spanish in 1916), a lively, colourful account of the Revolution. In the 1920s, writers began focusing once again on Mexican history. Artemio de Valle Arizpe (1888-1961) is the principal author to have analyzed the colonial period. Carlos Fuentes (1928), author of *Where the Air Is Clear, The Death of Artemio Cruz* and *The Old Gringo,* has attained celebrity status.

The most internationally renowned Mexican author is Octavio Paz (1914-1998), awarded the Nobel Prize for Literature in 1990. In addition to producing numerous essays, works of poetry and translations, Paz has also been a lecturer, a diplomat and a journalist. He is the author of *The Labyrinth of Solitude* (1950), among others. Along with Alfonso Reyes (1889-1959), he is considered Mexico's master essayist.

Today, a number of talented young authors belonging to the group *Espiga amotinada,* founded in 1980, are breathing new life into Mexican literature. These include Augusto Shelley, Juan Buñuelos and Oscar Olivas.

Outstanding authors from the Yucatán include poet and essayist Wilberto Cantón (1925-1979), who was awarded numerous prizes for his body of work; and playwright, professor and film critic Miguel

Barbachanco Ponce (1930). Journalist, historian and narrator Héctor Águilar Camil (1946), who has written a great deal about the Mexican Revolution, won the national prize for journalism, the *Premio nacional de Periodismo,* in 1986.

Painting

Magnificent pre-Columbian frescoes adorned many Mayan temples in Mexico. Traces of the reds, oranges and famous Maya blue that once covered the walls are still visible. Shortly after the Spanish conquest, European artists began teaching in Mexico City, in a school founded by the Franciscans.

Colonial art flourished in the 17th century, when numerous painters managed to integrate European art into their own style. Works from this period grace churches, cloisters and museums in many towns.

The Mexican baroque was born in the late 18th century, and proved remarkably immune to any native influence. Mexican painters continued to be influenced by the European masters right up until the 20th century. It wasn't until the Revolution of 1910 that an original, uniquely Mexican movement took shape:

Diego Rivera

Diego Rivera (1886-1949) painted huge frescoes inspired by the Italian Renaissance, as well as Mayan and Aztec art, and which depicted the social and political realities of Mexico. He married painter Frida Kahlo (1910-1954). Kahlo, confined to a wheelchair from the age of 18 onward, painted lucid images fraught with anguish. She has only recently attained a certain level of renown.

Rufino Tamayo

Painter Rufino Tamayo (1899-1991), of Zapotec origin, is considered the master of modern art. He refused to use his art for any political ends whatsoever. Inspired by various modern trends, especially cubism, he also borrowed elements from popular Mexican art.

muralism (the Minister of Education at the time, José Vasconselos, allowed painters to use the walls of schools and other public buildings).

The birth of muralism was marked by an exhibition of secessionist artists, organized by Gerardo Murillo (1875-1964), who liked to be called Dr. Atl. Political caricaturist Guadalupe Posada (1851-1913) is considered the precursor of this trend, characterized by the use of pre-Columbian motifs and colours and the renunciation of Spanish elements. The paintings glorified the country's Amerindian heritage and the Revolution. A manifesto denouncing paintings in museums was published in 1923. Diego Rivera, David Alfaro Siqueiros and José Clemente Orozco were three of the leading painters of this period.

Religion and Holidays

Mexico's largely Catholic population is very devout as a whole. The churches, always full, ring with the sounds of the faithful lifting their voices in song. The year is punctuated with religious holidays. The Catholic Church, which established itself here in the early days of the Spanish conquest, was very powerful, controlling education and interfering in politics and everyday life.

In keeping with their mixed roots, Mexicans, when practising their religion, combine traditional Catholic rituals with the mystical beliefs of the Amerindians. For example, they worship the dead (*Día de los Muertos*). Religious festivities, very important here, are colourful events that draw large crowds.

December 30 to January 6
Twelfthtide
(*Fiesta de Los Tres Reyes Magos*)

January 1
New Year's Day
(*Año Nuevo*)
Major festivities all over the country and agricultural fairs in rural areas.

January 6
Epiphany
(*Día de los Reyes*)
On this day, children receive gifts. At many social gatherings, a ring-shaped cake with a tiny doll hidden in it is served; the person who gets the piece of cake containing the doll has to host another gathering on February 2, Candlemas.

January 17
San Antonio Abad's Day
On this day, domesticated animals are honoured all over Mexico. Animals and livestock are decorated and blessed in the local churches.

February 2
Candlemas
(*Candelaria*)
Festivities, parades and bullfights. The streets are decorated with lanterns.

February 5
Constitution Day
(*Día de la Constitucíon*)
Commemoration of the constitutions of 1857 and 1917, which contain the fundamental laws of present-day Mexico.

Variable
Pre-Lenten Carnival
Music, dancing and parades in many seaside resorts, including Cancún, Isla Mujeres and Cozumel.

February 24
Flag Day

March 21
Benito Juárez's Birthday
A holiday in honour of the beloved former president (1806-1872), born of Zapotec parents. He effected numerous reforms during his time in office, including the abolition of Church privileges, the introduction of civil weddings and public schools, and industrialization.

March 20, 21 or 22
Vernal equinox
For about 15 minutes on this day, the sun shines down on the great pyramid at Chichén Itzá in such a manner as to create the spectacular illusion that a snake is crawling down the edge of the monument, all the way to the ground. This phenomenon also occurs during the autumnal equinox (September 20, 21 or 22).

March 27 to April 3
Holy Week
(Semana santa)
Holy Week, which starts on Palm Sunday, is the most important religious celebration in Mexico and is marked by festivities all over the country.

First Sunday in April
Easter

April
Regata Sol a Sol
A regatta between Florida and Cozumel, with numerous festivities to mark the occasion.

May 3
Holy Cross Day
(Día de la Santa Cruz)
On this day, construction workers put decorated crosses on top of the buildings they are erecting. Holy Cross Day is also celebrated with picnics and fireworks.

May 5
Battle of Puebla
(Cinco de Mayo)
Commemoration of the Mexican army's victory over Napoleon III's troops in Puebla in 1862.

May 15
San Isidoro Labrador
Festivals held in Panaba, near Valladolid, and in Calkini, southwest of Mérida.

May
Various festivities held on Isla Mujeres.

June
Fishing tournaments in Cozumel and Cancún.

June 24
St. John the Baptist's Day
(Día de la San Juan Bautista)
Fairs, religious festivities and swimming.

Portrait

August
Cancún Cup
Lancha (canoe) races in
Cancún.

September 15-16
Independence Day
(public holiday)
Mexico's Declaration of
Independence (1810) is
celebrated throughout the
country. At 11pm, on Sep-
tember 15, *El Grito* (The
Call), a re-enactment of
Father Hidalgo's famous
appeal to his compatriots to
rise up, is presented on the
central square of most
towns. The president opens
the traditional ceremonies
on Constitution Square, in
Mexico City. Nearly all institutions and places of business are closed on these
two days. Parades during
daytime and fireworks at
night.

September 20, 21 and 22
Autumnal equinox
(see March, vernal equinox)

September 27
Columbus Day
(Día de la Raza)
(public holiday)
Festivities commemorating
the blending of the indigenous and European peoples
of Mexico.

October 23 to November 2
Cancún festival

October 31
Hallowe'en
In the Yucatán, candles are
placed on tombstones. The
first of eight days devoted
to remembering the dead.

November 1
President's State of the Nation address
(Informe Presidencial)
(public holiday)
The Mexican president de-
livers this annual speech
before Congress.

November 1 and 2
All Saints' Day
(Día de los Muertos)
On these two days, the
country celebrates death
with festivities that combine
Christian and native traditions. Skulls and skeletons
made of sugar and minia-
ture coffins are sold everywhere, and there are pro-
cessions to the cemeteries,
where the altars and tombstones are elaborately decorated. This *fiesta* offers
Mexicans a chance to evoke
the memory of their dearly
departed.

November 20
Anniversary of the Mexican
Revolution (public holiday)
Commemoration of the
beginning of the civil war,
which lasted 10 years (from
1910 to 1920) and claimed
the lives of millions of Mexicans.

December 1-8
Numerous festivities held on Isla Mujeres.

December 12
Festival of the Virgin de Guadalupe
This is Mexico's most religious holiday, celebrating the country's patron saint. Pilgrims from all over the country converge on the cathedral in Mexico City, where a shroud mysteriously imprinted with the saint's image is displayed.

December 16-24
Posadas
Processions and festivities commemorating Joseph and Mary's trip to Bethlehem. Music fills the streets and *piñatas* are broken open.

December 25
Christmas *(Navidad)*
This family holiday is celebrated at home.

Practical Information

It is relatively easy to travel all over Mexico, whether you are alone or in an organized group, but to make the most of your trip it is best to be well prepared.

This section is intended to help you plan your trip to Cancún and Cozumel. It also includes general information and practical advice designed to familiarize you with local customs.

Entrance Formalities

Before leaving, make sure to bring all of the documents necessary to enter and leave the country. While these formalities are not especially demanding, without the requisite documentation it is impossible to travel in Mexico. Therefore, take special care of official documents.

Passport

To enter Mexico, you must have a valid passport. This is by far the most widely accepted piece of identification, and therefore the safest. If your passport expires within six months of your date of arrival in Mexico, check with your country's embassy or consulate as to the rules and restrictions applicable.

As a general rule, the expiration date of your passport should not fall less than six months after your arrival date. If you have a return ticket, however, your passport need only be valid for the duration of your stay. Otherwise, proof of sufficient funds may be required. For travellers from most Western countries (Canada, United States, Australia, New Zealand, Western European countries) a simple passport is enough; no visa is necessary. Other citizens are advised to contact the nearest consulate to see whether a visa is required to enter Mexico. Since requirements for entering the country can change quickly, it is wise to double-check them before leaving.

Your passport is a precious document that should be kept in a safe place. Do not leave it in your luggage or hotel room, where it could easily be stolen. A safety-deposit box at the hotel is the best place to store important papers and objects during your stay.

Travellers are advised to keep a photocopy of the most important pages of their passport, as well as to write down its number and date of issue. Keep these copies separate from the originals during your trip and also leave copies with friends or family in your own country. If ever your passport is lost or stolen, this will facilitate the replacement process (the same is true for citizenship cards and birth certificates). In the event that your passport is lost or stolen, contact the local police and your country's embassy or consulate (see addresses further below), in order to be reissued an equivalent document as soon as possible. You will have to fill out a new application form, provide proof of citizenship and new photographs, and pay the full fee for a replacement passport.

Minors Entering the Country

In Mexico, all individuals under 18 years of age are legally considered minors. Each traveller under the age of 18 is therefore required to present written proof of his or her status upon entering the country, namely, a letter of consent signed by his or her parents or legal guardians and notarized or certified by a representative of the court (a justice of the peace or a commissioner for oaths).

A minor accompanied by only one parent must carry a signed letter of consent from the other parent, which also must be notarized or certified by a representative of the court.

If the minor has only one legally recognized parent, he or she must have a paper attesting to that fact. Again, this document must be notarized or certified by a justice of the peace of a commissioner for oaths.

Airline companies require adults who are meeting minors unaccompanied by their parents or an official guardian to provide their address and telephone number.

Tourist Cards

Upon your arrival in Mexico, after your proof of citizenship and customs declaration form have been checked, the customs officer will give you a blue tourist card. This card is free and authorizes its holder to visit the country for 60 days. Do not lose it, as **you must return it to Mexican immigration when you leave the country**. Take the same precautions as you did with your passport, by recording the tourist card number somewhere else – on your airline ticket, for example. In case of theft or loss of your tourist card, contact Mexican immigration at ☎5-842892.

Airport Departure Tax

Except for children under two years of age, all passengers taking international flights out of Mexico are required to pay a tax of about \$15 US. The major airlines often include this tax in the ticket price; ask your travel agent.

Customs

On the way to Mexico, flight attendants will hand out a questionnaire to all air passengers; this is a customs declaration form, which must be completed before your arrival. If you have items to declare, your luggage will be searched. If not, you will have to activate a random "traffic light". A green light permits travellers to pass without searches; a red light means a search.

Of course, it is strictly forbidden to bring any drugs or firearms into the country. Any personal medication, especially psychotropic drugs, must have a prescription label. If you have any questions regarding customs regulations, you can call the customs office at Cancún airport, ☎*(98) 860073*.

Embassies and Consulates

Embassies and consulates can provide precious information to visitors who find themselves in a difficult situation (for example, loss of passport or in the event of an accident or death, they can provide names of doctors, lawyers, etc.). They deal only with urgent cases, however. It should be noted that costs arising from such services are not paid by these consular missions.

Foreign Consulates and Embassies in Mexico

Australia
Ruben Darío 55, Col. Polanco, 11560 - Mexico D.F.
☎*(5) 531-5225*
≈*(5) 203-8431*

Belgium
Avenida Alfredo de Musset, n° 41
Colonia Polanco 11550 Mexico D.F.
☎*(5) 280-0758*
≈*(5) 280-0208*

Canada
Calle Schiller, n° 529
(Rincón del Bosque), Colonia
Polanco, 11560 - Mexico, D.F.
☎*(5) 254-3288*
☎*91-800-70-629* (toll free)
≈*(5) 254-8554*

Consulate:
Plaza Caracol II, 3er piso, local 330
Boulevard Kukulcán, km 8.5, Zona
hotelera, 77500 Cancún, Quintana
Roo, Mexico
☎*(98) 83-3360*
☎*(98) 83-3361*
≈*(98) 83-3232*

Germany
Calle Lord Byron no. 737, Polanco
Chapultepec, 11560 Mexico D.F.
☎*(5) 2832200*
≈*(5) 2812588*

Honorary Consul:
Punta Conoca no. 36, block 24
77500 Cancún
☎*(98) 841598*
☎*(98)8411898*

Great Britain
Lerma 71, Col. Cuauhtémoc
06500 Mexico D.F.
☎*(525) 207-2089*
≈*(525) 207-7672*

Consulate:
Kukulkán Blvd., km 16.5, Cancún
Quintana Roo
☎*(98) 85-1166*

Holland
Montes Urales Sur no. 635, piso 2
Lomas de Chapultepec
11000 Mexico D.F.
☎*(5) 2028453*
☎*(5) 2028854*
≈*(5) 2026148*

Consulate:
Hotel Presidente, Avenida Kukulcán
Km 7.5, 77500 Cancún
☎ *(98) 830200*
⇰ *(98) 32515*

Italy
Avenida Paseo de las Palmas, n° 1994
Lomas de Chapultepec, C. P. 11000
Mexico D.F.
☎ *(5) 596-3655*
⇰ *(5) 596-7710*

New Zealand
Jose Luis Lagrange 103, 10th floor,
Colonia Los Morales, Polanco
11510 Mexico D.F.
☎ *(5) 281-5486*
⇰ *(5) 281-5212*

Norway
Avenida Virreyes no. 1460, Colonia
Lomas, Virreyes, 11000 Mexico D.F.
☎ *(5) 403486*
⇰ *(5) 2023019*

Spain
Galileo, n° 114, corner Horatio Col.
Polanco, 11550 - Mexico D.F.
☎ *(5) 282-2271*
☎ *(5) 282-2974*
⇰ *(5) 282-1520*
⇰ *(5) 282-1302*

Consulate:
Oasis Building, Avenida Kukulcán,
Km 6.5, Cancún
☎ *(98) 832466*
⇰ *(98) 832870*

Switzerland
Torre Optima, 11. Stock, Avenida
Paseo de las Palmas, n° 405, Lomas
de Chapltepec, 11000 - Mexico, D.F.
☎ *(5) 520-8535*
☎ *(5) 520-3003*
⇰ *(5) 520-8685*

Consulate:
Avenida Kukulcán, Km 17, Cancún
☎ *(98) 818000*
⇰ *(98) 818080*

United States
Paseo de la Reforma, n° 1305
06500 - Mexico, D.F.
☎ *(5) 211-0042*
⇰ *(5) 511-9980*

Consulate:
Kukulkán Blvd.,Plaza Caracol #11,
Cancún, Quintana Roo
☎ *(98) 83-0172*

Mexican Embassies and Consulates Abroad

Australia
49 Bay Street, Double Bay
Sydney, NSW 2028
☎ *(02) 326-1292*

Belgium
Avenue Franklin-Roosevelt 94
1050 Bruxelles
☎ *(32-2) 629-0777*
⇰ *(32-2) 649-8768*

Canada
45 O'Connor Street, Office 1500
Ottawa, Ontario, K1P 1A4
☎ *(613) 233-8988*
☎ *(613) 233-9572*
⇰ *(613) 235-9123*

Consulate:
2000, rue Mansfield, Bureau 1015
10th floor, Montréal, Québec, H3A 2Z7
☎ *(514) 288-2502*
⇰ *(514) 288-8287*

Practical Information

Consulate:
Commerce Court West, 99 Bay Street
Toronto, Ontario, M5L 1E9
☎ *(416) 368-2875*
⇀ *(416) 368-3478*

Germany
Adenaueralle 100, 53113 Bonn
☎ *(228) 91-48-60*

Great Britain
8 Halkin Street, London SWIX 7DW
☎ *(0171) 235-6393*

Italy
Vla Lazzaro Spallanzani 16
00161 Rome
☎ *(6) 441-151*
⇀ *(6) 440-3876*

New Zealand
111-115 Customhouse Quay
8th floor, Wellington
☎ *(644) 472-5555*

Spain
Carrera de San Jéronimo 46
28014 Madrid
☎ *(91) 369-2814*
⇀ *(91) 420-2292*

Switzerland
Bernastrasse, n° 57, 3005 -Berne
☎ *(31) 351-1875*
⇀ *(31) 351-3492.*

Note:
there are honorary consulates of Mexico in Zurich
and Lausanne; their ad-
dresses are available from
the embassy in Berne.

United States
1911 Pennsylvania Avenue, N.W.
20006 - Washington D.C.
☎ *(202) 736-1000*
☎ *(202) 736-1012*
⇀ *(202) 797-8458*

Consulate:
27 East 39th Street, New York
N.Y. 10016
☎ *(212) 217-6400*
⇀ *(212) 217-6493*

Consulate:
2401 W. 6th St.
Los Angeles CA, 90057
☎ *(213) 351-6800*
☎ *(213) 651-6825*
⇀ *(213) 351-6844*
⇀ *(213) 383-4927*

Consulate:
300 North Michigan Ave., 2nd floor
Chicago, IL 60601
☎ *(312) 855-0056*
☎ *(312) 855-0066*
⇀ *(312) 855-9257*

Tourist Information

In Mexico, the government
offers travellers a telephone
information line in English
that covers formalities (customs, visas), road direc-
tions, road conditions,
weather, etc. Toll free:
☎ *91 800 90392*

Cancún Tourist Office:
Avenida Tulum #29

Mexican Tourist Associations Abroad

The purpose of these offices is to help travellers prepare a trip to Mexico. Office staff can answer visitors' questions and provide brochures.

Before departure, Canadians can contact the Mexican Ministry of Tourism, toll free at ☎1-800-263-9426, for any travel-related inquiries. It is also possible to order brochures and maps of the region to be visited.

North America

Mexico Hotline
☎1-800-44-MEXICO
☎1-800-446-3942

Canada
1, Place Ville-Marie, Bureau 1931
Montréal, Québec, H3B 2C3
☎(514) 871-1052,
≈(514) 871-3825

2 Bloor Street West, Office 1801
Toronto, Ontario, M4W 3E2
☎(416) 925-2753
≈(416) 925-6061

United States
21 East 63rd Street
third floor, New York, NY 10021
New York N.Y. 10021
☎(212) 821-0313
≈(212) 821-0367

2401 West 6th Street
Los Angeles CA 90057
☎(213) 351-2069
☎(213) 351-2075/76
≈(213) 351-2074

70 East Lake Street, Suite 1413
Chicago, IL 60601
☎(312) 855-1380
☎(312) 565-2778

Europe

Germany
Wiesenhüttenplatz 26
d-60329 Frankfurt am Main 1
☎(496) 925-3413
≈(496) 925-3755

Great Britain
60-61 Trafalgar Sq.
London WC2 N5DS
☎(171) 173-1058
≈(171) 930-9202

Italy
Via Barberini, n° 3, 00187 - Rome
☎(6) 483-630
≈(6) 621-089

Spain
Calle Velázquez, n° 126
28006 - Madrid
☎(91) 561-1827
≈(34-1) 411-0759

Getting to Cancún and the Riviera Maya

By Plane

Many agencies offer convenient holiday packages that

include airfare and accommodation. Such packages are usually put together for the major tourist centres of the country, notably Cancún and Cozumel.

Another option is to buy airfare only and to reserve your own accommodations or find a place to stay once there. Accommodation options are plentiful, and this way travellers can visit more of the area, choosing lodgings from day to day. Outside of high seasons (Christmas holidays and Holy Week), it is usually not difficult to find a room, as much in more out-of-the-way spots as in the popular tourist centres. Reservations remain the surest approach nonetheless.

The Yucatán Peninsula has two international airports, one in Cancún and one in Cozumel. There are smaller airports in Chichén Itzá, Playa del Carmen and Mérida. As well, daily domestic flights are offered to Acapulco, Mérida and Mexico City.

Cancún International Airport (☎98-860028) is about 20km southwest of the hotel zone. It is one of the most modern airports in Mexico owing to recent renovation work. In addition to an exchange bureau and a duty-free shop, it has a few stores, restaurants and bars where the prices, just as in any place with a high concentration of tourists, are higher than those in town.

There is a shuttle service between Cancún and the airport, called Transfert, that costs approximately $10 US. This service is often included in the price of holiday packages. The buses are spacious and surprisingly punctual. On the way to the airport, be careful as it is possible that the shuttle will arrive at your hotel early and leave for the airport without waiting. To avoid this catastrophe, be 30 min ahead of schedule and wait for the shuttle outside.

Note that taxis are only authorized to bring travellers to the airport from the hotel zone or the town, and, conversely, public buses may only take tourists from the airport to their hotels.

Many car rental agencies have counters at the airport. To avoid excessive costs, it is preferable to rent a car before departure and to shop around. Most established agencies may be reached from all over the Americas by toll-free numbers. When comparing prices, take account of taxes, free mileage and insurance. Here are the names and numbers of agencies located at the Cancún airport:

Monterrey Rent
☎*(98) 860239*

Economovil
☎*(98) 860082*

Avis
☎*(98) 860222*
☎*1-800-321-3652*

Budget
☎*(98) 86660026*
☎*1-800-268-8970*

Hertz
☎*(98) 860150*
☎*91-800-263-0678*

National Tilden
☎*91-800-361-5334*

Cozumel International Airport (☎*987-2-2081*) is close to four kilometres northeast of San Miguel. It has a restaurant-bar and a few souvenir shops, tour operators on the upper floor, and car-rental agencies.

Unlike in Cancún, there is no public transit system in Cozumel, but countless taxis roam the island and offer reasonably priced service. A shuttle from the airport costs about $5 US.

More affluent travellers and those who cannot endure overland or boat travel can fly with Mexicana or Aeromexico to Cancún,

Mérida, Playa del Carmen and Chichén Itzá.

Mexicana
Avenida Coba 39, Cancún
☎*98-874444*
☎*91 800 50220*
~*98-874441*

Aeromexico
Avenida Coba 80, Cancún
☎*98-841097*
☎*91-800-37-6639*

Flights to Cancún from Cozumel leave every hour and cost about $40 US. Flights to Chichén Itzá leave twice daily and tickets are also about $40 US.

Practical Information

By Land

Until the 1950s, Mexico did not have a highway system that covered the whole of the country's tortuous topography. Since then, road work has constituted an essential element of the integration of isolated regions into the national economy.

A large proportion of new Mexican highways is a product of the private sector. Modern, safe, four-lane toll highways now link the large cities of the country. While they are very expensive, these new roads represent immense progress compared to older roads, which are often poorly maintained and crowded with trucks and buses.

Getting in and around Cancún and the Riviera Maya

By Car

Planning one's itinerary depends on the distances that separate the attractions one wishes to see. For example, did you know that the hotel zone in Cancún is 22-km long and it can take up to 45 min to reach downtown? Roadwork is also common and can slow traffic considerably, which can be very unpleasant under a tropical sun.

Car Rentals

Renting a car in Mexico is not a simple affair. Expect rates to be high and choice to be limited. All of the large car rental agencies operate in Mexico, including many American and some Mexican companies. Renters must be at least 21 years old and possess a valid driver's license and a recognized credit card. Clients must sign two credit card slips, one for the rental and one to cover potential damages, which is common practice in Mexico. Toll-free telephone numbers of car-

rental agencies are listed in the section "Getting to Cancún and the Riviera Maya" (see p 51).

Expect to pay an average of $50 per day (unlimited mileage is not always included) for a small car, not including insurance and tax. Choose a car in good condition, preferably new. A few of the local agencies have lower rates, but their cars are often in poor condition and they offer limited service in case of breakdown.

At the time of the rental you must subscribe to a Mexican automobile insurance policy, as your own policy is not valid in Mexico. Deductibles are very high *(about $1,000)*. Before signing a rental contract, be sure that methods of payment are very clearly stated. When you sign, your credit card should cover the cost of the rental and the insurance deductible, should it be necessary.

It is far better to reserve a rental car from home: it costs less and the paperwork is simpler. To guarantee the rate that is offered ask for confirmation to be faxed to you.

Table of Distances (km)
Via the shortest route

	Cancún						
	202	Chichén Itzá					
	315	113	Mérida				
	1651	1445	1332	Ciudad de México			
	69	256	384	1582	Playa del Carmen		
	132	193	306	1519	63	Tulum	
	158	44	157	1489	212	149	Valladolid

Example: The distance between Playa del Carmen and Cancún is 69 km.

© ULYSSES

Driving and the Highway Code

For years now the government has been pouring millions of pesos into highway infrastructure in this region. Highways and main road are therefore well paved and in generally good condition. The main arteries in the area of Cancún and Cozumel are Highway 307, which runs along the coast from Punta Sam, north of Cancún, past Tulúm to Chetumal, and Highway 180, which runs from Cancún to Mérida via Valladolid and Chichén Itzá. The 70km-long section of Highway 307 between Playa del Carmen and Tulúm has been the object of extensive repair and widening work since January 1997.

Travelling on secondary roads remains a perilous endeavour. They are often covered in loose stones and overgrown with weeds. Some are paved, but the majority are strewn with holes of various sizes, and must therefore be navigated slowly and carefully. These roads meander through small villages where it is especially important to drive slowly as pedestrians and animals can appear without warning. Speed bumps, also called silent policemen, have been placed on these roads to slow drivers in towns and are often poorly indicated.

Road signs are rare (speed limits, stops, and right of way are all poorly indicated). It is not uncommon for directions to be inscribed on a piece of cardboard hung from a tree, and drivers must often simply ask passersby for help.

Traffic is rarely busy on these roads, except in downtown Cancún and in the hotel zone. Elementary driving rules are often not respected – Mexicans drive fast and do not always check their blind spots when passing. Turn signals are also a rarity, as is the use of seatbelts.

Since most roads have neither lights nor adequate marking, it is strongly recommended to avoid night driving. The risk of robbery increases at night: never pick up hitchhikers after dark, avoid pulling over on the shoulder, and lock your doors.

The speed limit is 110kph on four-lane highways and 90kph on two-lane roads.

Accidents

As some Mexican roads are poorly lit and marked, avoid driving at night off the main streets. Look out for speed bumps and potholes. Slow down at level crossings. Authorities do not take parking violations lightly. Always remember to lock the doors of your car.

In case of an accident or of mechanical failure, pull onto the shoulder and raise the hood of the car. Assistance from other motorists should be quick in arriving. Main roads are patrolled by "green angels" (Los Angeles Verdes), government towtrucks driven by mechanics who speak English. This service is free, except for parts and gasoline, and operates 24 hours a day (☎91-800-90392).

The Police

Police officers are posted along highways to monitor motorists. They have the power to stop anyone who commits an infraction of the highway safety code, or simply to check a driver's papers. In general, they try not to bother tourists, but it can happen that certain officers will try to extract pesos from foreign motorists. If you are sure of not having committed any infraction, there is no reason to disburse any sum. Occasionally, tourists are stopped long enough to have their papers checked. As a rule police officers are obliging and helpful should you have trouble on the road.

Gasoline

Gasoline is sold by the litre, in two grades: Nova (blue pumps) is leaded gasoline with an octane rating of 81, and Magna Sin (green pumps) is unleaded. Magna Sin is easy to find. Look for a PEMEX sign (Petroleos Mexicanos, the state gas-station monopoly).

A gas station attendant usually receives a tip of a few pesos. There are no self-service stations. The price of gasoline seems high to Americans, but for Canadians it is more or less average, while it is low for Europeans. One last tip: fill up whenever you have the opportunity as gas stations are rather rare.

By Scooter

It is possible to rent scooters by the hour or by the day in many places for $25 to $30 per day. Isla Mujeres and Cozumel are especially suited to this mode of transportation. In Cancún traffic is too busy and fast for scooters.

By Taxi

Taxis run 24hrs a day and, in general, have quite reasonable rates, despite the fact that they are higher in resort areas than in the

Practical Information

towns of the interior. It is best to ask the price of a trip before boarding a cab, since most do not have meters. There are usually a few taxis waiting for customers outside of hotels. If there are not, ask a reception clerk to call one. The trip from the furthest hotel in the hotel zone in Cancún to downtown should cost about $10.

By Public Bus

Public buses, known as *camiónes* in Mexico, travel the hotel zone in Cancún. You will never have to wait more than three minutes, unless there is traffic. The fare is about five pesos, regardless of the distance travelled. Official bus stops are indicated by blue signs, although a wave of the hand will also stop the bus. In downtown Cancún, buses serve major intersections. Service is 24hrs.

These buses are not necessarily uncomfortable, except for the fact that the competition among the different companies is pretty heavy. Generally, buses barely slow down to allow passengers to board and take off again as quickly as possible. A tip: hold on tight! Elderly or frail people should definitely avoid this mode of transportation in Cancún.

Prepare the exact fare or tickets before boarding a bus, as drivers do not provide change. The driver must remit to passengers a receipt, which they may be asked to produce during the trip. Ask for it, if it is not offered.

In Cozumel, there is no public bus service.

By Boat

Ferry services for foot passengers and automobiles link many points in the Yucatán Peninsula.

From Puerto Juárez to Isla Mujeres: there is a ferry service just north of Cancún; eight departures daily in both directions, 20-minute crossing: ☎(98) 30216

From Playa del Carmen to Cozumel: two companies make the crossing. Nine departures daily in both directions, 45-minute crossing.

By Bus

The network of Mexican coach services is very developed, linking all of the villages. Fares are incredibly inexpensive (*the trip between Cancún and Tulúm, for example, costs about $3*), and service is frequent and rapid. Buses are generally relatively new and air-conditioned. Since second-class tickets do not offer much of a discount, opt for first class. Be forewarned that even modern buses can have poorly equipped washrooms: for longer trips, bring your own toilet paper and washcloths. Also bring a sweater since bus companies do not skimp on the air-conditioning.

Buses leave Cancún practically every hour for Mérida, Playa del Carmen, Tulúm and Chichén Itzá.

Hitchhiking

Risky business! It is uncommon and highly inadvisable, although possible, to hitchhike in Mexico. Hitchhikers can end up spending a very long time on the roadside waiting for motorists to stop.

Excursions and Guided Tours

Since Cancún is the most common departure point for excursions to Chichén Itzá and Tulúm, bus companies and tour operators swarm the city. Sales counters are usually found in hotel lobbies. Here is one of the largest agencies:

ExpoCancún
Paseo Poktapok, Edificio Green 16
☎ *837-721*
ExpoCancún organizes excursons to Isla Mujeres, Chichén Itzá, Tulúm, Xcaret and Cozumel, horseback rides, underwater tours, etc. ExpoCancún can also bring tourists to Isla Contoy, Mérida and Akumal.

Insurance

Travel

Travel insurance should be purchased before setting off on a trip. The insurance policy should be as comprehensive as possible, because health care costs add up quickly, even in Mexico. When purchasing the policy, make sure it covers medical expenses of all kinds, such as hospitalization, nursing services and doctor's fees (at fairly high rates, as these are expensive), as well as sports injuries and those related to pre-existing medical conditions. A repatriation clause, in case necessary care cannot be administered on site, is invaluable. In addition, you may have to pay upon leaving the clinic, so you should check your policy to see what provisions it includes for such instances.

Practical Information

Take the time to read the fine print in any policy before signing it. Ask questions, and compare a good sample of competing plans. Keep in mind that the various people who are authorized to sell travel health insurance are not necessarily experts in the field, despite their best intentions. Communicate directly with insurance companies to clear up any questions about a policy.

During your stay in Mexico, you should always keep proof that you are insured on your person to avoid any confusion in case of an accident.

Cancellation

Cancellation insurance is usually offered by the travel agent when you buy your airplane ticket or holiday package. It permits reimbursement for the ticket or package in the case of cancellation of a trip due to serious illness or death. People with no health problems do not really need this type of protection.

Theft

Most Canadian home insurance plans protect the insured for theft, including incidents of theft that occur outside the country. To submit a claim, a police report must be obtained. Depending on your coverage, it is not always useful to take out additional insurance. Europeans should check whether their policies cover them when they are abroad, as this is not automatically the case.

Health

Precautions

Three months before departure, visit your family doctor (or a travel clinic) to find out what precautions to take and whether any vaccinations are recommended. As a general rule vaccination against hepatitis A and boosters for standard vaccinations are recommended for people travelling to Mexico. For trips outside of major population centres, protection from malaria is also necessary.

In Mexico, hospitals are generally not as well equipped as clinics, which are recommended for non-emergency care. In tourist centres there are always English-speaking doctors.

Because medical facilities are sometimes rudimentary make sure (if possible) that quality control tests have been properly carried out before any blood transfusion.

Avoid walking barefoot outdoors since parasites and minuscule insects can work their way through the skin and cause various problems, such as dermatitis and fungal infections.

Montezuma's Revenge

Mexico is a wonderful country, but unfortunately some travellers succumb to the famous traveller's diarrhea commonly known as *turista* or "Montezuma's revenge". It is important to keep in mind that this condition is not caused uniquely by bacteria found in water, but rather by a combination of factors including fatigue due to altitude, time difference and climate.

Take these simple precautions to avoid illness:

- Wash hands frequently and without fail before eating.
- Contain your culinary curiosity for the first few days of your trip.
- Do not buy food from street vendors.
- During the first days of your vacation, avoid fruits and vegetables that cannot be peeled, dairy products, meat

and uncooked fish (*ceviche*)
- Brush your teeth with purified bottled water (*agua purificada*), for example Crystal brand water which is very inexpensive and available almost everywhere.
- Drink at least two litres of bottled water per day. Be sure that the bottle is sealed when you buy it.
- Try not to overdo it in the first few days of your trip. Fatigue will make you more vulnerable to illness.
- Increase your exposure to the sun gradually.
- Do not consume more alcohol than you ordinarily would.
- Always ask for drinks to be served without ice (*¡sin hielo, por favor!*), which might be made from unpurified water.

Practical Information

If, despite all of these precautions, you are a victim of "Montezuma's revenge" (usually within three days after arrival), remember, before resorting to antidiuretics like Lomotil or Imodium, that your body is reacting this way to rid itself of intestinal bacteria. Therefore, nature must take its course for a reasonable period of time.

Basic treatment for *turista* is simple. Avoid drinking for at least half an hour after a "crisis", and then drink only a few sips of bottled water every 15min. A solution of one litre (four cups) of water, two to three teaspoons of salt and one teaspoon of sugar can help. Do not eat until you are well; your intestinal flora will thank you for it! Once you are feeling better, avoid spicy food, foods rich in fibre, and acidic foods. Pasta, papaya, boiled carrots and rice are all recommended. A cup of chamomile tea (*manzanilla*), which is very popular in Mexico, will do wonders for an upset stomach. Avoid any activity, stay in the shade, and drink lots of water since once diarrhea has passed another enemy lurks: constipation.

In extreme cases, for example if you have suffered from diarrhea for more than two days combined with vomiting, fever and weakness, when there is a high risk of dehydration, medication is recommended. Antibiotics may even be necessary for very serious symptoms, in which case it is best to consult a doctor. Keep the address and telephone number of a nearby clinic with you (it can be very difficult to communicate with front-desk clerks when you have a fever of 40°C!).

Insects

Insects, which are plentiful just about everywhere in Mexico, can be the source of some discomfort, especially at sunset and during the rainy season. To avoid being bitten, cover up well in the evening (when insects are most active), avoid perfume, wear light colours (apparently light colours repel insects) and arm yourself with a good insect repellant (a minimum DEET concentration of 35%). During mountain and forest hikes, shoes and socks are very useful for protecting legs and feet. It is also recommended to bring a balm for soothing the irritation caused by insect bites. Insect-repellant coils make evenings on the patio, or in a room with open windows, more pleasant.

The Sun

Despite its benefits, the sun also causes numerous problems. Always use sunblock to protect yourself from the sun's harmful rays. Many of the sunscreens on the market do not provide adequate protection. Before setting off on your trip, ask your pharmacist which ones are truly effective against the dangerous rays of the sun. For the best results, apply the cream at least 20 minutes before going out in the sun. Overexposure to the sun can cause sunstroke, symptoms of which include dizziness, vomiting and fever. It is important to keep yourself well protected and avoid prolonged exposure, especially during the first few days of your trip, as it takes a while to get used to the sun's strength. Even after a few days, moderate exposure is best. A hat and pair of sunglasses are indispensable accessories in this part of the world.

First-aid Kit

A small first-aid kit can be useful in many situations. Prepare one carefully before your departure. Be sure to include a sufficient quantity of every medication that you take regularly, in its original container, as well as a valid prescription for each in case you lose or run out of it. It can be difficult to find certain medications in Mexico. Drugs such as Imodium or motion-sickness medication should also be bought prior to departure. Good-quality condoms are also difficult to find on site.

A minimally equipped first-aid kit should include a thermometer, acetaminophen, a good sun screen, adhesive bandages in a variety of formats, disinfectant swabs, tablets for stomach upset and motion sickness, contact-lens cleaner and spare glasses. If you have only one pair of glasses, bring your prescription so that it may easily be replaced if need be.

Climate

Like most tropical countries, Mexico has two principal seasons, a rainy season and a dry season. In general, precipitation and temperatures increase from June to October, while from November to May it is cooler and dryer.

In the Yucatán, the proximity of the coasts has a definite influence on the temperature and on the humidity level. During the summer, regions bordering the Caribbean and the Gulf of Mexico stay cool because of the trade winds, whereas in the jungle of the interior the air is hot and heavy. Rain showers are common in April and May and between September and January, when temperatures hover at about 30°C. The risk of hurricane is high in September and October, and the sky is often cloudy. Winter is the most pleasant season in the area.

Practical Information

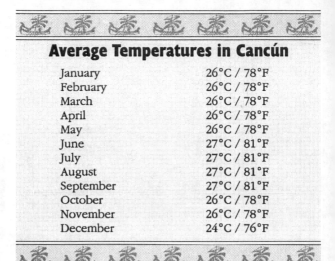

Average Temperatures in Cancún

January	26°C / 78°F
February	26°C / 78°F
March	26°C / 78°F
April	26°C / 78°F
May	26°C / 78°F
June	27°C / 81°F
July	27°C / 81°F
August	27°C / 81°F
September	27°C / 81°F
October	26°C / 78°F
November	26°C / 78°F
December	24°C / 76°F

Packing

Luggage

For carry-on luggage chose a bag with shoulder straps and pockets that close properly, that is big enough to hold a cosmetics bag, a book and a bottle of water. A side pocket is handy, especially at the airport when it comes time to deal with paperwork (passport, airplane ticket, etc.). This bag will also be practical for day trips.

Since you will undoubtedly return with suitcases full of pottery, jewellery, blankets and other marvels found during your trip, it is best to pack light. A good trick is to bring an empty flexible travel bag in which to pack your clothing and to save your hard cases for fragile souvenirs. The ideal hard suitcase has a combination lock, wheels and a strap. Choose high-quality cloth bags made of water-proof, tear-proof nylon.

Clothing

The first thing to do before piling clothes into suitcases is to envision what sorts of activities await, for example, visiting a church, an evening in a fancy restaurant, dancing, or climbing the temple of Chichén Itzá

on hands and knees...
Choose permanent-press,
fast-drying clothes that
match (in the neutral tones
that are the mainstay of any
traveller's wardrobe).

The type of clothing visitors
should pack varies little
from one season to the
next. In general, loose,
comfortable cotton and
linen clothing is most practical. For walking in the
city, it is better to wear
shoes that cover the entire
foot, since these provide
the best protection against
cuts that can become in-
fected. For cool evenings, a
long-sleeved shirt or
sweater can be useful. Remember to wear rubber
sandals on the beach.
When visiting certain sights
(churches for example), a
skirt that hangs below the
knees or a pair of pants
should be worn, so don't
forget to include the appropriate article of clothing in
your suitcase. If you intend
to go on an excursion into
the countryside, take along
a pair of good walking
shoes. Finally, don't forget
to bring a sunhat and sunglasses.

Safety and Security

Mexico is not a dangerous
country, but, just as anywhere else, robbery is a
risk. Remember that in the
eyes of the majority of peo-

ple here, whose income is
relatively low, travellers
possess quite a few luxuries
(cameras, leather suitcases,
video cameras, jewellery...)
which represent a good
deal of money. It is obviously appropriate to follow
the normal rules for per-
sonal safety. Avoid count-
ing money in the open, and
refrain from wearing osten-
tatious displays of jewellery. Keep electronic equipment in a nondescript bag
slung across your chest.
Conceal travellers' cheques,
passport and some cash in
a money belt that fits under
your clothing; this way if
your bags are ever stolen
you will still have the papers and money necessary
to get by. In the evening
and at night avoid poorly lit
streets. Get directions before venturing off to ex-
plore new areas. Remem-
ber, the less attention you
attract, the less chance you
have of being robbed.

If you bring valuables to
the beach you will have to
keep an eye on them,
which will not be very relaxing. A better option is to
leave these objects in the
safety-deposit
box
provided
by your
hotel.

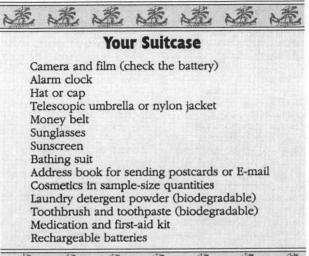

Your Suitcase

Camera and film (check the battery)
Alarm clock
Hat or cap
Telescopic umbrella or nylon jacket
Money belt
Sunglasses
Sunscreen
Bathing suit
Address book for sending postcards or E-mail
Cosmetics in sample-size quantities
Laundry detergent powder (biodegradable)
Toothbrush and toothpaste (biodegradable)
Medication and first-aid kit
Rechargeable batteries

Money and Banking

Currency

The country's currency is the nuevo peso or peso. The peso sign is $MEX or NP$. There are 10, 20, 50, 100, 200 and 500 peso bills and 1, 5, 10, 20 and 50 peso coins, as well as 5, 10, 20 and 50 centavo pieces. Prices are often also listed in US dollars, especially in Cancún and Cozumel, which can be confusing since both currencies are represented by the dollar

sign. Make sure that amounts on credit card receipts are clearly preceded by "NP". Also, there are still a few old pesos in circulation, and they are only worth 1% of the new peso. In a place like a dimly lit bar, someone might try to swindle you by slipping you your change in old pesos.

For the purpose of this book, we have indicated prices in US dollars preceded by the $ sign and in pesos succeeded by the word pesos.

It is a good idea to exchange the value of 20 to

30 US dollars before leaving for Mexico. The exchange offices at the airport will be closed if your flight arrives at night and you will be forced to wait until the next day to settle tips and taxi fares, or even to buy bottled water. The restaurant at your hotel might also be closed, and your arrival would then be a real nightmare.

Although dollars are accepted in major hotels, it is advisable to use pesos during your trip. You will not risk having your money refused, and you will save money too, since most merchants that accept dollars offer poor exchange rates.

Banks

The two largest Mexican banks are Banamex and Bancomer. These are linked to the Cirrus and PLUS networks, and its automatic teller machines even offer menus in English as well as Spanish. Some automatic teller machines offer money in pesos or US dollars. Banks are open Monday to Friday, from 9am to 5pm.

US Dollars

It is always best to travel with cash or travellers' cheques in US currency, since, in addition to being easy to exchange, it benefits from the best exchange rate.

Exchanging Money

For the best rate of exchange, make a cash withdrawal on your credit card; this will save you about 2%, which is generally more than the interest you'll have to pay when you get back. For the same reason, it is best to pay for purchases with your credit card whenever possible. If you make a deposit in anticipation of your trip, you can even avoid interest charges altogether. Most automatic teller machines accept Visa, MasterCard, Cirrus and Plus. This solution relieves you of having to buy travellers' cheques before your vacation, and of having to run around to Mexican banks to cash them during your trip. Also, automatic teller machines are open 24 hours a day. Losing your credit card, however, can be problematic. A variety of financial options (credit cards, travellers' cheques, Mexican cash) is the safest approach.

Exchange offices *(casas de cambio)* have longer hours of operation, well into the evening, and faster service than banks and are located all over the cities. Banks often have better exchange

Practical Information

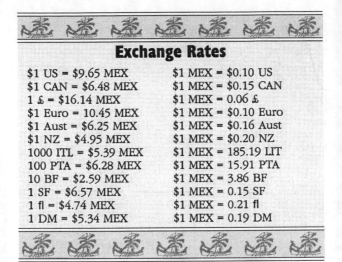

Exchange Rates

$1 US = $9.65 MEX	$1 MEX = $0.10 US
$1 CAN = $6.48 MEX	$1 MEX = $0.15 CAN
1 £ = $16.14 MEX	$1 MEX = 0.06 £
$1 Euro = 10.45 MEX	$1 MEX = $0.10 Euro
$1 Aust = $6.25 MEX	$1 MEX = $0.16 Aust
$1 NZ = $4.95 MEX	$1 MEX = $0.20 NZ
1000 ITL = $5.39 MEX	$1 MEX = 185.19 LIT
100 PTA = $6.28 MEX	$1 MEX = 15.91 PTA
10 BF = $2.59 MEX	$1 MEX = 3.86 BF
1 SF = $6.57 MEX	$1 MEX = 0.15 SF
1 fl = $4.74 MEX	$1 MEX = 0.21 fl
1 DM = $5.34 MEX	$1 MEX = 0.19 DM

rates, however. There is ususally no service charge. You can check the Internet for up-to-date exchange rates at *www.xe.net/currency* An electronic calculator that has a conversion function can also be helpful.

Mexican currency is subject to major fluctuations, and has been devalued numerous times in recent years. The exchange rates for various foreign currencies are listed in the exchange-rate box.

Traveller's Cheques

It is always wise to keep most of your money in travellers' cheques, which, when in US dollars, are sometimes accepted in restaurants, hotels and shops. They are also easy to exchange in most banks and foreign exchange offices. Be sure to keep a copy of the serial numbers of the cheques in a separate place, so if ever they are lost, the company that issued them can replace them quickly and easily. Nevertheless, always keep some cash on hand.

Credit Cards

Most credit cards are accepted in a large number of businesses, especially Visa and MasterCard. American Express and Diner's Club are less commonly accepted. Smaller stores often do not accept credit cards, so be sure to carry some cash along with credit cards and traveller's cheques.

When registering at your hotel, you may be asked to sign a credit card receipt to cover potential expenses during your stay. This is common practice in Mexico.

When using a credit card for purchases, check bills carefully and destroy copies yourself.

Mail and Telecommunications

Mail

It costs about 10 pesos to send a postcard or letter to Europe, and countries in North, South and Central America.

Post offices are generally open from 9am to 6pm, Monday to Friday, and Saturday mornings. It is also possible to send mail from the reception desks of most hotels. Stamps are normally available wherever postcards are sold.

Telephone

Calling Mexico from Abroad

From North America:
Dial 011 (for the international operator) + 52 (the country code for Mexico) + the area code + local number.

From Great Britain, New Zealand, Belgium and Switzerland:
Dial 00 (for the international operator) + 52 (the country code for Mexico) + the area code + local number.

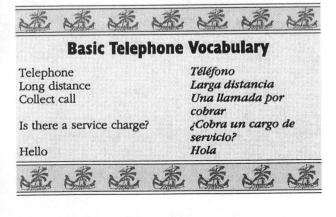

Basic Telephone Vocabulary

Telephone	*Téléfono*
Long distance	*Larga distancia*
Collect call	*Una llamada por cobrar*
Is there a service charge?	*¿Cobra un cargo de servicio?*
Hello	*Hola*

From Australia:
Dial 0011 (for the international operator) + 52 (the country code for Mexico) + the area code + local number.

Calling Abroad from Mexico

As a general rule, it is more economical to call collect; the best option for Canadian, American and British citizens wishing to call someone in their native country is through a direct collect-call service (eg. Canada Direct). It is recommended that you not make calls abroad from hotels as these charge guests up to $4 US, even for collect and toll-free calls. Local calls from hotels can cost up to 3 pesos per call, while at phone booths they cost 50 centavos.

In addition, be wary of the service *Larga Distancia, To call the USA collect or with credit card Simply Dial 0* that is advertised throughout the area and at the airport. This business, which is also identified by a logo depicting a red maple leaf, sometimes confuses Canadian visitors who mistake it for Canada Direct. In reality it is a completely separate business, which charges exorbitant rates for every call. Calls to North America with this service cost no less than 23 pesos per min-

ute and calls to Europe cost 27 pesos per minute, when the caller pays cash. Credit card payment is even more expensive.

Note that the toll-free numbers (*1-888* or *1-800*) mentioned in this guide are only accessible in North America.

Direct Access Numbers

Canada Direct
☎*01-800-123-0200*

AT&T (CAN)
☎*95-800-010-1991*

AT&T (US)
☎*95-800-462-4240*

Sprint (US)
☎*95-800-877-8000*

MCI (US)
☎*95-800-674-7000*

BT (GB)
☎*98 800 4400*

Dialling Direct

To call North America:
Dial 00-1 + the area code + the local number.

For other international calls:
Dial 00 + country code + area code + local number. For long-distance calls within Mexico, dial 0 + local number.

Country Codes

Australia	*61*
Belgium	*32*
Germany	*49*
Great Britain	*44*
Holland	*31*
Italy	*39*
New Zealand	*64*
Spain	*34*
Switzerland	*41*

Operator Assistance

- for local calls, dial 0
- for international calls, dial 09
- for calls within Mexico, dial 02
- for information, dial 04
- for an English-speaking operator, dial 09
- for the time, dial 03

Area Codes

Campeche	*981*
Cancún	*98*
Chetumal	*983*
Cozumel, Playa de Carmen and Isla Mujeres	*987*
Mérida	*99*
Mexico City	*5*
Valladolid	*985*

Fax

Faxes may be sent from post offices at the cost of about $1.75 per page, plus long distance charges, if applicable, at the rate of $3 per min.

Internet

The following companies provide Internet access:

Internet Cancún
Avenida Uxmal 65B, Cancún
☎(98) 872601
≈(98) 843809
info@Cancun.rce.com.mx
Contact: Juan Bou Riquer

ImageNet
Avenida Nader 138, SM 3
CP 77500, Cancún
☎(98) 847144
≈(98) 269270
flavio@imagenet.com.mx
Contact: Flavio Reyes Ramírez.

Accommodations

Many types of accommodation are available to tourists in this region, from modest *palapas* to international calibre luxury hotels. Usually, hotel reception employees speak at least a modicum of English. It is customary to leave $1 per bag for the porter and $1-$2 per day for the room-cleaning service, which may be left at the end of your stay or daily, well in view on the dresser. A tip upon arrival will guarantee excellent service.

Given that departure formalities are usually time-consuming, budget a few extra minutes for a delay at the reception desk. If you

Practical Information

are planning to check out after 1pm, check with the reception desk staff. Most hotels accept extensions of one or two hours for check-out times if they have been forewarned. Once the bill is settled you will be given a pass *(pase de salida)* that you must remit to the bellhop upon departure.

Most larger hotels accept credit cards, while smaller hotels rarely do.

Rates

The rates mentioned in this guide are for a standard room for two people during the high season. A tax of 17% is added to these prices.

$ = less than $50 US
$$ = $50 to $80 US
$$$ = $80 to $130 US
$$$$ = $130 to $180 US
$$$$$ = more than $180 US

Hotels

There are three categories of hotels. Near downtown areas are low-budget, minimal-comfort hotels. Rooms usually include a washroom and a ceiling fan. The second category includes moderately priced hotels that generally offer simply decorated, air-conditioned rooms. These are found in resort areas and in

larger towns or cities. Finally, superior quality hotels have been established in Cancún's hotel zone and in Playa del Carmen, Cozumel and Isla Mujeres. These surpass all others in luxury and comort. Among the hotels of this category, there are many large international chains, notably Jack Tar Villge, Camino Real, Hyatt Regency and the Sheraton.

Most establishments have their own water purification systems, indicated by a sticker on the bathroom mirror; if you do not see this sticker, inquire at the reception desk. Otherwise, hotels often provide free bottled water, placed in the washroom.

Most hotels offer satellite television, giving guests remote controls upon arrival, which must be returned. Beach-towel rental is also strictly monitored and there are expensive fees for guests who do not return towels at the end of each day.

Finally, some hotels offer all-inclusive packages, including two or three meals a day, as well as domestic drinks, taxes, and service (see further below).

Apartment Hotels

Apartment hotels are full-service hotels with rooms that include equipped kitchenettes. For longer stays in Mexico this is an economical option. Apartment hotels are especially practical for families travelling with children, who can eat at their convenience without having to suffer through their parents' long restaurant meals.

Time-Shares

Sales of time-share apartments in Mexico are soaring. In fact, Mexico ranks second in the world after the United States for the total number of time-share residences. This system, whereby hotel stays of a set number of weeks per year extending over several years are sold, has been the subject of much discussion.

Vacationers are often harrassed by salespeople who pop up at every street corner, especially in Cancún. Those who grant them an audience are generally offered appealing gifts to participate in an information session (meals, helicopter tours, free accommodation, cash). These offers are always "without obligation", but not without pressure... If you are able to listen to an hours-long sales pitch without being drawn in, take advantage of these offers to visit fabulous resorts. Remember that if it sounds too good to be true, it probably is.

Haciendas

Haciendas are grand colonial homes that once belonged to the founding land-owners of Mexico. These are vast, magnificently decorated residences with interior courtyards. Some have been converted into hotels.

Cabañas

Cabañas can be found pretty much throughtout the Cancún-Tulúm corridor and consist of rooms in little detached buildings that are generally inexpensive and that sometimes include a kitchenette.

Palapas

These little circular rooms with thatch roofs are the traditional homes of the

Maya. There are smaller ones, with only room for a hammock, and larger ones, with double beds and closets. This is the most economical type of lodging and is very popular in Playa del Carmen.

Bed and Breakfasts

The comfort of the bed and breakfasts found here varies greatly from one to the next and usually does not include a private bathroom.

Youth Hostels

Youth hostels, offering dormitories of single beds and cafeterias or common kitchens, are available in the region.

Campgrounds

Campgrounds are rare in Cancún and Cozumel. The best area for camping is the Cancún-Tulúm corridor where little seaside hotel owners will let you put up a tent or hang a hammock for $2. These deals are negotiated rather informally, although there is an organized campground in Playa del Carmen that can accommodate recreational vehicles.

All-inclusive Packages in Cancún

In recent years, a formula of all-inclusive holiday packages has become popular in Cancún: for a fixed rate, for stays of one or two weeks, the hotel provides three meals per day and national drinks. This formula seems to be a good deal for the client, but it does have several disadvantages. Imagine having 21 meals in one week at the same restaurant. Usually the "all-inclusive" hotels offer two or three restaurants, but actually guests eat most meals in a cafeteria from a buffet table that does not vary much from day to day.

On the other hand, since restaurants are relatively inexpensive in Mexico, a budget for three meals per day outside the hotel, as well as for drinks, in US dollars would be as follows:

Breakfast	*$5*
Lunch	*$8*
Dinner	*$12*
Drinks	*$5*
TOTAL	*$30*

An all-inclusive package thus provides a savings of $140 US per week, hardly worth depriving oneself of the pleasure of the area's range of restaurants, of choosing where to eat every day according to your mood, and of the joy of discovery. Is the luxury of whimsy not one of the main reasons people travel? In fact, most guests at all-inclusive hotels go out at least a few times and spend part of their $140 savings anyway.

For some, another major inconvenience of an all-inclusive package is that most guests tend to spend all day at the hotel, and staff organize activities for them that are often disruptive and noisy, such as pool aerobics, volleyball tournaments, or dance competitions with blaring American music. Most of the time these activities have nothing at all to do with the Mexico travellers come to discover.

Restaurants and Food

There is a multitude of excellent restaurants in this region, some specialized in Mexican cuisine and others in international cuisines, notably Italian and French. There are also a few vegetarian restaurants. Outside of the resort towns, though, restaurants serve only local cuisine.

Use your judgement when choosing a restaurant – if it is packed, it is probably for a good reason. Marvellous discoveries are waiting to be made outside your hotel. This guide includes a large selection of the best spots.

Meals take longer in Mexico, since the service is often slower and because it is customary to spend longer at the table. You will have to ask for the bill (la cuenta, por favor!), and you will without doubt have to wait a bit to get your change. This custom is thought of as polite, so there no sense being impatient.

Prices

Prices described below refer to a meal for one person, including an appetizer, an entrée, and dessert.

$ = less than $10 US
$$ = $10 to $20 US
$$$ = $20 to $30 US
$$$$ = more than $30 US

Tipping

The term propina incluida signifies that the gratuity is included in the price. Usually, it is not included, and, depending on the quality of service, diners should budget for 10% to 15% of

Practical Information

Basic Restaurant Vocabulary

Restaurant	*restaurante*
Table	*mesa*
Menu	*menú*
An order of...	*una orden de...*
Dish	*plato*
Meal	*comida*
Snack or appetizer	*botana* or *antojito*
Breakfast	*desayuno*
Lunch	*comida*
Dinner	*cena*
Beverage	*bebida*
Dessert	*postre*
Fork	*tenedor*
Knife	*cuchillo*
Spoon	*cuchara*
Napkin	*servilleta*
Cup	*taza*
Glass	*vaso*

Essential Phrases

May I see the menu?
¿Puedo ver el menú?

I would like...
Quisiera...

The bill (check) please
La cuenta, por favor

I don't eat meat
Yo no como carne

Where are the
washrooms?
*¿Dónde están los
sanitarios?*

I am vegetarian
Yo soy vegetariano

the total. Contrary to the
practice in Europe, the tip
is not included in the total,
but rather must be calcu-
lated and remitted to the
waiter by the diner. Service

and tip are one and the same thing in North America.

Mexican Cuisine

Tortillas, tacos, empanadas, enchiladas, so many terms can be confusing to those encountering Mexican cuisine for the first time. Since prejudices die hard (dishes are too spicy, for example), too often visitors faced with new, unfamiliar flavours opt for international cuisine. Although some local dishes can prove particularly spicy, Mexican cuisine offers an infinite variety of dishes, from the mildest to the hottest. As a guide through the delicious meanderings of Mexican cuisine, we have assembled a gastronomic glossary below.

Mexican dishes are often served with rice *(arroz)* and black or red beans *(frijoles)*, and a basket of hot tortillas is placed on your table. Of course, the hot sauce *(salsa)* is never very far and there are many kinds. Traditionally, salsa is prepared by mashing tomatos, onions, coriander and different spices together with a mortar.

Breakfast is *desayuno* in Spanish, *almuerzo* means lunch and *cena* dinner. The *comida corrida* is served in the late afternoon, around 5pm or 6pm, and it consists of a daily menu, which is usually reasonably priced. Mexicans do not tend to eat a lot in the evening, so don't be surprised if you go to a village restaurant after 6pm and it's closed.

Ceviche
Raw shrimp, tuna or sea pike, "cooked" only in lime juice. In Mexico, onions, tomatoes, hot peppers and coriander are added.

Chicharrón
Fried pork rind, usually served with an apéritif.

Chile
Fresh or dried peppers (there are more than 100 varieties) that are prepared in a thousand different ways: stuffed, or as stuffing, boiled, fried, etc.

Empanadas
Thin corn pancakes in the shape of turnovers, stuffed with meat, poultry or fish.

Enchiladas
Rolled and baked tortillas (see further below), enchiladas are generally stuffed with chicken, covered with a spicy sauce, sliced onions

and cream, and sometimes sprinkled with cheese.

Fajitas
Strips of marinated chicken grilled with onions. Fajitas are usually served with tomato sauce, cream and vegetables, and can be wrapped in a tortilla.

Gazpacho
A delicious and refreshing cold soup made with tomatoes, peppers, celery, onions, olive oil, cucumbers, lemon juice and garlic. Gazpacho is sometimes served with croutons.

Guacamole
Salted and peppered purée of avocado mixed with diced tomatoes, onions, fresh peppers and a bit of lime juice. Even when this dish is not on the menu, do not hesitate to ask for *guacamole con totopos* (with corn chips), a very common dish that makes a refreshing appetizer or snack.

Huevos Rancheros
Two or three fried eggs served on a corn tortilla and covered with a spicy tomato sauce. Huevos rancheros are sometimes served with potatoes on the side. This is a good dish for those with strong stomachs who want to start the day off with a good breakfast.

Mole
This term designates a category of creamy sauces composed of mixtures of spices, nuts, chocolate, tomatoes, tortillas, peppers, onions, and other foodstuffs varying by region. The most famous of these are Mole Poblano and Mole Negro Oaxaqueno, both made with a base of chocolate and spices. These sauces accompany poultry and meat.

Nopales
Cactus leaves (without the spines, of course!) cooked in water or served in a soup or salad. The juice of these is also offered at breakfast.

Pozole
A corn and pork stew with radishes, onions, coriander and lime juice. There are two varieties, red and green. The red is hotter.

Quesadillas
A sort of crepe stuffed with cheese and cream.

Sopa de Lima
A hot soup made with chicken, lemon or lime, and mixed with pieces of corn tortillas.

Tacos
A sort of rolled corn crepe often stuffed with chicken, but also frequently with other preparations. Stalls on the street make tacos with

Recipes

Guacamole (Avocado dip)
serves 6

2 large avocadoes
1 small onion, finely chopped
1 to 2 sliced hot peppers
1 large tomato, peeled and chopped
fresh or dried coriander
lime juice
salt

Guacamole should not be prepared in a blender because its texture is not supposed to be homogeneous. In a bowl, mash the avocadoes with a fork and sprinkle them with lime juice. Carefully mix the avocado, onion, peppers, tomato and coriander. Add a pinch of salt and serve immediately with tacos.

Cruda (Mexican sauce)
Makes about a cup and a half (350 ml)

1 medium tomato, not peeled
1 onion, finely diced
2 tbsp. coarsely chopped coriander
3 finely chopped hot peppers
1/2 tsp. bitter orange juice
75 ml cold water

Cruda is a chunky, refreshing sauce for tortillas and is often served with eggs for breakfast, and with roasted meat and tacos in the evening. Chop the tomato and mix it with the other ingredients. This sauce can be prepared up to 3hrs ahead of time, but it is best eaten right away so that it doesn't lose its crunchy texture.

Practical Information

marinated, grilled meat which is served on a tortilla with your choice of salsa and vegetables.

Tamales
Corn husks stuffed with meat, poultry, or fish. Many vegetables and spices are also added to the stuffing, varying according to region. Tamales are cooked wrapped in banana-tree leaves.

Topos
These are a rough equivalent to North American potato chips. Made with corn here, they may be round or triangular.

Tortillas
As opposed to Spanish tortillas (made with eggs and potatoes), Mexican tortillas are flat pancakes with a corn-flour base, cooked on an unoiled griddle. Generally they accompany other dishes. Traditionally made by hand, today tortillas are mass produced in food-processing factories. Tortillas are also increasingly being made using white flour.

Tacos, quesadillas and burritos can be made with corn tortillas or flour (especially tacos and quesadillas). The corn tortillas can be hard or soft, depending on your taste.

Mexican Drinks

Beer

Several companies brew beer in Mexico, among them the famous Corona, Dos Equis (XX) and Superior. All three are good, but the most popular is Corona. Many hotels and restaurants also carry imported beers.

Wine

Local wines are inexpensive and generally good. Try Calafia, L.A. Cetto or Los Reyes.

Tequila

The Mexican national drink is squeezed from the bulbous base of the agave, a plant indigenous to Mexico that looks like a pineapple. The juice collected is then slowly fermented producing a dry, white alcohol. The recipe for tequila was invented in the Sate of Jalisco, probably in the 18th century. As any Mexican will tell you, not all tequilas are the same: the taste of tequila varies from more pungent white varieties, to golden *añejos* with a mellower flavour, close to brandy. The best brands are Orendain, Hornitos, Herradura Reposado and Tres Generaciones.

Margarita and Sangrita

The Mexican margarita is probably stronger than the one with which most travellers are familiar. It is made of tequila, Cointreau, lime, lemon and salt. Try a *sangrita*, grenadine with juice extracted from bitter oranges that chases little sips of tequila.

Kahlúa

Kahlúa is a coffee liqueur originally distilled in Mexico and now produced in Europe as well.

Xtabentún

Many regions have a local liqueur. In the Yucatán it is *Xtabentún* (pronounced shta-ben-toun), a subtle, honey-based, anise-flavoured liqueur.

Shopping

What to bring home

It is always fun to bring interesting local products home from a vacation. Tequila, *Xtabentún*, and Mexican vanilla are all excellent choices. Mexican crafts are colourful and original. Every region has a hand-painted pottery industry, hand-woven and hand-embroidered fabrics, ceramics, fine leather goods, and various silverwork and silver jewellery. The silver content of an item is indicated by the stamp, ".925", which signifies that the metal is 92.5% pure. *Huipils* (dresses), *guayaberas* (shirts), hammocks and braided baskets are also good gift ideas. Lovely *piñatas* (papier-mâché stars or animals filled with candy for children to break open at Christmas) are another option. Terracotta nativity figurines (nacimientos) are also very popular.

Huge seashells can be found on the wilder beaches between Cancún and Tulúm (no need to get swindled in Cancún's fancy shops). Do not forget to carefully clean shells before packing them; a fishmonger can do this for you.

The export of antique art objects, which are considered national treasures, is illegal. When purchasing reproductions, be sure that their status is well indicated to avoid headaches at customs.

Duty-Free Shops

Duty-Free shops are found in airports and basically

Practical Information

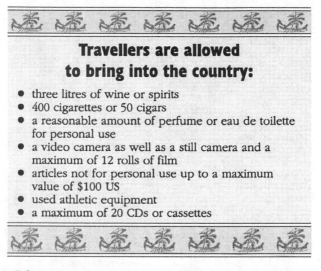

Travellers are allowed to bring into the country:

- three litres of wine or spirits
- 400 cigarettes or 50 cigars
- a reasonable amount of perfume or eau de toilette for personal use
- a video camera as well as a still camera and a maximum of 12 rolls of film
- articles not for personal use up to a maximum value of $100 US
- used athletic equipment
- a maximum of 20 CDs or cassettes

sell foreign products, such as perfume, cigarettes and liquor. Purchases must be made with US dollars. Prices in general are not especially advantageous since merchants take advantage of the tax break to increase profits.

In Mexico it is common to turn down the first price offered by a merchant and bargain over desired merchandise. A distinction is drawn, however, between fancy shops and poor artisans who sell their wares on the sidewalk at rock-bottom prices. In the latter case, bargaining is basically equivalent to an insult. Bargaining only has currency in stores outside of shopping malls. Shops are open from 9am or 10am to 1pm or 2pm, and from 4pm or 5m to 9pm or 10pm, seven days a week. In large shopping malls, where colonies of tourists gather, stores rarely close for lunch.

Be careful not to make purchases in excess of the maximum permitted by your country's customs authorities. Also think of the weight of your suitcases. Some shops can ship items that are too cumbersome for you to carry in your luggage.

Street Vendors

The tenacity of Mexican street vendors is legendary.

If you display the least bit of interest in vendors' wares, expect them to latch onto you. The best way to avoid being bothered is to demonstrate total indifference to their merchandise and, when approached, to answer firmly but politely, "*no, gracias*".

Festivals and Holidays

All banks and many businesses are closed on holidays, and the country seems to slow down. Be sure to do your banking ahead of time.

January 1
Año Nuevo
(New Year's Day)

January 6
Día de los Reyes Magos
(Epiphany) and the anniversary of the founding of Mérida

February 5
Día de la Constitución
(Constitution Day)

February 24
Día de la Bandera
(Flag Day)

March 21
Día de Nacimiento de Benito Juárez (Benito Juárez's Birthday)

May 1
Día del Trabajo (May Day)

May 5
Cinco de Mayo
(anniversary of the Battle of Puebla)

2nd Sunday in May
Día de la Madre
(Mother's Day)

September 1
First day of the new congressional session

September 16
Día de la Independencia
(Independence Day)

2nd Monday in October
Día de la Raza
(Colombus Day)

November 1
Día de Todos Santos
(All Saints Day)
Informe Presidencial
(president's address to the nation)

November 1 and 2
Día de los Muertos
(Day of the Dead)

November 20
Día de la Revolución
(Revolution Day)

December 12
Día de Nuestra Señora de Guadeloupe (festival of the Virgin of Guadeloupe)

December 25
Día de Navidad
(Christmas Day)

Practical Information

Banks and government offices are also closed during Holy Week, particularly on the Thursday and the Friday preceding Easter (Holy Week begins Palm Sunday). Many offices and businesses are closed during Christmas Week, between December 25 and January 2.

Miscellaneous

Taxes

Mexico has a value-added sales tax of 10% called the "IVA" *(impuesto de valor agregado)*, payable by tourists and residents alike, and applicable to most items. The IVA is often "hidden" in restaurant bills, the price of store merchandise and organized trips. Other taxes are levied on telephone calls, in restaurants and in hotels.

Tour Guides

Near tourist centres, many people who speak some English introduce themselves as tour guides. Some of these people are barely competent, so be skeptical. The tourist information office is a good place to find out about competent guides, or to check the credentials of somebody who has offered you guide service. These guides sometimes demand large sums in remuneration for their services, so, before embarking on a tour with one, be clear that you have agreed on exactly what services will be rendered for exactly what payment, and only pay at the very end of the tour. This Ulysses Guide permits you to travel and tour independently.

Alcohol

The legal drinking age in Mexico is 18 years. The sale of alcohol is illegal after 3am, on Sunday, and on holidays.

Smokers

Restrictions on smoking are increasingly common. Smoking on buses is prohibited, although this rule is not respected to the letter, and people are very tolerant. Smoking in all other public areas is permitted.

Electricity

Local electricity operates at 110 volts AC, as in North America. Plugs have two flat pins, so Europeans will need both a converter and a wall socket adapter.

Women Travellers

Women travelling alone in the Yucatán should not have any problems. In general, locals are friendly and not too aggressive. Although men treat women with respect and harassment is relatively rare, Mexicans will undoubtedly flirt with female travellers – politely, though. Dress is at women's discretion in Cancún, except in restaurants and churches. In smaller villages, foreign women stand out, especially when their dress is more revealing (short skirts, for example). Of course, a minimum amount of caution is required; for example, women should avoid walking alone through poorly lit areas at night. If you do run into trouble, simply approach other, friendly looking women and explain the situation.

Time Zones

Mexico is divided into three time zones. The country switches to daylight-saving time between the first Sunday in April and the last Sunday in October (clocks are put ahead one hour). The Yucatán is one hour behind Eastern Standard Time and six hours behind Greenwich Mean Time.

Newspapers and Magazines

Among the most prevalent publications in the Yucatán are a number of small magazines in which information is disseminated through advertisements. Their content, laid out in journalistic style, is nothing more than publicity. Updates consist of replacing cover photographs. These magazines are essentially useful for the maps they include.

The most popular of these magazines is incontrovertible *Cancún Tips*, which covers in brief all of the topics in a traditional travel guide. Tourist information offices distribute this magazine as though it were an official government publication. *Cancún Tips*, published quarterly and available for free in Spanish and in English, has the advantage of being easy to consult. A more substantial version, with more in-depth articles, is distributed in hotel rooms (along with the Bible and the phone book).

Other magazines of this ilk include *Cancún Nights, Mexican Carribean, La Iguana* in Cozumel and *Destination Playa del Carmen*. If each of these publications targets a different readership, they all have one thing in common: they are all free and crammed full of discount coupons that can somewhat reduce the high cost of vacationing in the Cancún-Cozumel region.

For more substance and information on current events, *Por Esto* is a very interesting daily paper, published in Spanish, that is available everywhere for three pesos. It covers in detail subjects related to the main economic base of the region: tourism (union crisis in a hotel, opening of a major new attraction, etc.). Slightly more highbrow, *Chronica de Cancún* publishes an interesting culture insert on Saturdays, entitled *"cada siete"*, which includes information on local celebrities and artists.

Finally, *Novedades de Quintana Roo*, a large-format magazine, provides indepth coverage of political and national issues.

Weights and Measures

Mexico uses the metric system. Here are a few equivalencies.

Weights
1 pound (lb)
= 454 grams (g)

1 kilogram (kg)
= 2.2 pounds (lbs)

Linear Measure
1 inch
= 2.2 centimetres (cm)

1 foot (ft)
= 30 centimetres (cm)

1 mile
= 1.6 kilometres (km)

1 kilometres (km)
= 0.63 miles

1 metre (m)
= 39.37 inches

Land Measure
1 acre = 0.4 hectare
1 hectare = 2.471 acres

Volume Measure
1 U.S. gallon (gal)
= 3.79 litres

1 U.S. gallon (gal)
= 0.83 imperial gallon

Temperature
To convert °F into °C: subtract 32, divide by 9, multiply by 5

To convert °C into °F: multiply by 9, divide by 5, add 32.

Outdoors

A veritable paradise for divers, and watersports lovers in general, the coasts of the Yucatán Peninsula provide the necessary geography for other activities as well, for the most part on the very grounds of hotels: golf, cycling on bicycle paths, bird-watching, hiking in various national parks, tennis...

This region, with its large recreation centres (Xel-Há and Xcaret) and world-famous diving areas (Cancún and Cozumel), has much to offer.

This chapter lists the most popular outdoor activities, providing an overview of the sporting options in the area. In chapters devoted to specific regions, the sections "Parks and Beaches" and "Outdoor Activities" include additional, more detailed and precise information on outdoor activities

Parks

The natural assets of this region have been protected by the establishment of numerous national parks. Isla Contoy, north of Isla

Mujeres, is a haven for marine birds. An observation tower and an interpretive centre have been constructed on the island for the better admiration of these avian species.

The national park of Tulúm conceals fabulous Mayan ruins in its 672ha. The area is covered in mangrove swamps and coastal dunes, and its turquoise waters are inviting for swimming and scuba diving.

The Sian Ka'an biosphere reserve is situated a few kilometres south of the Mayan ruins of Tulúm and spans close to 100 kilometres of shoreline. It comprises a multitude of bays, lagoons and coral reefs that are part of the second largest barrier reef in the world, and is inhabited by many aquatic species. Twenty-three ancient Mayan sites have been found in this reserve. Animal species such as the puma, the ocelot, the spider monkey and the toucan live here. A day trip into the reserve is possible with Amigos de Sian Ka'an, a private, non-profit organization, for approximately $100 US (**☎849583**).

Río Lagartos, on the north coast of the Yucatán, is a very special ecological reserve because it is the principal Mexican nesting ground of pink flamingoes, which form large colonies, and also of herons.

Outdoor Activities

Swimming

The east coast of the Yucatán (including Cancún, Tulúm, and Cozumel) has some of the calmest waters in Mexico, although ground swells are not completely unheard of here. Access is unlimited to these beaches the waters of which cover the palette of blues and greens and the white sands of which stay cool underfoot. These limpid waters, dotted with coral reefs, shelter abundant marine wildlife.

Since the coast of the State of Quintana Roo is actually one long beach, it is possible to walk for long periods in perfect solitude. In Cancún, expect a completely different picture: the city is literally overrun during the high season.

In general, in Cancún, the beaches of the western shore are quieter than those of the east coast, and their calmer waters (protected from the wind) are ideal for swimming. The more exposed east coast is battered by constant waves and wind, although it is possible to discover stunning cliffs and bays that are safe for swimming.

When the waves are very strong, regardless of where you are, avoid swimming altogether or do so very cautiously. Remember that few establishments provide lifeguard service. A flag system on the beaches indicates the degree of risk for would-be swimmers, sort of in the fashion of traffic lights. A red or black flag indicates danger; a yellow flag is cautionary; a blue or green flag signals that the situation is normal; ideal swimming conditions are represented by white flags.

Although the practice seems to be tolerated in Cancún and Playa del Carmen, most of the time it is strictly forbidden to sunbathe nude or topless and doing so will certainly cause quite a stir among residents and hotel employees, not to mention a few tourists.

Scuba Diving

Underwater adventurers are catered to by many diving centres, mainly found in Cancún, Playa del Carmen and Cozumel, and reefs are numerous in this region.

Certified divers can explore the secrets of the Yucatec coastline to their heart's content. Others can still experience breathing underwater, but must be accompanied by a qualified guide, who will supervise their descent (to a depth of 5m). There is little danger; however, be sure that the supervision is adequate. Some instructors take more than one diver down at a time, which goes against the rules.

Equipment can easily be rented from the different centres along the coasts, but it can be expensive. If you have your own equipment you'll save money by bringing it along, especially if you are planning several days of diving.

Cozumel is world famous for the crystalline clarity of its waters, the richness of its marine life and its excellent facilities. Greater than half

Outdoors

of the island's visitors come to it of for one reason, and one reason only: diving. Isla Mujeres is equally highly rated. Cancún's many dive shops organize guided excursions to the best diving spots around the city.

Scuba diving makes it possible to discover fascinating sights like coral reefs, schools of multi-coloured fish and amazing underwater plants. Don't forget that this ecosystem is fragile and deserves special attention. All divers must respect a few basic **safety guidelines** in order to protect these natural sites: do not touch anything; do not take pieces of coral; do not feed the fish; be careful not to disturb anything with your fins, and, of course, do not litter. If you want a souvenir of your underwater experience, disposable underwater cameras are available.

A Fragile Ecosystem

Coral reefs are formed by minuscule organisms called coelenterate polyps, which are very sensitive to water pollution. The high level of nitrates in polluted water accelerates the growth of seaweed, which in turn takes over the coral, stops it from growing and literally smothers it. Sea urchins (whose long spikes can cause severe injuries) live on the coral and play a major role in controlling the amount of seaweed that grows on the coral by eating what the fish cannot. An epidemic threatened the survival of many reefs in 1983, when the waters became so polluted that sea urchins were affected and seaweed flourished in the Caribbean waters. Scientific studies have since proved the importance of urchins to the ecological balance, and the species has thus been restored on certain reefs. However, these little urchins cannot solve the problem on their own. Pollution control is essential if the coral reefs, upon which 400,000 organisms depend, are to survive.

Snorkelling

It doesn't take much to snorkel: a mask, a snorkel and some fins. Anyone can enjoy this activity, which is a great way to develop an appreciation for the richness of the underwater world. Not far from several beaches, you can go snorkelling around coral reefs inhabited by various underwater species. Remember that the basic rules for protecting the underwater environment (see scuba diving section) must also be respected when snorkelling.

Windsurfing, Jet-skiing and Waterskiing

These activities require calmer waters than the rough seas that bathe the coast of Cancún and surround Cozumel. The calm waters of the lagoon of Nichupté in Cancún, or of Bahía Mujeres, on the west coast, are therefore recommended.

If you have never tried these activities, there are a few safety measures to be aware of: choose a beach where the water is calm, watch out for swimmers and divers, don't head too far from shore (if you get into trouble don't hesitate to wave your arms to signal your distress); wear shoes so that you don't cut your feet on the rocks.

Cruises

Excursions aboard sailboats and yachts offer another enchanting way to freely explore the sea's sparkling waves. Some centres organize trips, while others rent sailboats to experienced sailors. You will find a few addresses throughout the guide.

Non-divers can appreciate the marvellous scenery of the deep sea without getting wet thanks to observation submarines and glassbottom boats that allow for discovery of marine fauna and coral reefs.

Fishing

It is possible to participate in day-long or half-day sport fishing tournaments that depart from Cancún, Cozumel and Playa del Carmen as long as you reserve a few days in advance with an outfitter. Mackerel, swordfish, tuna and red snapper are abundant in the area. Prices are between $240 and $300 per boat, per day.

Golf

The State of Quintana Roo is home to a few golf courses. Among these, Pok-Ta-Pok in Cancún was designed by world-famous landscape architect Robert Trent Jones Jr. and offers an ocean view as well as the peculiarity of Mayan ruin obstacles.

The undulating grounds of Playacar (in Playa del Carmen), one of the best-rated courses in the country, laid out by Robert von Hagge, are also worth a few tee-offs. Other courses can be found in Cancún at the Caesar Park hotel, the Melia Cancún and the Resort Course of Puerto Aventuras. The Cancún Palace Hotel offers an original 36-hole mini-putt.

Bird-watching

The national parks as well as the outskirts of the large archaeological sites of the Yucatán are preferred locations for the observation of winged wildlife. A great variety of birds may be admired in the tropical forest of Sian Ka'an, on Isla Contoy (where 97 species are protected), as well as at Xaman-Há, an ornithological reserve near Playa del Carmen that shelters about 30 bird species including toucans and parrots.

Bicycling

In Cancún it is practically impossible to cycle elsewhere but on the 14km bicycle path that is laid out along the west side of the hotel zone from Punta Cancún to downtown. This path, which runs alongside a busy two-lane road, is also used by roller-bladers and joggers, and is poorly lit at night. In Cozumel and Isla Mujeres, bicycles may be rented for between $5 and $8 per day. Do not overestimate your stamina – the

Frigate bird

Unexpected meetings often provide astonishing ornithological discoveries: merging with the landscape, a perched male frigate bird will suddenly swell his scarlet throat to seduce a female and successfully attract the eyes of onlookers.

To ensure the success of your expedition, bring binoculars, insect repellent and a camera with a telephoto lens.

sun beats down hard on this region and the roads are far from easy terrain. The best time for cycling is the very early morning, before temperatures peak. Avoid riding at nightfall since many roads are unlit.

Horseback Riding

There are few rental stables, Rancho Buenavista in Cozumel and Rancho Loma Bonita in Cancún among them. It is possible to ride at Xcaret for $30 per hour. For more information, consult the "Outdoor Activities" sections of the chapters on areas of interest to you.

Tennis

Some hotels have tennis courts at guests' disposal. Many of these are lit for evening play. Unfortunately, in most cases balls and rackets are not furnished by these establishments and the courts are in very poor condition.

Outdoors

Cancún

Before the Mexican government decided to transform a strip of sand inhabited by about a hundred Mayan fishermen into a major tourist resort, Cancún was a peaceful, isolated paradise.

As they went about their usual business, the local fishermen surely had little idea that scores of bureaucrats were studying all sorts of computer-compiled data indicating, beyond the shadow of a doubt, that Cancún had the potential to attract more tourists season after season than anywhere else in Mexico.

In a little over 20 years, Cancún mushroomed into a town of 30,000 inhabitants, with about a hundred hotels able to accommodate a total of two million tourists year-round in some 19,000 rooms, as well as hundreds of restaurants and shops.

It all began in the 1960s, when Mexico became aware of its own tourist potential. In 1967, Cancún was officially chosen as the site on which to develop the infrastructure for a mega-project, thanks to its long, white-sand beach, subtropical climate, turquoise Caribbean waters and proximity to the region's other tourist spots.

Construction was begun on roads, aqueducts and hotels in 1974, but the place remained relatively unknown until the mid-1980s, when a whirlwind of activity hit the area: hotels sprouted up like mushrooms and Cancún became a tourist resort par excellence.

Cancún has been designed to please its major clientele, US tourists, who account for 60% of all visitors to the city. It's just like home for them here, with the same big restaurant and hotel chains, the same supermarkets, the same music in the nightclubs. Everything is tailor-made to suit their tastes. Furthermore, English often prevails over Spanish in conversation. This divests the place of much of its exotic charm, but obviously appeals to many people: Cancún is one of the most popular Mexican destinations for foreign tourists.

Cancún is made up of Ciudad Cancún (Cancún City) and the Zona Hotelera (Hotel Zone). It is one of the only cities in the world where residents and tourists are so clearly separated. The 22.5km-long Hotel Zone is covered with gigantic, international-class hotels. These stand side by side between the sea and a wide road.

Most residents of Cancún City work in the local hotels, bars and restaurants, and most were born elsewhere; only the children and adolescents are Cancún natives.

Cancún is a convenient gateway for travellers wishing to explore the Mayan ruins at Chichén Itza and Tulúm, and to immerse themselves in the traditional Yucatec lifestyle, which can

Chichén Itzá is awe-inspiring, not only for its majestic grace but for its magnificently preserved architecture providing details about life in this great city. - *Tibor Bognar*

Two temples with bas-reliefs of Chac reach up to the sky.
- Alain Legault

be traced directly back to the ancient Maya.

Finding Your Way Around

The Hotel Zone, for its part, is simply a strip of land, and thus seems like an easy place to find your way around. However, it is altogether possible to confuse the Laguna Nichupté with the Caribbean, making it hard to know whether to turn left or right! As you will probably be getting around by bus, ask the driver for directions in case of doubt.

In downtown Cancún, street names and numbers are rarely indicated. It is therefore wise to bring a map along on all outings, even though the city is not very big. Picking out a few landmarks is a good trick.

The city is divided into *supermanzanas*, which are like districts. The addresses are thus followed by the letters SM and the appropriate number. Each SM has its own postal code.

Cancún International Airport

Cancún International Airport (☎*860028*) is located about 20km southwest of the Hotel Zone. Thanks to recent renovations, it is now one of the most modern airports in Mexico. In addition to a currency exchange office and a duty-free shop, it houses several stores, restaurants and bars, whose prices, as in any airport, are slightly higher than in town.

Several car-rental agencies have counters at the airport. To avoid paying through the nose, it is best to reserve a car from home and compare rates. Ask for the agency to fax you a confirmation of the rate and your reservation. Most big companies have toll-free (*1-800* or *1-888*) numbers that can be used anywhere in North America. When comparing rates, make sure to factor in the taxes, the number of free kilometres offered and any insurance fees. Here are the names and numbers of the agencies with branches at the airport:

Monterrey Rent
☎*860239*

Economovil
☎*860082*

Cancún

Avis
☎860222
☎1-800-321-3652

Budget
☎860026
☎1-800-268-8970

Hertz
☎860150
☎1-800-263-0678

National/Tilden
☎1-800-361-5334

Dollar
☎860133
☎1-800-800-4000

Entering and Leaving the City

If you rent a car at the airport, which is located 16km south of the city, it will take you only about 15min to get downtown. If you are going to the Hotel Zone, take Paseo Kukulcán, which you will see right after you get on Avenida Tulúm. Within a few minutes, you will be at the bottom end of the Hotel Zone, which is shaped like a "7".

There is a shuttle service between the airport and downtown Cancún (about $10). The return trip is included in some vacation packages. The buses are spacious and surprisingly punctual. Be careful on the day of your departure, as the shuttle driver might get to the hotel early and leave immediately for the airport without waiting for you. To avoid this catastrophe, be ready 30 min before the shuttle is scheduled to arrive and wait for it outside.

It should be noted that taxis are only allowed to take travellers to the airport, while public buses can only carry tourists from the airport to their hotel.

If you are driving to Tulúm (or farther south) from the Hotel Zone, you will save yourself a lot of time by avoiding the downtown area. Drive to the southern tip of the Hotel Zone, toward Punta Nizuc, then continue to Avenida Tulúm, where you will see a sign showing the way.

To get to Valladolid, Chichén Itzá or Mérida, take Avenida Uxmal (Route 180) from downtown Cancún.

If you want to go to Isla Mujeres, you will have to take the ferry at Puerto Juárez, 3km north of Cancún. To get there by bus, go to the terminal at the intersection of Avenidas Tulúm and Uxmal. There are frequent departures, and it's only a 5km trip. Another much more expensive but more convenient option is to take *The Shuttle* which leaves from Playa Tortugas, in the northern part of the Hotel Zone.

Taxis run from the airport to the Zona Hotelera for $32, so sharing it costs less.

In Town

There are four main avenues in downtown Cancún: Cobá and Uxmal run east-west, while Tulúm and Yaxchilán run north-south. The latter two are the most commercially developed, with scores of shops, restaurants, hotels and exchange offices.

The best place to catch a bus to the hotel strip is near the traffic circle at the corner of Cobá and Tulúm.

By Car

Unless you are truly allergic to public transportation, renting a car to travel back and forth between your hotel and downtown Cancún is a needless expense and is sure to cause you all sorts of headaches. There is frequent bus service, the fares are cheap and the downtown area is

not that big. You will waste a lot of time looking for parking – and trying to find your way! Furthermore, the car-rental rates are fairly high in Cancún. If you do rent a car for an excursion, you will undoubtedly have to drive through the city. Bear in mind that the speed limit is 40 kph. There is a Pemex service station on Route 307, between Cancún and the airport. Make sure to fill up your tank, as gas stations are hard to find in this region.

The major car-rental agencies have branches at the airport and downtown, as well as in certain hotels:

Avis
Playa Maya Fair, Blvd Kukulcán
☎830-044

Budget
Avenida Tulúm 231
☎840-730

Hertz
Reno 35
☎876-634

By Taxi

The local taxis have no meters, so the fare depends on the distance covered, the cost of gas and your bargaining skills. The staff at the front desk of your hotel can tell you what the

Cancún

going rates are. A trip from the Hotel Zone downtown or vice versa generally costs $8 and up. The farther your hotel is from downtown, of course, the more you will have to pay. Always determine the fare with the driver before getting in the taxi. There is a taxi drivers' union (☎831840), where you can obtain information or file a complaint.

By Bus

Bus station
Corner of Avenidas Tulúm and Uxmal
☎841378
☎843948
The bus station is open 24hrs a day and offers service to a whole slew of destinations, from the capital, México City, to Chetumal, on the Belize border. The fares for first-class and second-class buses are almost the same.

Within Cancún City and the Hotel Zone, the bus fare is 4.5 pesos *(about $0.50)*. Several bus companies are competing fiercely for the lucrative tourist market, and their vehicles tear up and down the Paseo Kukulcán, which runs through the Hotel Zone. If they are not full and you are not at one of their official stops, you can sometimes flag one down one with a wave of your hand. Most buses run around the clock.

Practical Information

Tourist Office

Quintana Roo tourist office
Mon to Fri 9am to 9pm
Avenida Tulúm, between the Multibanco Comerex and City Hall
☎848073
The staff here can provide some helpful information. They are sure to give you the latest edition of the complimentary publication *Cancún Tips*, which is full of advertisements but nonetheless contains some pertinent information, as well as some very useful maps of the city.

Post Office

Post office
Avenida Sunyaxchén
near Avenida Yaxchilán
☎841418
It is open from 8am to 5pm on weekdays and from 9am to 1pm on weekends. Most hotels in the Zona Hotelera sell stamps and can mail your letters or postcards.

Telephone

You need a Ladatel phone card to use the public

telephones, which are all over the place but don't always work very well. If you are tempted to use the phone in your room, bear in mind that there is an exorbitant charge for each call. Hotels even collect a 60% surcharge for overseas calls! Pick up a Ladatel card as soon as you arrive, in case you need to make a call. Cards are sold at many shopping centres, as well as certain exchange offices.

Banks and Exchange Offices

You can cash travellers' cheques at the front desk of your hotel, at a bank or at any of the numerous exchange offices *(casas de cambio)* downtown and in the Hotel Zone. Exchange offices usually offer better rates than banks and stay open later, until 9pm. Banks are open on weekdays from 9am to 5pm. Here are two you might try:

Banamex
Avenida Tulúm, next to City Hall
☎845411

Bancomer
Avenida Tulúm 20
☎844400

There is an exchange office at the airport, but it is not always open and better rates are available downtown.

Safety

Emergencies
☎06

Fire Department
☎841202

Police Station
In the Palacio Municipal Avenida Tulúm, SM5
☎841913

Hospital Americano
open 24hrs
Calle Viento 15
☎846133
Offers assistance in English.

Total Assist
open 24hrs
Clavelas 5
Offers assistance in English.

Exploring

Long before it became the great seaside resort it is today, the site of Cancún was described by explorer John Lloyd Stephens, who "discovered" it in 1842. Among other works, Stephens wrote *Incidents of Travel in the Yucatán* (1843), which describes his archaeological discoveries in the Yucatán. The city of Cancún as such was built in the 1960s, and is thus very new. It is quite poor and of little architectural interest.

Cancún

Its only real charm is its inhabitants. On the other hand, many Mayan ruins have been excavated in the area, mainly between Punta Cancún and Punta Nizuc, along the shore in the Hotel Zone. Cancún's main tourist attractions are its long beach washed by the Caribbean, its renowned golf courses and its luxury hotels.

The Hotel Zone (Zona Hotelera)

Cancún's Mayan ruins, major shopping centres and Centro de Convenciones (convention centre) are all located in the Hotel Zone, where the hotels and other buildings are lined up in the shape of a "7". There are no residential buildings in this area, and it is hard to walk around here, as the traffic moves at high speeds and the sidewalks are not always well-maintained. If you decide to tour the Zona Hotelera on foot, bear in mind that the distances are considerable; bring along some change so that you can hop on a bus when you feel like it. You can also stop in at any of the hotels along the way and take a little rest in one of its bars or restaurants.

If you set out from downtown Cancún, your first stop will be the **Golf Pok-Ta-Pok** (*Paseo Kukulcán, between km 6 and 7*), where two small Mayan ruins have been integrated into the course. You have to ask for permission to visit the ruins at the club entrance, and walk for about 15min. Another, less interesting set of ruins, **Ni Ku**, is integrated into the architecture of the Camino Real hotel, on the Punta Cancún beach, in the angle of the "7". Right nearby, you will see the **Centro de Convenciones** (*Paseo Kukulcán, Km 9, ☎830199*), a modern building where many cultural events and all sorts of other gatherings are held; it contains several restaurants, shops and service businesses.

On the ground floor of the Centro de Convenciones, there is a small museum devoted to Mayan history called the cultural centre of **El Instituto Nacional de Antropología e Historia** (*$3; free admission Sun, Tue to Sun 9am to 5pm; guided tours in English, French, German and Spanish; Paseo Kukulcán, Km 9.5; ☎833671*), the national institute of anthropology and history. It displays over 1,000 interesting Mayan relics, such as decorated terracotta vases and jade masks, found all over Quintana Roo.

The ruins of **Yamil Lu'um** (*Paseo Kukulcán, Km 12, on the grounds of the Sheraton*

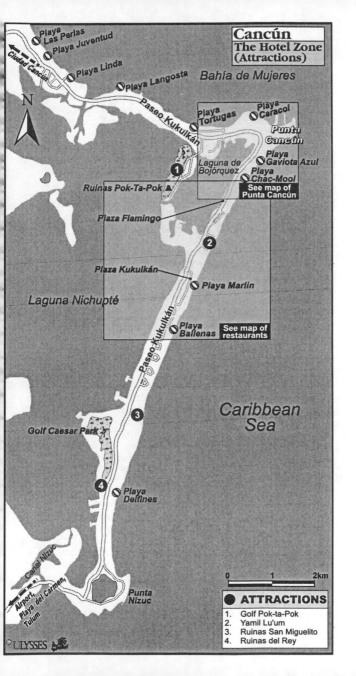

Cancún
The Hotel Zone
(Attractions)

Playa Las Perlas
Playa Juventud
Ciudad Cancún
Playa Linda

Bahía de Mujeres

Playa Langosta

Paseo Kukulkán

N

Playa Tortugas
Playa Caracol

Punta Cancún

Playa Gaviota Azul
Playa Chac-Mool

See map of Punta Cancún

Laguna de Bojórquez

1

Ruinas Pok-Ta-Pok

Plaza Flamingo

2

Laguna Nichupté

Plaza Kukulkán
Playa Marlín

Paseo Kukulkán

Playa Ballenas

See map of restaurants

Caribbean Sea

3

Golf Caesar Park

4
Playa Delfines

Canal Nizuc

Airport, Playa del Carmen, Tulum

Punta Nizuc

0   1   2km

● **ATTRACTIONS**
1. Golf Pok-ta-Pok
2. Yamil Lu'um
3. Ruinas San Miguelito
4. Ruinas del Rey

© ULYSSES

hotel), believed to date back to the 13th or 14th century, stand on the highest point in the Hotel Zone. The small, square structure no doubt served as an observation post. These ruins are easy to reach. As the site is completely exposed to the sun, visitors are advised to wear a hat and sunglasses.

Continuing southward, you will see the ruins of **San Miguelito** *(Paseo Kukulcán, Km 16.5)*, a tiny structure made up of stone columns. Right across the Paseo Kukulcán, in front of the El Pueblito hotel, lie the **Ruinas Del Rey** *(around $3; free admission Sun; every day 8am to 5pm)*, the most extensive Mayan ruins in Cancún. Made up essentially of two squares surrounded by platforms and stone houses, this grouping was fully excavated and opened to tourists in the mid-1970s, but had already been visited by a number of archaeologists at the beginning of the 20th century. The site is now part of the Caesar Park hotel, whose golf course lies alongside it.

Around Cancún

El Meco

The ruins of El Meco lie between Puerto Juárez and Punta Sam, on the left side of Highway 307, north of Cancún. Built between AD 250 and AD 600, this site probably originated as a fishing village. It includes a main temple, known as El Castillo, a number of stone buildings and various sculptures, including snakes' heads.

Isla Holbox ★★

Yes, there are actually places on the Yucatan Peninsula that haven't yet been penetrated by mass tourism. Located 169km north of Cancún, Isla Holbox is a peaceful oasis devoid of tourist development. Here, under the relentless tropical sun, time slowly and lazily rolls by with the waves. There are no hotels, but if you don't mind sleeping in a spartan room devoid of all the usual comforts, the local residents will be more than happy to rent you one at a low price. Otherwise, camping is permitted. The rustic restaurants on the island wonderfully prepare whatever the sea brings in. The island covers a distance of 30km from east to west and is inhabited by a handful of fishers. What is there to do on Isla Holbox? Nothing, besides swimming, fishing, relaxing, living and existing.

To get to Isla Holbox, first you have to go to the small village of Chiquila. There are buses going to Chiquila from Cancún, but schedules are irregular. So if there are no buses going to Chiquila on the day you want to go, the best way to get there is to rent a car or share a taxi. If you are going by car, follow the *vieja carretera* Merida-Cancún. As you approach Chiquila, there are few signs indicating the town, so you will have to stop someone on the way to give you directions. Once in Chiquila, you will have to leave your car there and then take the ferry *(daily at 8am and 2pm)* from the pier to Isla Holbox.

If you can brave the stifling heat and the humidity, you can also bicycle to Isla Holbox while working up a sweat. Bicycles and motorcycles are permitted on the ferry.

Cruises

Finally, as Cancún is a major seaside resort, one of the most pleasant things to do here is to take a cruise. Most boats take passengers to Isla Mujeres, located a little to the north. These cruises generally include live music, dancing, games and a meal served with plenty of drinks. Some boats don't actually stop at Isla Mujeres but simply go around it, so make sure to check before boarding. Most excursions start at Playa Tortugas, on Paseo Kukulcán. The following companies offer a variety of outings:

The Shuttle (☎ 846433) plies back and forth between Cancún and Isla Mujeres four times a day offering not only transportation to the island but also an interesting cruise. Departures are from Playa Tortugas.

From 6pm to 11pm, the ***Caribbean Carnaval Night Cruise*** (☎ 843760 or 872184) offers a tropical cruise and show for 400 passengers, complete with a limbo competition, music, dancing and a buffet.

Have you always dreamed of taking an evening cruise aboard a boat with a nightclub ambiance, complete with a casino, a buffet and karaoke? If so, the ***Pirate's Night Adventure*** (☎ 831488) will be right up your alley. The boat sets out from Playa Langosta.

Cancún

Captain Hook's Galleon
(☎ *667716*) offers water
activities and a paella buffet
during the day. There is no
charge for children under
12 accompanied by their
parents. At night, the boat
is transformed into a seafood restaurant, and then a
nightclub until 1:30am.

From Monday to Saturday,
you can enjoy a quiet dinner cruise on the Laguna
Nichupté aboard the
Columbus (☎ *831488*), a replica of Christopher Columbus's three-masted ship.

The *Cancún Queen* (☎ *852288*)
is a paddle-wheeler that
offers cruises accompanied
by games, tropical drinks,
fine food and mood music.

The *Fiesta Maya* (☎ *844878*)
travels to Isla Mujeres and
back, with a brief stop on
the island, where passen-
gers can go for a dip. The
cruise includes a buffet
meal and live music.

Beaches

As you already know,
Cancún's Hotel Zone is
shaped like a "7". In the
north part, which is more
sheltered from the wind,
the beaches are
much calmer than those to
the south, which face onto

the Caribbean. The water in
the southern part is
rougher, and you have to
watch out for the strong
currents. There, as everywhere else in Mexico, the
beaches are public, and
everyone can use them (in
principle, at least). It is
advisable to stay out of the
sun between 11am and
3pm, and to keep an eye
on the coloured flags on
the beaches, which indicate
whether or not it is safe to
go swimming. A blue or
green flag means that the
sea is safe; yellow that you
should be careful and red
that you are better off staying on dry land.

Playa Las Perlas

The beach closest to downtown Cancún, Playa Las
Perlas lies at the northwest
end of the Zona Hotelera.
Like the neighbouring
beaches as far as Punta
Cancún, it is sheltered from
the wind, but its waters are
not as clear as those of
Playa Tortugas and Playa
Langosta, farther east.

Playa Juventud

This beach lies in front of
the Causa Joven (see p 114)
the region's only youth
hostel, hence its name.
Naturally, the crowd here is
fairly young, with a taste

for water sports and late-night partying. Playa Juventud has the advantage of being located just 2km from downtown Cancún.

Playa Linda

Located atkm 4, between Playa Juventud and Playa Langosta, this beach lies at the border of the Zona Hotelera and Ciudad Cancún, where the Nichupté bridge links the island beaches to the mainland. Windsurf ing buffs can have a blast here, sheltered from the strong winds. Playa Linda is a 10min bus ride from downtown Cancún.

Playa Langosta

One of the prettiest beaches in Cancún, Playa Langosta (Km 5) has a small, rocky area that quickly turns into a lovely strip of white sand. Located near the Casa Maya hotel, it is literally covered with palapas.

Playa Tortugas

Boats regularly shuttle back and forth between this beach and Isla Mujeres. Playa Tortugas remains fairly peaceful, despite the region's unbridled develop-

ment. It offers one of the loveliest views of the Bahía de Mujeres (Bay of Women).

Playa Caracol

This beach forms the bend of the Hotel Zone. Located near the most luxurious hotels and the Convention Centre, peaceful Playa Caracol, the beach of choice among Cancún's older crowd, skirts gently round the Camino Real hotel and Punta Cancún, then links up with Playa Chac-Mool.

Playa Chac-Mool

This beach, like the rest of the area stretching from Punta Cancún to Punta Nizuc, was hard hit by Hurricanes Gilbert (1988) and Roxanne (1995). On the up side, its splendid view of the Carib-bean remains unal-tered, and it is lo-cated near the commercial activ-ity in the Hotel Zone. There used to be a restaurant right on the beach, which helped make this a popular spot with Cancún residents, who still flock here with their fami-lies on weekends. A statue of the Mayan god Chac-Mool stands on the dune

Cancún

overlooking the beach, watching over the swimmers.

Playa Ballenas

South of Playa Chac-Mool, between Km 15 and Km 16, Playa Ballenas is relatively deserted, due to the strong winds that sweep this part of the Hotel Zone. The hotels here are among the most luxurious and most modern on the island, and passersby are closely watched.

Playa Delphines

This lovely beach, located between Km 20 and Km 21, is fairly empty, since it is almost impossible to find a shady spot here, not to mention a restaurant. Most of the people who come here are guests of the big hotels nearby. There are some Mayan ruins, the Ruinas del Rey, on the other side of the road.

Laguna Nichupté

The Hotel Zone stretches around the vast Laguna Nichupté, where tourists have a ball water-skiing and sailing. The area's numerous boat-rental and tour agencies are making a mint.

Punta Nizuc

Located near the southern end of the Hotel Zone, near Club Med, Punta Nizuc is popular for its coral reefs, which are less impressive than those off Cozumel and Chetumal but nonetheless interesting. Furthermore, the mangroves lend the spot a jungle feel. Local authorities are considering reducing tourist access to the beach in order to protect the trees.

Outdoor Activities

Watersports

Cancún is one of the best-equipped cities in the world as far as water sports are concerned. Everything revolves around the water here, and all the gear necessary for snorkelling and scuba diving is available at most big hotels in the Zona Hotelera. There are also scores of rental outfits, as well as full-service marinas, on the Laguna Nichupté, for example.

Introductory scuba courses are available, but make sure to check the instructor's qualifications before putting your trust in him or her.

The following places rent out equipment for diving, sailing, jet-skiing, water-skiing and sometimes even sportfishing. They also offer a variety of excursions.

Aqua World Marina
7am to 10pm
Paseo Kukulcán, Km 15.2
☎852288
☎852299
This marina is one of the biggest in the area. For hygiene reasons, you will be given a new snorkel for your outing.

Aqua Tours Adventures
7am to 9pm
Paseo Kukulcán, Km 6.5
☎830400
☎830403
This outfit offers daily deep-sea fishing excursions and gourmet cruises.

Aqua Fun
8am to 5pm
Paseo Kukulcán, Km 16.5
☎852930
Head to Aqua Fun For sailing lessons and canoe and pedal-boat rentals. The locker-room is free.

Jungle Cruise
8am to 8pm
at the Marina Barracuda
Paseo Kukulcán, Km 14
Jungle Cruise organizes daily jet-skiing expeditions through the mangroves to

the reef at Punta Nizuc, at the southern tip of the Hotel Zone, near Club Med.

Marina Punta del Este
Paseo Kukulcán, Km 10.3
☎871600
☎871592
For an outing on calm waters, you can climb aboard one of the little motor boats at this marina, then ride alongside the tropical jungle and take in the natural sights.

Underwater Sightseeing

Atlantis
$80-90, including one meal
☎833021
www.goatlantis.com
This submarine plunges into the depths of the Caribbean Sea between Cancún and Isla Mujeres.

Two glass-bottomed boats crisscross the waters off the shores of Cancún, offering passengers a chance to check out the coral reef:

Subsee Explorer
$40
☎852288

Cancún

Nautibus
$35 for 1.5hrs
☎*833552*

Golf

Pok-Ta-Pok golf course
Cancún golf club
Paseo Kukulcán, Km 7.5
☎*831230*
In the Laguna Nichupté, a peninsula has been skilfully landscaped by Robert Trent Jones, Jr. to evoke a Mayan city. The result is this internationally renowned, 18-hole golf course. Right next to it, moreover, are the ruins of a real Mayan temple. In addition to this outstanding course, there are two tennis courts, a swimming pool and a restaurant. Visitors can take lessons and rent all the necessary equipment at the club. The green fees are $65 for 18 holes and $40 for nine, not including equipment rentals. The course is open from 6:30am to 4pm, and you have to reserve at least one day in advance.

Caesar Park hotel
Paseo Kukulcán, Km 17
☎*818000*

Meliá Cancún hotel
Paseo Kukulcán, Km 12
☎*850226*

Both these hotels have an 18-hole golf course. Though less spectacular than the Pok-Ta-Pok course, they both offer a magnificent view, the former of the Laguna Nichupté, the latter of the ocean. You do not have to be a hotel guest to play on either course.

Cancún Palace hotel
Paseo Kukulcán, Km 14.5
☎*850533 ext. 6655*
Cancún has something to offer fans of miniature golf as well! You can putt-putt here from 11am to midnight on a course inspired by Mayan pyramids.

Fishing

The waters around Cancún are teeming with over 500 species of fish. A deep-sea fishing trip costs between $350 and $550 US, depending on how long you stay out. Aqua Tours and Aqua World, which have offices around the Laguna Nichupté, offer a variety of expeditions. The fishing season runs from March to July.

In-line Skating

This sport still hasn't really caught on in Cancún. It should be stressed that the sidewalks in the Hotel Zone are ill-suited to in-line skating, due to the deep diagonal lines that the municipal authorities insist on carving into them. There is, however, a place where skaters can glide about at ease: the bike path that runs along the Zona Hotelera to downtown Cancún.

Rent-a-Roll
Paseo Kukulcán, opposite
the La Boom nightclub
It has recently become possible to rent skates in Cancún, thanks to this outfit which also rents mopeds.

Jogging

There is not really any pleasant place in Cancún to jog, unless you run barefoot by the sea. Throughout the Hotel Zone, there is heavy, potentially dangerous traffic on Paseo Kukulcán, and the downtown streets are in pitiful condition. Die-hard joggers can try the bike path early in the morning.

Cycling

The bike path that runs alongside the Hotel Zone is constantly growing. Though it is partially protected from the sun by a few trees, the best time to use it is still very early in the morning or in the late afternoon. The path is not lit at night.

Go-Karting

Karting International Cancún
every day 10am to 11pm
Km 7.5
This is a 1000m go-kart track along the highway linking Cancún City to the airport. Its little race cars can travel at speeds of 25, 80 and even 130kph. There is bus service from Avenida Tulúm, in Cancún, to the race track.

Accommodations

Cancún City is linked to the Hotel Zone by a small bridge near Playa Linda. When referring to Cancún, therefore, it is necessary to distinguish between the city itself, on the mainland, and the Zona Hotelera, a strip of sand about 20km long and shaped like a figure "7", which skirts round the Laguna Nichupté. From the far end of the hotel strip, the bus-ride to the city can take up to 45min.

Cancún boasts a number of very luxurious hotels, some ranking among the loveliest in the world. Generally speaking, a hotel in town will be less expensive than one of equal quality in the Hotel Zone. When choosing a place to stay, you have to decide if you are going to spend most of your time on the beach or would rather check out the restaurants and nightclubs downtown. As many downtown hotels provide their guests with free transportation to the beach, staying in town can be an economical and attractive option for some.

The Hotel Zone, for its part, tries to be self-sufficient by creating a somewhat unreal urban environment with its bars, restaurants and shopping centres. Many hotels in the zone also offer all-inclusive packages during the high season.

Ciudad Cancún (Cancún City)

Blue Bay Club and Marina
$
≡, ⊗, ≈, ⊙, ℜ
Carretera Punta Sam, Km 2
☎ *801068*
This hotel, on the road leading to Punta Sam, about 13km north of Cancún City, is affiliated with the Blue Bay Village, located in the Hotel Zone. This five-story hotel has 202 rooms with a colonial decor. During the day, guests can enjoy all sorts of water sports, and at night Latin music fills the air at the nightclub. It is very easy to get to and from Cancún from here, as there is frequent bus service around the clock.

Posada Lucy
$
≡, ℜ, *K*
8 Gladiolas, SM22
☎ *844165*
This establishment has 33 quiet little rooms with salmon-pink walls which are sheltered from the noise of the street. They offer a nice view of the ocean. Some of the rooms in the adjacent building can be rented by the month.

Cancún

● **ATTRACTIONS**

1. El Mero

◯ **ACCOMMODATIONS**

1. Best Western
   Plaza Caribe
2. Blue Bay Club
3. Holiday Inn Centro
4. Howard Johnson
5. María De Lourde

Antillano
$$

≡, ≈

Avenida Tulúm at Claveles

☎*841532*

⇆*841878*

One of the oldest downtown hotels, the Antillano has 48 pretty, comfortable rooms with wooden furniture and ceramic-tile floors. This attractively decorated and well-kept hotel also houses a bar and a shop.

Best Western Plaza Caribe
$$

≡, ≈, ℜ

Avenida Tulúm, at Avenida Uxmal 36

☎*841377*

⇆*846352*

The Best Western has 150 rooms in the heart of all the downtown action and nightlife, as well as a small but very pretty L-shaped pool. The Tulúm cinema, the bus station and the Comercial Mexicana market are all near by.

Holiday Inn Centro Cancún
$$

≡, ≈, △, ⊘, ℜ

Avenida Nader 1

☎*874455*

⇆*847954*

In the heart of downtown Cancún, the Holiday Inn offers guests free transportation to the beach of the Crown Princess Club hotel.

Cancún

The hotel has an pretty, palm-tree shaded inner courtyard with a pool and a bar-restaurant, and its colonial atmosphere is very pleasant. In addition to a small grocery store, a pharmacy, a beauty salon and a travel agency, the hotel has a variety of services for businesspeople.

Howard Johnson Kokai Cancún
$$
≡, ≈, ℝ, ⊕, ℜ
Avenida Uxmal 26, SM2A
☎*843218*
≈*844335*
The 48 rooms here are relatively small but comfortable and well-equipped. The hotel also has a restaurant that specializes in Mexican cuisine. Guests are offered free transportation to the beaches in the Hotel Zone.

María de Lourdes
$$
≡, ≈, ℜ
Avenida Yaxchilán 80
☎*844744*
≈*841242*
Though its 51 rooms are rather nondescript, this hotel is located in the heart of the downtown action. The pool is small but quite pretty. A souvenir shop, laundromat and travel agency are all located on the premises.

The Hotel Zone (Zona Hotelera)

Causa Joven
$
≈
Paseo Kukulcán, Km 3
☎*831337*
Visitors on a tight budget can find refuge at this youth hostel, which has 300 beds in separate men's and women's dormitories. On Playa Juventud beach (see p 106), guests can play basketball and volleyball. It is also possible to camp here for $9 per person.

Carisa Y Palma
$
≡, ≈, K, △, ⊘
Paseo Kukulcán, Km 10
☎*830211*
≈*830932*
This property, built in the 1970s, has 122 rooms in two buildings set side by side. It is located near the Mini Tienda flea market and the Centro de Convenciones. Very well maintained, it looks virtually untouched by time. The rooms are charming, and the comfort of the clientele is clearly a top priority. Still, guests have to use the beach of the neighbouring hotels a few metres over, since the shore in front of the Carisa Y Palma is covered with big rocks.

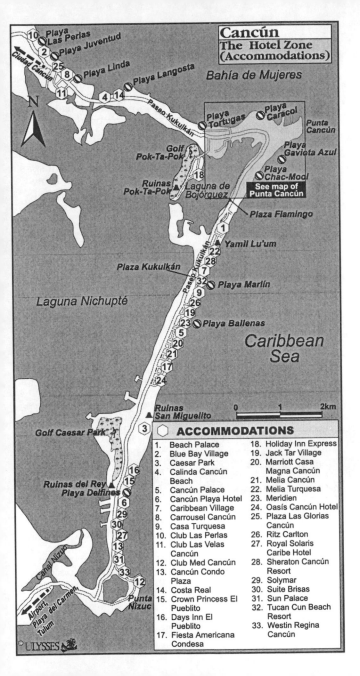

Cancún
The Hotel Zone
(Accommodations)

Bahía de Mujeres

Playa Las Perlas
Playa Juventud
Playa Linda
Playa Langosta
Playa Tortugas
Playa Caracol
Punta Cancún
Playa Gaviota Azul
Playa Chac-Mool
See map of Punta Cancún
Plaza Flamingo
Yamil Lu'um
Plaza Kukulkán
Playa Marlín
Playa Ballenas
Caribbean Sea
Paseo Kukulkán
Golf Pok-Ta-Pok
Ruinas Pok-Ta-Pok
Laguna de Bojórquez
Laguna Nichupté
Ruinas San Miguelito
Golf Caesar Park
Ruinas del Rey
Playa Delfines
Canal Nizuc
Punta Nizuc
Airport, Playa del Carmen, Tulum
Ciudad Cancún

N

0   1   2km

© ULYSSES

⬡ ACCOMMODATIONS

1. Beach Palace
2. Blue Bay Village
3. Caesar Park
4. Calinda Cancún Beach
5. Cancún Palace
6. Cancún Playa Hotel
7. Caribbean Village
8. Carrousel Cancún
9. Casa Turquesa
10. Club Las Perlas
11. Club Las Velas Cancún
12. Club Med Cancún
13. Cancún Condo Plaza
14. Costa Real
15. Crown Princess El Pueblito
16. Days Inn El Pueblito
17. Fiesta Americana Condesa
18. Holiday Inn Express
19. Jack Tar Village
20. Marriott Casa Magna Cancún
21. Melia Cancún
22. Melia Turquesa
23. Meridien
24. Oasís Cancún Hotel
25. Plaza Las Glorias Cancún
26. Ritz Carlton
27. Royal Solaris Caribe Hotel
28. Sheraton Cancún Resort
29. Solymar
30. Suite Brisas
31. Sun Palace
32. Tucan Cun Beach Resort
33. Westin Regina Cancún

Club Las Perlas

$

≡, ≈, ℜ

Paseo Kukulcán, Km 2.5

☎ *1-800-223-9815*

⇋ *830830*

Not to be confused with the smaller Imperial Las Perlas, Club Las Perlas is located right near downtown Cancún, at the beginning of the hotel strip, and is flanked on two sides by the Playa Las Perlas. The hotel has 194 rooms, each with a balcony; two tennis courts and two swimming pools with slides.

Condominiums Cancún Plaza

$

≡, ≈, *K*, ℜ

Paseo Kukulcán, Km 20

☎ *851110*

⇋ *851175*

This group of buildings containing over 200 rooms in all, has a mixed clientele of permanent residents and tourists. It is easy to get lost in this maze, with its attractive but complicated architecture. Bar and restaurant on the premises.

Costa Real Hotel and Suites

$

≡, ≈, ℜ

Paseo Kukulcán, Km 4.5

☎ *833955*

⇋ *833945*

Not all of the 262 rooms here have a view of the sea, but the hotel's outstanding location makes up for that. Built near a landing stage where boats pick up passengers throughout the day for excursions to Isla Mujeres, the Costa Real is a lovely hotel made up of seven pink buildings of varying shape and height. Baby-sitting and laundry services are available at a small extra charge. All sorts of social, artistic and water activities are organized for hotel guests.

Girasol

$

≡, ≈, *K*, ℜ

Paseo Kukulcán, Km 10

☎ *832151*

⇋ *832246*

The Girasol is located right next to the Carisa Y Palma, looks a bit neglected. The elevators, among other things, are a nuisance – you are better off taking the stairs! The restaurant of this "condo-hotel", located right next to the pool, offers several Yucatec specialties, and also serves as a bar. The rooms, spread over eight floors, all have a private balcony.

Sol Y Mar

$

≡, ≈, ℜ

Paseo Kukulcán, Km 19.5

☎ *851811*

Near the El Rey Maya ruins, on Delfines beach, the Sol Y Mar is a 150-room, pyramidal building, decorated in traditional Mexican style. Numerous sports can be enjoyed here: scuba diving, snorkelling, water-skiing, fishing, cycling and tennis. Depending on your finances, you can also play golf at the Caesar Park hotel's 18-hole course, located on the other side of Paseo Kukulcán.

Suites Brisas
$
≡, ≈, *K*, ℜ
Paseo Kukulcán, Km 19.5
☎850361
This is a hotel with 205 suites, each with a living-room/dining-room area and one bedroom. Though hardly extraordinary, these are nonetheless comfortable. The bathrooms have a shower but no bathtub. Hotel amenities include a restaurant, a swimming pool with a wading pool and a small grocery store.

Tucancún Beach Resort and Villas
$
≡, ≈, *K*, ℜ
Paseo Kukulcán, Km 13
☎850614
⇌850615
The design of this six-story earth-coloured building with white balconies is mildly reminiscent of a Mexican *pueblo* (little village). The rooms, with their rattan furniture and peach-coloured walls, all have a private balcony and a kitchenette. Near the round swimming pool, hammocks and *palapas* add to the typi-

cally Mexican ambiance of this 130-room hotel.

Aristos Cancún
$$
≡, ⊗, ≈, ℜ
Paseo Kukulcán, Km 9.5
☎/⇌830078
This establishment, which faces onto Playa Chac-Mool, is located right near the Centro de Convenciones and the shopping centres in this part of the Hotel Zone. It has 244 attractively decorated rooms on four floors; some offer a lovely view of the sea. Hotel amenities include two tennis courts; a swimming pool surrounded by palm trees and equipped with a slide; a gift shop and a small pharmacy, as well as a variety of services, such as car- and motorcycle-rentals.

Blue Bay Village
$$
≡, ≈, ℜ
Paseo Kukulcán, Km 3.5
☎830028
☎830904
⇌830904
This property has 160 rooms divided among several two- and three-story buildings facing onto the sea or the garden. The decor of the rooms is simple but decent. The hotel has three restaurants, three bars, a golf course and a small souvenir shop and offers scuba and Spanish lessons, among other ser-

Cancún

vices. Evening entertainment includes gambling, Mexican dance shows and competitions.

Calinda Beach Cancún
$$

≡, ≈, ℝ, ℜ

Paseo Kukulcán, Km 4.6

☎*831600*

⇌*831857*

www.hotelescalinda.com

Cylindrical in shape, The Calinda Beach Cancún bears no small resemblance to the Caesar Park, located at Km 17. There is another building adjacent to the pyramid, bringing the total number of rooms to 470, each with a view of the ocean or the Laguna Nichupté. This hotel spares no expense on activities and entertainment, offering its guests a marina, two tennis courts lined with palm trees, live music every night and festivities as often as possible. The Calinda Beach also has two restaurants and four bars.

Calinda Viva
$$

≡, ≈, ℜ

Paseo Kukulcán, Km 8.5

☎*830800*

⇌*832087*

The Calinda Viva is opposite the Plaza Caracol. It has 210 rooms and two large suites, all with a view of the sea, which is fairly calm in this area. There are a number of communicating rooms. A travel agency and car-rental agency can both be found on the premises, and a babysitting service and children's activities are available for a small additional charge.

Cancún Playa
$$

≡, ≈, ℝ, ℜ

Paseo Kukulcán, Km 18

☎*1-800-446-2747*

Not to be confused with the Condominiums Cancún Plaza, just a short distance away, the Cancún Playa has 388 modern, functional rooms with a view of the sea or the Laguna Nichupté. The building is shaped like a pyramid and laid out around a large L-shaped pool fringed with palm trees. There are six restaurants, four bars and two tennis courts on the premises.

Caribbean Village
$$

ℜ, ⊛, ≈

Paseo Kukulcán, km 13.5

☎/⇌*850-999*

Two steps away from the Plaza Kukulcán, the Caribbean Village is aptly named because it is a real all-inclusive resort offering everything for visitors so that they never have to leave the hotel. When seen from the sky, this hotel complex forms a Y. Myriad activities are offered to the clientele, who are mostly young Americans seeking fun under the hot Mexican sun.

All kinds of sports activities are organized around the pool, and there is a wide range of water-sports opportunities. Lavish buffets are offered for breakfast, lunch and dinner and three restaurants (Mexican, Portuguese and Italian) are reserved exclusively for guests of the hotel. There are also a car-rental service and travel agency on site.

Carrousel Cancún
$$

≡, ≈, ℝ, *K*, ⊛, ⊘, ℜ

Paseo Kukulcán, D-6

☎ *1-800-525-8588*

≈ *832312*

Just a few kilometres from downtown Cancún, the Carrousel Cancún faces onto Playa Linda, not far from a landing stage. This hotel has 149 rooms distributed among just three floors. Shaped like a "C", it wraps around a tennis court and a big pool. Its large, peaceful beach lies nestled in the curve of the Bahía de Mujeres. The hotel organizes a variety of water activities every day and presents shows in the evening.

Club Las Velas
$$

≡, ≈, ℜ

Paseo Kukulcán, Km 2.5

☎ *832222*

≈ *832118*

Attractively located on the Bahía de Mujeres, Club Las Velas looks like a small

coloniai town. As you stroll around the little houses scattered about here and there, you will feel as if you are in a village, an impression heightened by the fountains, squares and flower-filled gardens. Each of the 285 rooms has a bar, a television and a telephone. The hotel also has two swimming pools, two restaurants and two bars and organizes a number of activities, including windsurfing, volleyball, tennis and scuba diving.

Continental Villas Plaza
$$

≡, ≈, ℜ

Paseo Kukulcán, Km 11

☎ *831022*

≈ *851063*

You will find few hotels in Cancún that offer as many services and activities as the Continental Villas Plaza, which has 626 rooms, each with a balcony with a view of the sea or the lagoon. The hotel, a grouping of two- and three-story buildings, has five restaurants, two shops, a tennis court, a travel agency and a car-rental agency.

Crowne Princess Club
$$

≡, ≈, ℜ

Paseo Kukulcán, Km 18.5

☎ *851022*

≈ *850313*

When seen from above, this hotel is shaped much like the Hotel Zone itself, like a

Cancún

"7". Amenities include four restaurants; four swimming pools, one of which is covered; a beauty salon and four bars with live music in the evening. The hotel also offers children's activities.

Dos Playas
$$
≡, ≈, ℜ
Paseo Kukulcán, Km 6.5
☎ *830500*
⇌ *832037*

Located next to a small marina, Dos Playas has three small buildings containing a total of 125 rooms. Though the place looks a bit gloomy from the outside, the entryway is charming. The atmosphere is pleasant, particularly near the beach, where lots of catamarans and sailboats liven up the landscape. The hotel is equipped with two tennis courts and a pretty round pool. Some of the studios have closed rooms.

El Pueblito
$$
≡, ≈, ℜ
Paseo Kukulcán, Km 17.5
☎ *850422*
⇌ *850731*

As indicated by its name, El Pueblito is a little village made up of five pink and white buildings set on a gently sloping piece of land. On one side, the water from a fountain flows from the top of the property down to the swimming pool, and on the other, four

small pools of varying depths follow one after the other on their way downhill toward a round restaurant with a thatched roof. The 240 comfortable rooms all have a Mexican decor and a private balcony.

Holiday Inn Express Cancún
$$
bkfst incl; ≡, ≈
Paseo Pok-Ta-Pok
☎ *832200*
⇌ *832532*

Located near the Pok-Ta-Pok golf course, the Holiday Inn Express Cancún differs from the other hotels in that it faces onto the Laguna Nichupté. It has 119 rooms, each with a private balcony, on two floors. The building as a whole has a colonial look about it. The hotel has no restaurant, but there is a snack bar near the pool. A travel agency can also be found on the premises, and laundry service is available.

Kin-Ha Hotel and Condos
$$
≡, ≈, ☯
Paseo Kukulcán, Km 8
☎ *832377*
⇌ *832147*

Located near pretty Playa Caracol, the Kin-Ha has 166 condominiums with standard rooms and suites with one to four bedrooms. The lobby, furnished with comfortable sofas and armchairs, opens onto a terrace at the back. The beach, much deeper than those of other hotels, is studded with little round tables. Pedal-boats and other beach equipment are available for rent. The hotel also has a bar and a snack-bar. The Kin-Ha hosts a Mexican fiesta every Monday night, drawing large crowds.

Meliá Turquesa
$$
≡, ≈, ℝ, ℜ
Paseo Kukulcán, Km 12
☎832544
⇌851029

This pyramidal, white building, is located near Planet Hollywood and the Plaza Flamingo. All of its 444 rooms have a private terrace decked with plants. The hotel has a café, a seafood restaurant, three bars, two tennis courts and a large pool. Evenings are often enhanced by live music.

Plaza Las Glorias
$$
≡, ≈, ℜ, K
Paseo Kukulcán, Km 3.5
☎830811
⇌830901

Located near pretty Playa Caracol, the Playa Las Glorias has two modern buildings set face to face, and is located near downtown Cancún. Some of the 138 simply decorated rooms have a kitchenette.

This little hotel has a travel and car-rental agency, a small market and equipment for all sorts of water sports, making it a convenient place to stay.

Presidential Retreat
$$
≡, ≈, K, ⊛, ℜ
Paseo Kukulcán, Km 5.5
☎830555
⇌831822

At the Playa Langosta (see p 107), the three buildings of the Presidential Retreat house 170 well-equipped modern rooms that look out onto the Caribbean Sea. A 3m-high replica of the temple at Chichén Itzá greets guests at the hotel entrance.

Beach Palace
$$$
≡, ≈, ⊛, ☉, ℜ
Paseo Kukulcán, Km 11.5
☎831177
⇌850439

This hotel has 160 rooms decorated in traditional Mexican style. The bar, covered with a thatched roof, rises up out of the middle of the pool. Amenities include two restaurants, two bars, laundry service, a tennis court and a small gift and craft shop. The Yamil Lu'um ruins are nearby.

Cancún

 **Camino Real Cancún**
$$$
≡, ≈, ℝ, ℜ
Paseo Kukulcán, Km 8.5
☎*830100*
⇌*831730*
www.caminoreal.com/cancun

The Camino real at Punta Cancún was one of the first hotels built in Cancún. It boasts the best site possible, in the bend of the Hotel Zone, with a view of the ocean on both sides. It is also located right near the area's commercial and nighttime activity. It has 381 rooms with Mexican decor, six restaurants, two bars, a pool surrounded by stone towers and three tennis courts. A shop and a car-rental agency/tour operator can also be found on the premises.

Club Med
$$$
≡, ≈, ℜ
Punta Nizuc
☎*852409*

Club Med is somewhat isolated, compared to other hotels in the zone. First, it is located at the southern tip of the string of hotels, and second, it is a good distance from Paseo Kukulcán. It is made up of small, two- and three-story buildings decorated, like the 300 rooms they contain, in traditional Mexican style. Like all Club Meds, it is a fantastic place to enjoy all sorts of sports, including scuba diving, waterskiing,

tennis and golf. It also has two restaurants and a nightclub with a terrace facing onto the beach, where the atmosphere is extremely lively in the evening, thanks to the famous G.O.'s. Club Med is designed to meet the needs of couples and families as well as single travellers. It takes about 45min to get downtown by bus and about 30 to reach the Hotel Zone.

Fiesta Americana Cancún
$$$
≡, ≈, ℜ
Paseo Kukulcán, Km 9.5
☎*831400*
⇌*832502*

Along with the Camino Real and the Presidente, the Fiesta Americana was one of the pioneer hotels in Cancún. With its four attractively laid-out, peach-coloured buildings, it resembles a Mexican village, an effect heightened by the inner court, where a restaurant with a thatched roof is surrounded by a big, round pool and scores of palm trees.

Fiesta Americana Condesa Cancún
$$$
≡, ≈, ⊛, ⊘, ℜ
Paseo Kukulcán, Km 16.5
☎*1-800-FIESTA-1*
⇌*851800*

One of the newest hotels in the Fiesta Americana chain is the Condesa Cancún, which looks something like a beehive. It has two pueblo-style buildings containing a total of 502 rooms and suites. As soon as you walk in, you will be wowed by the luxuriousness of the lobby, with its marble floor and big paintings. The meandering curves of the vast swimming pool are surrounded by palapas. The hotel has four restaurants, three bars and three covered tennis courts. The beach isn't very big, but there's plenty of room to lie in the sun.

Hyatt Regency Cancún
$$$
≡, ⊗, ≈, ℝ, ⊘, ℜ
Paseo Kukulcán, Km 8.5
☎*831234*
⇢*831349*

This hotel, which is in the middle of the Hotel Zone, between the Camino Real and the Krystal, is a 14-story building topped by a glass atrium. Its 130 renovated rooms all have wall-to-wall carpeting, rattan furniture and a balcony with a view of the sea. The hotel also has three restaurants, three bars, two swimming pools, a tennis court, a travel agency, a beauty salon and a number of shops.

Jack Tar Village
$$$
≡, ≈, ℜ
Paseo Kukulcán, Km 14
☎*851366*
⇢*851363*

There is no shortage of water activities at the Jack Tar Village, which has its own little marina. Located next to the imposing Ritz-Carlton and the Plaza Kukulcán, this hotel has eight floors of rooms (150 in all), each with a view of the ocean or the Laguna Nichupté. Amenities include three restaurants, a lounge, three bars and a health club as well as an unusual swimming pool shaped like an "8".

Krystal Cancún
$$$
≡, ≈, ⊛, ⌂, ⊘, ℜ
Paseo Kukulcán, Km 9.5
☎*831133*
☎*1-800-231-9860*
⇢*831790*
kcancun@krystal.com.mex

The various brochures singing Cancún's praises often show a picture of some big, stone columns set in a semicircle. These surround the pool at the Krystal Cancún creating a very dramatic effect. The hotel itself is a rectangular building containing 321 rooms distributed among eight floors and decorated with rattan furniture. There are no balconies, but the rooms have big windows looking out onto the sea

or the lagoon. Four restaurants, five bars and two tennis courts surround the pool. The beach is not very big.

Le Méridien
$$$
ℜ, ⊛, ≈
Retorno del Rey, km 14
☎98812220
⇥98812201
meridienCancúna@cnet.net

A new hotel has opened in Cancún's Zona Hotelera which belongs to the internationally renown French hotel chain of the same name. Le Méridien stands out among the plethora of hotels in Cancún that try to meet the needs of the most demanding clients. The always-smiling staff are always there to serve you, and they are so courteous that they should be used as a model in international hotel management. The spacious rooms have a lovely view of the ocean and are decorated in the most discrete elegance possible. The Méridien's restaurant, Côté Sud (see p 134), will make your mouth water. The pool is amazing: it's on three different levels, and each level has a different temperature.

Miramar Misión Cancún Park
$$$
≡, ≈, ℜ
Paseo Kukulcán, Km 9.5
☎831755
⇥831136

All the 225 rooms at this hotel have a private balcony with a view of the sea or the lagoon. Though their decor is a bit outdated, they are fairly spacious and comfortable in a simple way. The hotel has two square pools set side by side, facing lovely Playa Chac-Mool. Other amenities include five restaurants and bars (including the Batacha, which features tropical music), a beauty salon with massage services, a shop and various services.

Oasis Cancún
$$$
≡, ≈, ⊘, ℜ
Paseo Kukulcán, Km 17
☎850867
⇥850131

This is one of the biggest hotels in Cancún with 960 rooms in four four- and five-story pyramids. Located near the El Rey and San Miguelito Maya ruins, this huge place covers more than 14ha. The renovated rooms all have stone-tile floors and a balcony. The enormous swimming pool is surrounded by palm trees and equipped with a "swim-up" bar. Other amenities include several restaurants and bars, a large nightclub, two tennis courts, a nine-hole golf course and a fully equipped gym.

Radisson Sierra Plaza Hotel Cancún
$$$ all-inclusive

≡, ≈, ℜ

Paseo Kukulcán, Km 10

☎ *832444*

⇄ *832486*

This 260-room hotel boasts quite an unusual site. The Laguna Nichupté breaks the string of hotels at this point, so the Sierra is surrounded by water, with Playa Chac-Mool and its heavy surf on one side and the calm lagoon on the other. The hotel has tennis courts, several shops and its own little marina.

Sheraton Cancún
$$$

≡, ≈, ℝ, ⊛, △, ⊘, ℜ

Paseo Kukulcán, Km 12.5

☎ *831988*

⇄ *850974*

Not far from the Plaza Kukulcán and right next to the Yamil Lu'um ruins stands the Sheraton, which has two buildings, one containing 314 rooms, the other 167. Amenities include a miniature-golf course, a garden with hammocks in it, a basketball court, four tennis courts and a large swimming pool shaped like an "8". The hotel takes up nearly a kilometre of beach.

Suites Sunset Cancún
$$$ all-inclusive

≡, ≈, ⊛, ℝ, ℜ

Paseo Kukulcán, Km 10

☎ *830856*

⇄ *830868*

Not far from the Plaza Caracol, nestled in the bend of the Hotel Zone, is the Suites Sunset Cancún, which has 220 modern rooms, most with a kitchenette. The rooms are decorated in pastel colours and have large windows looking out onto the lagoon or the ocean. There are about twenty palapas on the beach to protect guests from the harsh rays of the sun.

🐚 Caesar Park Cancún Beach & Resort
$$$$

≡, ≈, ℝ, ⊘, ℜ

Paseo Kukulcán, Km 17

☎ *818000*

⇄ *818082*

This complex looks a bit like the pyramid at Chichén Itzá. One of the loveliest and most expensive hotels in Cancún, it has 529 rooms, five restaurants, two outdoor whirlpool baths, a water sports centre and two tennis courts, which are lighted at night. All the rooms have a view of the ocean, voice-mail service and a clock-radio. Guests also enjoy access to the Caesar Park golf club, on the other side of the Paseo Kukulcán, right near the ruins of a Mayan temple.

Cancún Palace
$$$$
≡, ≈, ℝ, ⌂, ☺, ℜ
Paseo Kukulcán, Km 14.5
☎*850533*
≈*851593*

A combination hotel/timeshare condominium, the 424-room Cancún Palace, offers numerous amenities, including car rentals, a babysitting service, a souvenir shop, an exercise room, a sauna, four restaurants, three bars and two tennis courts. The beach is fairly small but well laid-out, and the view of the Caribbean is magnificent.

Casa Turquesa
$$$$
≡, ≈, ℝ, ⊛, ℜ
Paseo Kukulcán, Km 13.5
☎*852924*
≈*852922*
casaturquesa@sybcom.com

Reminiscent of the luxurious haciendas of the previous century, the Casa Turquesa is a small pink and white hotel with 33 lavishly appointed suites, each with a huge bed, a whirlpool bath and a private balcony. In front of the hotel, at the foot of a long flight of stairs and almost right in the sea, is a large pool surrounded by tents and palm trees. The Casa Turquesa is a member of the Small Luxury Hotels of the World association. The service is first-rate.

Fiesta Americana Coral Beach Cancún
$$$$
≡, ≈, ⊛, ☺, ℜ
Paseo Kukulcán, Km 9.5
☎*832900*
≈*833173*

This establishment, located near the Centro de Convenciones and the Plaza Caracol shopping centre, has been ranked one of the 100 best hotels in the world by Condé Nast Traveler magazine. The lobby is adorned with big palm trees and opens onto the Bahía de Mujeres. The 602 suites, divided between two peach-coloured buildings, are attractively decorated in pastel hues and offer a view of the ocean. The hotel has five restaurants, six bars and three tennis courts. The large and very elegant swimming pool is surrounded by *palapas* and palm trees, and the numerous specialized shops and daily activities program (volleyball, windsurfing and exercise classes) guarantee a delightful stay.

Hyatt Cancún Caribe
$$$$
≡, ≈, ℜ
Paseo Kukulcán, Km 10.5
☎*830044*
≈*831514*

Two stone jaguars greet guests at the entrance of the Hyatt, a curved building with 199 rooms, each with a magnificent view, a private balcony and a huge bathroom. The elegant lobby is decorated with a judicious blend of pink marble, palm trees, works of art and replicas of pre-Hispanic stone sculptures. Several shops; the Cocay Cafe restaurant, which serves theme buffets; the Creole restaurant Blue Bayou; two tennis courts; a travel agency and a beauty salon can all be found on the premises, along with a split-level pool.

Marriott Casa Magna Cancún
$$$$
≡, ⊗, ≈, ℝ, ☉, ℜ
Paseo Kukulcán, Km 14.5
☎852000
⇝851731

The Marriott, on Playa Ballenas, is a big, modern, six-story, white and beige building. The Mediterranean look of its architecture is accentuated by vaults and domes. The 450 rooms and suites all have a private balcony and are decorated with tropical motifs in pastel colours. Each is also equipped with an iron and ironing board. Waterfalls lend a cheerful atmosphere to the swimming pools, which are surrounded by four restaurants and four bars. The hotel also has several tennis courts and offers a full program of activities for kids (diving, tennis, marina, etc.).

Meliá Cancún Beach and Spa Resort
$$$$
≡, ≈, ℝ, ☉, ℜ
Paseo Kukulcán, Km 23
☎851114
⇝851263
meliavta@cancun.rce.com.mx

The glass roof of the Meliá Cancún, the Spanish chain's first Mexican hotel, looks a bit like the Louvre pyramid. This big glass and concrete building has 413 medium-sized rooms, each with a large terrace. Its vast inner court is literally overrun with vegetation. Amenities include a golf course, one pool with a "swim-up" bar and another that imitates the seashore with its sloping edge, as well as three tennis courts, five restaurants, four bars and a health club.

Presidente Intercontinental Cancún
$$$$
≡, ≈, ⊛, ☉, ℜ
Paseo Kukulcán, Km 7.5
☎830200
☎1-800-327-0200 from the US
⇝851085
www.interconti.com

This hotel has 298 huge rooms that combine a Mexican decor with modern comfort. One of the oldest hotels in Cancún, the Presidente was renovated and redecorated in 1988. Guests can enjoy all sorts of watersports here. The hotel also has a beauty salon, two swimming pools, several shops, two restaurants, a bar and a tennis court.

🐉 Ritz-Carlton Cancún
$$$$

≡, ≈, ⊛, △, ⊘, ℜ

Paseo Kukulcán
Retorno del Rey 36
☎*850808*
⇥*851015*

Like all hotels in this chain, the Ritz-Carlton Cancún is very elegant. It is located just a short distance from the Plaza Kukulcán, slightly elevated in relation to the Paseo Kukulcán. A glimpse of the lobby tells you all you need to know about this hotel. The marble floor of the richly decorated entryway offers a foretaste of the beauty of the 370 rooms, which are also very comfortable. Everything discreetly evokes the architecture and ambiance of a lavish Mexican home. The Ritz-Carlton boasts one of the finest restaurants in Cancún, the Club-Grill (see p 140), as well as an Italian restaurant, a health club, a beauty salon, three tennis courts and a number of shops.

Royal Solaris Caribe
$$$$

≡, ≈, ⊛, ⊘, ℜ

Paseo Kukulcán, Km 19.5
☎*850100*
⇥*850354*

This large, 480-room hotel, has a main building surrounded by several annexes. Facing onto Playa

Delfines, it stands right near the Ruinas del Rey (see p 104). A daily water sports program and a nightclub with live Latin music in the evening make for a very lively atmosphere.

Sun Palace
$$$$

≡, ≈, ⊛, △, ⊘, ℜ

Paseo Kukulcán, Km 20
☎*851555*
⇥*852040*

On the beach at the Sun Palace, the hotel managers bustle about making sure that nobody is bored! Guests can go kayaking, sailing, water-skiing and pedal-boating, and play volleyball, to name just a few possible activities. This yellow, seven-story building contains 227 bright, modern rooms and a small craft and gift shop. There are also several tennis courts on the premises, and near the pool, a big whirlpool bath (which can fit 40 people) with a fountain in the middle.

Westin Regina Cancún
$$$$

≡, ≈, ℝ, ⊛, △, ⊘, ℜ

Paseo Kukulcán, Km 20
☎*850086*
⇥*850774*
recan@westin.com

The 385 rooms here are attractively decorated and have a little area near the window where you can relax. The square pool is not very big, but the hotel has a private marina where guests can enjoy non-motorized activities at no extra charge.

Restaurants

Ciudad Cancún (Cancún City)

Boulangerie Pâtisserie
$
Behind the shopping centre Lote 33, local 10 SM 2, Ave. Tulum
☎807319
Good for a quick and simple bite to eat, this small

bakery/pastry-shop opens as early as 5am to serve you fresh chocolate or almond croissants, baguettes or rolls. There is no place to sit but there is a small park diagonally across the street where you can eat.

Internet Cafe
$
Ave. Tulum SM - 2, M - 1, lot 33 y 34
☎873167
This Internet café is right next to the Boulangerie Pâtisserie (see above). Despite the word café in its name, the place does not sell coffee. However, you can bring your own food and eat it on the terrasse after surfing the Net

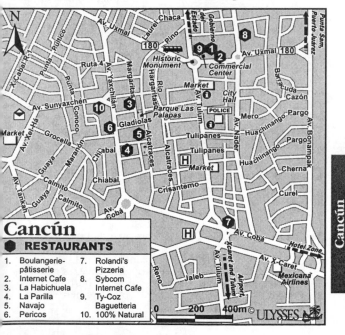

Cancún

● RESTAURANTS

1. Boulangerie-pâtisserie
2. Internet Cafe
3. La Habichuela
4. La Parilla
5. Navajo
6. Pericos
7. Rolandi's Pizzeria
8. Sybcom Internet Cafe
9. Ty-Coz Baguetteria
10. 100% Natural

Cancún

(20 pesos for 30 min). Some soft drinks are sold.

Sybcom Internet Cafe
Nader 42

If no computers are available at the Internet Cafe (see above), the Sybcom Internet Cafe is only two minutes away. The place is easy to miss because it's on the sunny side of the street, but inside it's modern and air-conditioned. Surfing the Net also costs 20 pesos for for the first 30 min, then only 38 pesos per hour. Coffee and soft drinks are served on arrival.

Ty-Coz Baguetteria
$-$$
Right next to the Boulangerie Pâtisserie

Right behind the shopping centre, the Ty-Coz Baguetteria looks like a charming little French bistro, and so does its menu which offers all the classics including ham-and-cheese croissants or baguettes, espresso and capuccino. European signs are plastered all over the walls, and even the sign for the bathroom says *toilette* instead of *baños*. Friendly service, and excellent value for the money.

Navajo
$-$$$
south of Parque de Las Palapas facing a small park

This restaurant offers an assortment of fortifying and refreshing juices and simple but succulent dishes such as omelettes, homemade pizza, salads, soups and *ceviche*, all of which can be savoured outside on the thatch-roofed terrasse.

Pericos
$-$$$
Ave. Yaxchilan
☎840821

This Mexican restaurant is recognizable by the old cart on its thatched roof. The decor is wild and crazy with strange murals, life-sized papier-maché skeletons playing cards at a table with a bottle of tequila, saddles on the barstools, designer chairs, hats on the ceiling and old black-and-white photographs on the walls. Even the bathrooms are specially decorated with deformed mirrors: the ones in the ladies room will please those who would prefer a more slender, sylphlike silhouette, while those in the men's room will make guys appear shorter or taller depending on how much they've had to drink.

Rolandi's Pizzeria
$$-$$$
Avenida Cobá 12, downtown
☎844047

This pizzeria belongs to the same owner as the Casa Rolandi (see p 138). Though the pizzas cooked in the wood-burning oven get top billing here, steak and seafood dishes also figure on the menu. This restaurant, open since 1978, has a simple, fun and colourful decor. Delivery available.

La Habichuela
$$-$$$$
Calle Margarita, facing
Las Palapas park, downtown
☎843158

This restaurant specializes in the tropical cuisine of the Caribbean, with a menu made up mainly of seafood dishes. A big mural, abundant greenery and numerous Mayan sculptures make for a lavish, relaxing ambiance. The specialty of the house is *cocobichuela*, shrimp and lobster in curry sauce, served in a half-coconut. In the evening, guests dine to the sounds of very soft jazz.

La Parilla
$$-$$$$
Avenida Yaxchilán 51, near Avenida
Cobá, downtown
☎845398

Seafood, Yucatec specialties and steak share the extensive menu at Parilla. This Cancún institution, open since 1975, is popular with tourists and locals alike, a testimony to the authenticity of its cuisine. This is also *the* place to discover the various facets of tequila, the national drink – the menu lists no fewer than 48 different kinds.

Zona Hotelera (The Hotel Zone)

Los Almendros
$-$$
Paseo Kukulcán, Km 19 opposite the
Centro de Convenciones
☎833093

This is a truly appealing little restaurant that serves Yucatec specialties like *sopa de lima* and chicken or pork cooked in banana leaves (*pollo pibil* or *cochinita pibil*). The *Paco en Salsa de Alcaparras* consists of thick slices of turkey in a sauce made of capers, olives, grapes and tomatoes. The specialty of the house is *Poc Chuc*, pork marinated in the juice of bitter oranges then grilled and served with black beans.

Bellini
$-$$
Plaza Caracol, 2nd floor
☎830459

Bellini is a small, modern café that serves simple dishes such as club sandwiches, pesto spaghetti and homemade cakes. This is just the place for those missing the flavours of home.

Petit Madrid
$-$$
on the ground floor of the
Centro de Convenciones
It is common practice for the Spanish to get together in the late afternoon for

Cancún

drinks and snacks. These appetizers, known as *tapas*, make up the bulk of the menu of the Petit Madrid. You can wash them down with beer, tequila, sangria or wine. The place is tiny, with only a few tables in a quiet spot right next to the theatre where the Ballet Folkloricó de Cancún (see p 140) performs every Saturday night. For a pleasant evening of discovery, you can combine the two.

Suchi Itto
$-$$
Plaza Forum by the sea
☎*834482*
For something a little lighter than quesadillas and tacos, go to this Japanese restaurant, which prepares all the classics of this country: sushis, tempuras, teriyakis.

Ok Maguey
$-$$$
Kukulcán Plaza
☎*850503*
A two-minute walk away from the Caribbean Village hotel (see p 118), Ok Maguey has a lively and casual atmosphere made even livelier when the mariachis come to sing romance under dark, starry skies. The interior decor looks like a colonial village and the staff is dressed in traditional Mexican costumes. The menu is typically Mexican and fairly consistent: *sopa*

de Lima, guacamole, quesadillas and the rest.

100% Natural
$-$$$
Av. Plaza Kukulcán
☎*852904*
Fresh, healthy food and a smile are guaranteed at 100% Natural, where mountains of fresh fruit, a variety of energy-boosting juices, simple but scrumptious vegetarian dishes, as well as chicken and seafood dishes, are served. The restaurant also has a small terrasse good for watching passersby on Paseo Kukulcán.

Pat O'Brien's
$-$$$
Flamingo Plaza, Km 11.5
☎*830418*
This is a seaside open-air bar-restaurant that serves decent meals that may not be great big culinary surprises, but are reasonably priced and won't put a strain on your budget. There is a breakfast buffet for $7, and a *table-d'hôte* breakfast for $10. The place livens up when the sun goes down and a waterfall is lit up by a huge, flickering flame. Things really get going after 9pm when a band starts to play and the dance floor fills up. From then on, the food plays second fiddle to the atmosphere. The bar serves great New-Orleans-style Hurricanes.

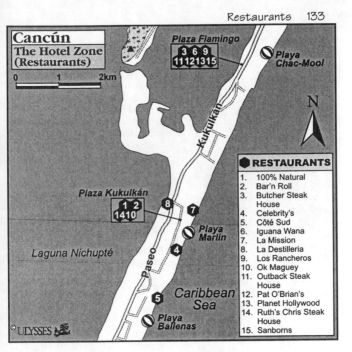

Cancún
**The Hotel Zone
(Restaurants)**

0   1   2km

Plaza Flamingo
3 6 9
11 12 13 15

*Playa
Chac-Mool*

N

Kukulkán

Plaza Kukulkán
1 2
14 10

8

7

*Playa
Marlín*

Laguna Nichupté

4

Paseo

*Caribbean
Sea*

5

*Playa
Ballenas*

©ULYSSES

⬡ RESTAURANTS

1. 100% Natural
2. Bar'n Roll
3. Butcher Steak House
4. Celebrity's
5. Côté Sud
6. Iguana Wana
7. La Mission
8. La Destilleria
9. Los Rancheros
10. Ok Maguey
11. Outback Steak House
12. Pat O'Brian's
13. Planet Hollywood
14. Ruth's Chris Steak House
15. Sanborns

Official All Star Cafe
$$
Paseo Kukulcán, Km 9.5
☎818110
This is a big sports shrine with a restaurant, a bar, a shop and video games. Top billing on the menu goes to the hamburger with a capital "H", served in seven different incarnations. Other fare includes spare ribs, pasta, salads, chicken wings and hot dogs. You can't escape the repeat broadcasts of all sorts of sporting events, as the giant screens scattered about are tuned into no fewer than 25 TV stations. The air-conditioning, furthermore, is much too effective!

Blue Bayou
$$-$$$
Hyatt Caribe hotel
Paseo Kukulcán
☎830044
If you are looking for a relaxed, romantic atmosphere, the Blue Bayou will fit the bill perfectly. From 9pm to 11pm, you can enjoy live jazz music while dining. The menu is made up of traditional Creole and Cajun cuisine.

Côté Sud
$$-$$$
Retorno del Rey, Km 14
☎812260
The chic restaurant inside
the Meridien hotel (see
p 124), Côté Sud is *the*
place for a memorable culinary experience. The house
speciality is obviously
French cuisine with a Mexican twist. All the dishes are
marvelously well-presented
and prepared originally and
elegantly with the freshest
of ingredients. Among the
splendid creations on the
menu are the fish tartare
with herbs, shrimps with
strips of smoked bacon,
mango duck *magret* with
potato and red onion
galettes, and classics like
grilled steak and *coquille St-
Jacques*. The simple but
elegant decor is ideal for an
intimate dinner or business
lunch and is on par with
the flawless service.

La Destillería
$$-$$$
Blvd. Kukulcán, Km 12.65
☎851087
Northwest of the Plaza
Kukulcán, La Destillería, a
replica of a Guadalajara
tequila distillery, has a fiery
orange facade. The chef
uses only the freshest ingredients to concoct traditional
Mexican dishes with re-
gional influences from
Campeche, Oaxaca, Puebla
and, of course, the Yucatan.
If you like tequila, there are
over 150 kinds on the

menu. There is a small
terrasse in back of the restaurant where you can en-
joy your meal and a view
of the ocean while being
cooled by sea-breezes,
which is the only form of
ventilation. On Mondays
and Wednesdays, the res-
taurant organizes information sessions about the process of making Mexico's
national drink, followed by
a tequila tasting and several
Mexican dishes, all for only
$5.

La Dolce Vita
$$-$$$
Paseo Kukulcán, Km 14.5
Laguna Nichupté
across from the Marriott hotel
☎850150
This fine Italian restaurant
was a hit with downtown
residents for over 10 years
before it started attracting
tourists. The terrace now
looks out onto the lagoon,
making it a very romantic
spot for dinner. The menu
features seafood and fresh
pasta made on the pre-
mises. The house specialty
is a lobster and shrimp dish
served on a bed of spinach
pasta in a white wine
sauce.

La Fisheria
$$-$$$
Plaza Caracol
☎831395
This seafood restaurant
serves the famous *ceviche*,
raw marinated fish in to-
mato sauce seasoned with

onion and coriander. Main dish selections include trout amandine, octopus in *chipotle* sauce, grilled lobster and the catch of the day. The pizzas, cooked in a wood-burning oven, are also worth the trip.

Iguana Wana
$$-$$$
Plaza Caracol
☎830829
This restaurant cooks up the simplest and best-known Mexican dishes: enchiladas, fajitas, chile, as well as seafood. Try the Iguana Wana giant shrimp, served in a garlic and lime sauce, and the enchilada trio (beef, chicken and cheese). You will dine to the sounds of salsa and merengue music.

La Misión
$$-$$$
Blvd. Kukulcán, Km 13.5
☎851706
This restaurant is located northeast of the Kukulcán shopping centre and two steps away from the Ok Maguey (see p 132) restaurant. However, La Misión is more upscale than its neighbour. Mexican and international cuisine are offered: filet mignon, chicken supreme, filet of fish, lobster, etc. Inside, the mirrors on the walls make the place seem larger, while outside on the small terrasse, a pianist entertains

those who prefer to dine in the open air.

Outback Steak House
$$-$$$
Plaza Flamingo
Blvd. Kukulcán, Km 11.5
☎833350
Meat-lovers might also want to keep this address in mind. This Aussie import is definitely a candidate for best steakhouse in Cancún. Fish and seafood are also on the menu. *Foster's*, Australia's national beer, is served here to quench your thirst.

Los Rancheros
$$-$$$
Plaza Flamingo
☎833975
This restaurant, which also serves typical Mexican cuisine, has a festive atmosphere. Guests enjoy mariachi music and a folk ballet show every evening starting at 8pm.

Rainforest Cafe
$$-$$$
Plaza Forum by the Sea
If you are looking for a family-style restaurant, the kids will definitely love the Rainforest Cafe. As its name suggests, the decor tries to recreate a tropical rainforest environment with colourful fish swimming in the giant aquarium, mechanically operated animals and rushing waterfalls. The menu lists pasta, sandwiches, chicken and salads. The only annoying thing is the

Cancún

souvenir shop selling tons of merchandise with the restaurant's logo.

Sanborns
$$-$$$
Plaza Flamingo

The late-night diner in the Zona Hotellera, Sanborns does not serve very creative dishes but is open 24hrs to satisfy any craving at any time of day or night. American travellers will feel at home here.

Santa Fe Beer Factory
$$-$$$
Plaza Forum by the Sea
☎834469
www.sfbeerfactory.com.mx

This restaurant shares a rear terrasse with the Hard Rock Cafe (see p 137, 142). This is the spot to try one of the many home-brewed beers, look at the ocean and let the sea-breeze gently caress your face. If you are hungry, they serve simple but salty Mexican dishes.

Yuppies Sports Café
$$-$$$
Blvd Kukulcán, km 9.5

Its name may be a little bit pompous, but this is a good place to chat with friends, have a bite to eat and watch your favorite team on the television.

Bogart's
$$-$$$$
Paseo Kukulcán, km 9.5
☎831133

One of the most popular restaurants in town, Bogart's is located inside the Krystal Hotel (see p 123). The menu features classic international cuisine, and the decor is reminiscent of North Africa, or shall we say Morocco – after all, the restaurant is named after the star of the film Casablanca, isn't it? Discrete, personalized service.

El Mexicano
$$-$$$$
Centro Comercial La Mansión Costa Blanca
near the Plaza Caracol and the Centro de Convenciones
☎832220

Musicians and dancers will entertain you while you dine at El Mexicano, a popular restaurant with tourists who like mariachi- and folk-ballet shows. If you are looking for quiet, keep looking! There is lots of noise, lots of colour, lots of everything here! The culinary traditions of various parts of Mexico are represented on the menu, which is made up mainly of fish and seafood dishes and nice, thick steaks. Caribbean shrimp (*camarones caribeños*), fished in the area, are prepared in a variety of ways.

Faro's
$$-$$$$
Plaza Lagunas
☎*832080*

Decorated entirely with colours and objects evocative of the sea, Faro's specializes in seafood. You will have a hard time choosing among dishes like shrimp with tequila, filets of fish *à la maya* and the big Faro's fisherman's platter.

Hard Rock Cafe
$$-$$$$
Plaza Lagunas
☎*833269*

Like Planet Hollywood (see further below), the Hard Rock is a world-wide institution. There is one in every big city on earth, including Cozumel. Burgers and sandwiches make up the bulk of the menu. The blaring rock music might not appeal to everyone.

Mango Tango
$$-$$$$
Paseo Kukulcán, Km 14.2
☎*850303*

Right near La Dolce Vita and the Ritz-Carlton, the Mango Tango has an extremely varied menu. Try the big Mango Tango salad (shrimp, avocado, chicken and mushrooms), the fettuccine with shrimp or the grilled fish served with slices of pineapple or banana. Reggae music and dancing are also on the menu until the wee hours.

Planet Hollywood
$$-$$$$
Plaza Flamingo
☎*850723*

Various stars of the big screen have opened restaurants like this one all over the world. This chain serves overpriced burgers, steaks and spare ribs, as well as Chinese and Italian food in a relaxed, even lax, atmosphere. At night (from 11pm on), the music plays full blast, and people work up a sweat on the dance floor.

Savio's
$$-$$$$
Plaza Caracol
☎*832085*

Savio's is a two-storey restaurant located in a brightly lit building. The restaurant specializes in Northern Italian cuisine and serves such dishes as bruscheta, fettuccini primavera, Neopolitan lasagna and veal cutlets. And since the sea is right nearby, fish and seafood dishes make up a significant part of the menu.

Angus Butcher Steak House
$$$-$$$$
Blvd Kukulcán, km 9.5
☎*834301*

Great big juicy steaks are served here. The softly playing jazz music gives this place a warm and mellow atmosphere.

Cancún

Casa Rolandi
$$$-$$$$
Plaza Caracol
☎*831817*

Credit for the delicious, authentic Italian cuisine at this restaurant goes to owner and chef Mirco Giovanni. All the pastas are fresh and made on the premises. The menu includes *antipasti* (appetizers), risotto, lasagna, lamb chops with thyme, pizza cooked in a wood-burning oven and every kind of pasta imaginable! The simplicity and tastefulness of the decor evoke the Mediterranean. Service is available in Spanish, English, Italian, German and French.

Celebrity's
$$$-$$$$
Blvd. Kukulcán, km 10.5
☎*852924*

Stars of all stripes frequent Celebrity's. The chefs concocts a variety of international and local dishes. The staff are extremely courteous. The chic and sober decor is perfect for a business lunch or an intimate dinner when the lights are dimmed and reflected in the radiant smiles of diners gazing at each other across the table.

Hacienda El Mortero
$$$-$$$$
Paseo Kukulcán in the Krystal Cancún hotel

This chic restaurant is an exact replica of an 18th-century *hacienda*, one of those luxurious homes owned by big landowners. This chic restaurant is very popular, thanks to its Mexican specialties and mariachi music, so reservations are recommended.

Lorenzillo's
$$$-$$$$
Paseo Kukulcán, km 10.5
☎*831254*

You have to go through an alley to get to this restaurant, where you will see the thatch-covered dining room decorated like a yacht club with life buoys, rudders and fishing nets. Lobster is the house speciality, and you get to choose one from the tank. Fish, meat and seafood dishes are also on the menu. This restaurant is very popular despite its high prices.

Ruth's Chris Steak House
$$$-$$$$
Plaza Kukulcán

This steakhouse is very popular with Americans for its big, juicy steaks, just like they make 'em back home. The decor is bland but the portions are enormous, and the meat is always fresh and served the way you like it. Pork ribs, marinated chicken and grilled shrimp

Punta Cancún

Bahía de Mujeres

Playa Tortugas

Playa Caracol

Plaza Caracol

Centro de Convenciones

Plaza Lagunas

Forum by the Sea

Playa Gaviota Azul

Paseo Kukulkán

Laguna de Bojórquez

Caribbean Sea

Playa Chac-Mool

N

0   500   1000m

RESTAURANTS	ACCOMMODATIONS
1. Bellini	1. Aristos Cancún
2. Bogart's	2. Calinda Viva Cancún
3. Casa Rolandi	3. Camino Real
4. Faro's	4. Carisa Y Palma
5. Hard Rock Cafe	5. Continental Villas Plaza
6. Official All Star Cafe	6. Fiesta Americana Cancún
7. La Fisheria	7. Fiesta Americana Coral Beach
8. Lorenzillo's	8. Girasol
9. Los Almendros	9. Hyatt Cancún Caribe
10. Petit Madrid	10. Hyatt Regency Cancún
11. Rainforest Cafe	11. KinHa Condo Hotel
12. Santa Fe Beer Factory	12. Krystal Cancún (R)
13. Savio's	13. Miramar Misión Park Plaza
14. Suchi Itto	14. Presidente Intercontinental Cancún
15. Yuppies Sport Cafe	15. Sierra Radisson Plaza Hotel
	16. Suite Sunset Cancún
	(R): Property with restaurant (see description)

© ULYSSES

are also offered

Club Grill
$$$$
Paseo Kukulcán, Km 13.5
☎ *850808*

One of the chicest and most expensive restaurants in Cancún is Club Grill, the restaurant of the Ritz-Carlton. The cuisine is a sophisticated variation on the theme of French, Creole and Yucatec cuisine (try the seafood "Club-Grill"). The plush decor (beige and gold, deep chairs with armrests, round tables, fine tablecloths, elegant place settings, flowers on the tables, etc.) and professional service contribute to the restaurant's reputation.

Entertainment

Cultural Activities

Ballet Folklórico de Cancún
☎ *830199*

This company puts on a show every Saturday night at the Centro de Convenciones. A dozen or so dancers and as many singers perform traditional dances from the various Mexican states (the old folk's dance, the stag dance, the bottle dance, etc.). The show is preceded by a buffet-style Mexican meal.

Plaza de Toros
3:30pm
200 pesos
Paseo Kukulcán
near Avenida Bonampak
☎ *848372*

Imported from Spain, *corridas* are a tradition in Mexico. In Cancún, these bullfights are held every Wednesday at the Plaza de Toros. To entertain the audience beforehand, traditional Mexican songs and dances are performed, along with a *Charrería*, a stunt which involves jumping from one galloping horse to another. The corrida is carried out in the purest Spanish style, with the matador decked out in a colourful costume.

Two local movie theatres show popular Hollywood films:

Tulúm
Avenida Tulúm 16, SM2
☎ *843451*

Cinemas Kukulcán
Plaza Kukulcán, Paseo Kukulcán
Km 13, 2nd floor
☎ *853021*

Bars and Nightclubs

Ciudad Cancún
(Cancún City)

Cancún's heart beats to the rhythm of the Latin, disco, dance and rock music played in its scores of crowded bars. Generally, the nightclubs are pretty empty until 11pm, but stay packed from midnight to dawn. The following are among the most popular:

Azucar
cover charge
11:30pm to 4am, closed Sun
Camino Real hotel
☎*830100*
One of the chicest and most pleasant places to spend the evening in Cancún is the Camino Real hotel, which often books excellent Cuban bands so that couples can kick up their heels to boisterous salsa music. You can also simply have a seat, savour the music and the sophisticated decor, or take in the dazzling view of the sea. T-shirts and shorts are not appropriate attire here.

La Boom
about $10
Paseo Kukulcán, Km 3.5
☎*830404*
This nightclub has very elaborate sound and lighting effects, making it a popular dance club. There are different contests every

night, and numerous video screens liven up the atmosphere.

Christine
from 10pm on; no cover charge Sun; ladies enter for free Tue and Thu
next to the Krystal Hotel Paseo Kukulcán
☎*831133*
At Chrisine, there is a different theme every night. Tuesday: wet T-shirt contest; Thursday: 1970s and 1980s music; Friday: male beauty contest. The place is aiming at a certain level of sophistication, and shorts and jeans are not allowed, though long bermuda shorts are tolerated.

Dady'O
around $10
from 10pm on
Paseo Kukulcán, Km 9.5
at the Plaza Caracol
☎*83333*
Big stucco walls lend this nightclub a distinctive look. The big dance floor and laser-light show make it a very popular spot. The evening gets off to a mellow start with jazz around 9pm, then the beat picks up at just the right pace, with all types of music getting their due, the culmination being house music. This bar seems to attract a very young crowd. There is also a small restaurant *($)* in case you get hungry.

Cancún

Dady Rock
from 8pm on
Paseo Kukulcán, Km 9.5
☎*831626*
This nightclub is located right near its big brother, the Dady'O. It is both a restaurant and a bar where rock bands entertain a young crowd from 11pm onward.

Hard Rock Cafe
every day 11am to 2am
Plaza Lagunas, Paseo Kukulcán
☎*832024*
The huge dance floor of the Hard Rock Cafe attracts fans of classic rock. Live bands often perform around 11pm.

Pericos
Av. Yaxchilán
☎*840821*
This restaurant (see p 130) is a good place to enjoy a little entertainment while dining. Patrons can have some wine and a good time listening to the musicians who take the stage in two theatres.

Planet Hollywood
11am to 1am
Plaza Flamingo
Paseo Kukulcán, Km 11.5
☎*832955*
This is a combination restaurant, bar and store popular for its Hollywood atmosphere:
patrons are swept up by the soundtracks of films like *Gone with the Wind*, and cinematic hits from Hollywood's golden age are shown on four giant screens.

Señor Frog's
Paseo Kukulcán, Km 9.5
☎*832188*
A restaurant and nightclub rolled into one, Señor Frog's is a very lively place with loud music that attracts a young crowd. From 10pm on, dance music and reggae rule here.

Zona Hotelera
(The Hotel Zone)

Bar'n Roll
$-$$
Plaza Kukulcán
☎*853133*
With a name like this, you already have some idea of what kind of place this is and what to expect. Caricatures of famous people in the music world decorate this establishment. Salty, fattening food, like chicken wings and nachos, is served, as well as beer and an interesting selection of cocktails with amusing names such as
Strawberry Dylan, Sex Morrison and *Dunhill Lennon*. The latest sporting events are broadcasted on several televisions.

La Tequilería
Ave. Playas no 79
☎*846615*

This establishment offers 232 kinds of tequila, several kinds of mescal and several brand-name cigars. There is a small terrasse that is not shaded, but you can escape the heat by going upstairs where there are fans in front of the windows.

Shopping

Cancún is a real shopping city, with no fewer than 12 malls, not to mention all the little craft shops both downtown and in the Hotel Zone. One advantage of the latter is that the prices are negotiable.

Ki Huic
9am to 10pm
Avenida Tulúm 17
☎*843347*

One of the largest craft shops, Ki Huic is highly recommended.

Plaza Bonita
SM8, at the corner of Avenidas Zel-Ha and Tankah

This is an interesting group of stores and other businesses laid out around a fountain in the heart of downtown Cancún. Pretty handcrafted items can be purchased here at very reasonable prices.

Plaza Kukulcán
Paseo Kukulcán, Km 13
☎*852200*

This is a large shopping mall that is air-conditioned, spotlessly clean and has lots of shops. You can find just about anything here, including many souvenir shops where the prices are high, a number of restaurants, a Cancún Tips tourist information counter, a pharmacy, a movie theatre, a bowling alley, a video arcade, etc.

Plaza Caracol
8am to 10pm
Paseo Kukulcán, Km 8.5 located right near the Centro de Convenciones close to Punta Cancún

This mall is more inviting and livelier than Plaza Kukulcán, it is also close to a number of good restaurants.

La Fiesta
Paseo Kukulcán, Km 9
☎*832100*

This is a big shopping centre for handicrafts, silver jewellery and leather goods. Despite what its ads say, the prices are quite high here.

Cerámica Oliver
60 Calle 21, SM64
☎*805941*

For lovely ceramics handcrafted by a local artist, head to this boutique, where you will find some amazing mobiles representing holiday themes and aspects of daily life. The shop is inconveniently located far from the Zona Hotelera and therefore hard to get to.

Gift Show
Centro de Convenciones.
At this event, which is held towards the end of the year and is open to the public, you might come across some unique items, mainly local handicrafts.

Isla Mujeres ★★

Isla Mujeres: Island of Women. This name was given to the island in 1517 by Francisco Hernández de Córdoba, who at the time was leading a Spanish expedition in search of labourers for the gold mines of Cuba.

So much is attested to by Bishop Diego de Landa in his famous historical tract *Relaciónes de las Cosas de Yucatán* (Description of the Affairs of the Yucatán), written in 1566. Córdoba was apparently inspired by the many statues representing the female figure that were found in the Mayan temples of the island, the majority of which were certainly erected in homage to Ix-Chel, the goddess of the moon and of fertility. It seems that the Maya never actually inhabited the island, that it served solely as the destination of pilgrimages.

During the 17th and 18th centuries, pirates and traffickers of all sorts paid homage daily to the "God of concupiscence" at the island and then left the place to fishermen, who were its only visitors until the first tourists started to appear, about 20 years ago. During the Second World War, the Allies constructed a naval base here, which is used today by the Mexican government.

The island is 8km long and 800m across at its widest point. The enchanting charm of this locale is a combination of many white-sand beaches, lagoons, coral reefs teeming with marine life, and swaying coconut trees.

The town of Isla Mujeres has about 10,000 residents and 15 criss-crossing streets, spread out on the northern end of the island. Wrought-iron balconies and whitewashed walls contribute to its altogether Mexican atmosphere. Most of the restaurants, hotels and shops of the island are concentrated in this little city, and it is a good idea to visit it outside of the tourist rush hour (mainly between noon and 3pm), when guides arrive leading throngs of visitors from Cancún and Cozumel.

The beaches and the coral reefs are generally in the southwest, facing the mainland. On the other side of the island the sea is so rough that it is unsafe for watersports.

The rest of the island is covered in attractions described in the pages that follow.

Finding Your Way Around

By boat

The port is in the northern part of the island, in the town of Isla Mujeres, facing Calle Morelos. A ferry, an inexpensive option for foot passengers that is much used by area residents, arrives almost every hour from Puerto Juárez (**☎7-0253**), which is a few kilometres north of Cancún and is accessible by bus from the station in Cancún, or by car north along Highway 180. If there are not enough passengers to fill the boat, the ferry may be delayed until the next scheduled departure time. The one-way fare costs around 4 pesos and the trip takes between 30 and 40 min.

Caribbean Express and *Caribbean Miss,* more comfortable and faster boats, also leave from Puerto Juárez. The first departure is at 7:30am and the return trip from Isla Mujeres leaves at 8pm. The crossing, twice as fast as the ferry, costs around 14 pesos for the round trip. Which ever boat you board, supply yourself with seasickness medication and eat lightly at least one hour before boarding, since the sea is rough.

The passenger ferry schedule (changes frequently):

Departures from Puerto Juárez for Isla Mujeres:

5:30am, 7:30am, 8:30am, 9:30am, 10:30am, 11:30am, 1:30pm, 3:30pm, 4:30pm, and 5:30pm

Departures from Isla Mujeres for Puerto Juárez:

6:30am, 7:30am, 8:30am, 9:30am, 10:30am, 11:30am, 1:30pm, 2:30pm, 3:30pm, 4:30pm, and 5:30pm

At Punta Sam *(Hwy. 180, 5 km north of Cancún)* there is a car ferry that is slightly more comfortable than the Puerto Juárez ferry. The fare is 10 pesos for foot passengers and 40 pesos for cars. It is recommended to arrive an hour ahead of departure time and to line up immediately with ticket in hand.

Departures from Punta Sam for Isla Mujeres:

8am, 11am, 2:45pm, 5:30pm and 20:15pm

Departures from Isla Mujeres for Punta Sam:

6:30am, 9:30am, 12:45am, 4:15pm, 7:15pm

Other boats regularly leave Playa Linda or Playa Tortuga, beaches in the hotel zone of Cancún, as part of organized cruises. Isla Mujeres is situated 11km from the coast and the crossing takes about 45min. Many agencies organize such cruises to Isla Mujeres, and some have transformed this short crossing into an elaborate excursion including meals and open bar, snorkelling and bands. Of course these expeditions are more expensive than simple ferry crossings, but they can be very pleasant. Before boarding be sure that the boat is going to land at the island, as some cruises just go around it. Arrive at least a half-hour early to get a good seat.

The following companies organize cruises to Isla Mujeres from Cancún:

The Shuttle
☎846333

Isla Mujeres Shuttle
☎ *833448*

M/V Aqua II
☎ *871909*

In the City

The city of Isla Mujeres occupies the northern tip of the island and comprises approximately 15 streets – unless one is very distracted, it is impossible to get lost. The main street is Avenida Rueda Medina, which leads south to Parque Nacional de El Garrafón, to the beaches, to the Mayan temple Ix-Chel and to the lighthouse. Very pretty Playa Coco is situated north of the village. The town square is between Avenidas Morelos and Bravo.

By Car

A car is more of a headache than a convenience on Isla Mujeres. The small size of the island does not justify the time and the cost of the crossing. Nonetheless, if you cannot do without a car, the ferry landing is just facing Avenida Rueda Medina, the only road that travels the entire island from north to south. There is a gas station on this street near the port at the corner of Avenida Abasolo.

By Taxi

Taxi fares are set by the municipality and are posted in plain sight near the port. Nevertheless, be sure to agree on a price with the driver before boarding a cab.

Some sample fares:

From the city
to Parque Nacional de El Garrafón: *34 pesos*
to Playa Landero: *17 pesos*
to Playa Atlantis: *20 pesos*
to Playa Norte: *10 pesos*
to Las Colonias: *7 pesos*

By Bus

The island's public bus (☎ *7-0529*) has no fixed schedule, but rather matches the ebb and flow of crowds brought by the arrival and departure of boats in the port. It leaves from the Posada del Mar hotel, on Avenida Rueda Medina, and travels to Playa Lancheros. Stops are frequent and the trip can take a long time.

By Motorcycle

A motorcycle is definitely the most appropriate mode of transportation on Isla Mujeres. Motorcycles may be rented near the foot passenger ferry landing or

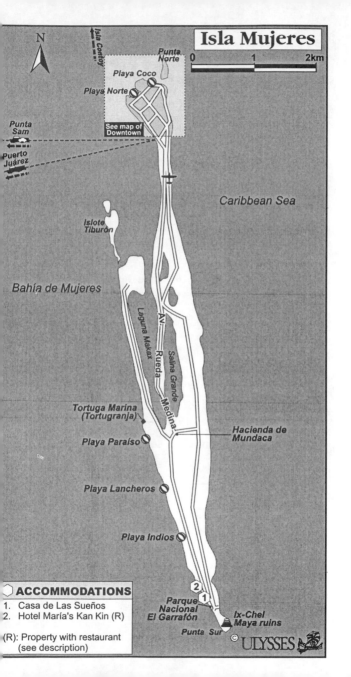

in the city. The hourly rate is about 80 pesos; budget for 200 pesos for a full day. A deposit will also be required. Before leaving be sure that the gas tank is full and that the vehicle is in good condition. As the roads are not well paved and are travelled by inexperienced tourists, ride slowly and carefully, and wear clothing that covers your arms and legs (you will not regret the long sleeves if you take a spill).

Motorcycle rental outlets:

Cardenas
Avenida Guerrero no. 105
☎7-0079

Gomar
Avenida F. Madero
☎7-0142

PPE'S Motorent
Avenida Hidalgo no. 19
☎7-0019
This establishment also rents golf carts for touring the island for 120 pesos per hour or 400 pesos per day.

By Bicycle

A good mode of transportation for the island, a bicycle allows you to explore every corner of it at your own pace. Be careful of heatstroke and wear a hat.

If your hotel does not rent bicycles, many little shops in town do, especially near the port. Test the bicycle of your choice before renting it ("May I try it?" = "*¿Puedo pruebar?*") to be sure that it rides well. A deposit of approximately 50 pesos and identification will be required. The fee for one hour is about 30 pesos; and around 80 pesos for a full day.

Isla Contoy

To get to Isla Contoy, first take the ferry to Isla Mujeres. Once there, one of the many travel agencies organizes trips to the island.

Practical Information

Tourist Information

The tourist information office is located at Avenida Hidalgo, near the park, facing the baseball field.

Tour Companies

La Isleña
corner of Morales and Medina
☎70036

**Sociedad Cooperativa
Isla Mujeres**
Avenida Rueda Medina north of the
landing
☎7-0274

Post Office

Mon to Fri 8am to 7pm
Sat 9am to 1pm
At the corner of Avenida Guerrero and
Calle López Mateos
☎7-0085

Banks and Exchange Offices

Atlantico
Avenida Rueda Medina
☎7-0005

Sureste
Avenida R. Medina no. 3
☎7-0104

Cunex
Avenida Hidalgo no. 12
☎7-0474

Pharmacy

Lily
Mon to Sat 8:30am to 9:30pm
Sun 8:30am to 3pm
Avenida F. Madero no. 18
☎7-0164

Hospital

☎7-0001

Police

☎7-0082

Photoshops

Foto Omega
Avenida R. Medina no. 1
☎7-0481

Publications

Isla Mujeres' equivalent to
Cancún's *Cancún Tips* is
Islander, a monthly magazine that is distributed in
the hotels and at the tourist
information office. If you
read a bit of Spanish you
can keep up with current
events with *Por Esto!*, a daily
distributed throughout the
state of Quintana Roo.

Exploring

Isla Mujeres

Isla Mujeres is greatly admired for the beauty of its
beaches, its coral reefs, its
temples and its landscape.
Many tourists staying in
Cancún come to these more
authentic and more relaxing
parts for a day or two of
peace. Moreover, the island
is home to very good res-

taurants, hotels that offer good value for your money and many craft shops.

In the City

The music reaches full swing twice a day at **Casa de la Cultura** *(Av. Guerrero,* ☎ *7-0307)*, where musicians, dancers, painters and other local artists express themselves in myriad media. English books are available on loan here.

The ruins of the century-old **Hacienda de Mundaca** are located about 4km south of the city along Avenida Rueda Medina, near Playa Lancheros. According to legend, this house was built at the beginning of the 19th century by pirate and slave-trader Fermín Antonio Mundaca to win the heart of a young island girl, *Triguena*. After some time living communally with Mundaca, she left for Mérida and married some-one else. Brokenhearted, Mundaca perished shortly thereafter. His tomb is in a little cemetery along Calle López Mateos, in the vil-lage. One side of his tomb-stone reads, "*como eres, yo fui*" ("as you are, I was") and the other reads, "*como soy, tu serás*" ("as I am, you will be"). Mundaca's re-mains are actually in Mérida, where he lived out his last days.

The Hacienda de Mundaca is composed of two main, decrepit buildings sur-rounded by gardens and lanes, of which only traces remain, enclosed by ram-parts. To reach it, follow the signs along Avenida Rueda Medina. There are also caged animals living in pitiful conditions.

The Southern Part of the Island

The **Tortugranja** ★★ *(14 pesos; every day 9am to 5pm)* is a turtle farm that can also be reached by following the road signs along Avenida Rueda Me-dina. The farm is near Hacienda de Mundaca, on a small, tortuous road. Given the rapid decline of the turtle population in the Caribbean, the environmen-tal organization Eco Caribe has taken on the responsi-bility of breeding, studying and saving threatened species. Every year the farm raises and protects thou-sands of little turtles until they grow to a sufficient size to be released safely into the ocean.

As explained at the begin-ning of this chapter, Isla Mujeres was named for the many statues representing female figures in the ruins of the **temple of the goddess Ix-Chel** ★. These ruins are at the southern tip of the island, on a cliff near the lighthouse, from which the view is unforgettable. In 1988 they were almost swept away by the terrible winds of Hurricane Gilbert, but the building's walls and the architecture are still visible. The temple, in addition to being the destination of pilgrimages, served as an astronomical observatory. In 1517 Córdoba recorded a rather complete description of the site. There is a pretty view from the cliff.

Parks and Beaches

Parks

Parque Nacional de El Garrafón ★ ★ *(40 pesos; every day 8am to 5pm; Playa Garrafón, about 6km south of the ferry landing,* ☎ *7-0082),* is a very popular spot with novice snorkellers due to its calm waters. The great number of visitors to this site has caused the fish to flee for less frequented waters. The once colourful coral reef is becoming less and less attractive due to damage. It can be dangerous to touch it.

It is recommended to arrive at the park very early in the morning if you would like to see more than the palm trees swaying. The greatest flow of visitors is between 10am and 2pm. For 20 pesos, snorkelling equipment may be rented on site. There are also an aquarium, a small museum, a seafood restaurant, a changing room, lockers (*12 pesos*) and showers in the park.

Once a refuge for pirates, buccaneers and filibusters who endlessly scoured the Yucatán coast for Spanish ships carrying gold and other riches, **Isla Contoy** ★ ★ is located 24km north of Isla Mujeres, now a refuge for birds, which will definitely attract avid bird-watchers. Among the numerous bird species that make their home in the mangrove swamps and lagoons on this tiny island, which is only 8km long and 800m wide, are herons, pelicans and frigates. Just for those who are interested, the nesting season for frigate birds runs from April until July.

Isla Contoy is also good for snorkelling. The island is rimmed with sandy beaches and coral reefs. Thus, the warm, crystal-clear waters that wash its beaches abound in all kinds and all shapes of colourful fish.

Beaches

Adjacent to the village of Isla Mujeres, **Playa Norte** stretches along the northwest coast of the island. People shun this rocky beach in favour of **Playa Los Cocos**, or Cocoteros, the most beautiful beach on the island. The sand at Playa Cocoteros is white and soft underfoot, and the calm turquoise sea offers magnificent scenery. Because of its beauty, it is much prized by visitors.

Playa Paraíso spreads out just near the turtle farm. Although rather small, it is a pretty beach with ample shade and various shops and fast-food stands.

Playa Lancheros is near Hacienda Mundaca and its calm waters are perfect for swimming. Free local celebrations are sometimes organized here on Sundays.

Playa Indios, south of Playa Lancheros, offers basically the same services and appeal as its neighbour but has the advantage of being less frequented.

Outdoor Activities

Fishing

Bahía Dive Shop
Av. Rueda Medina no. 166
near the port
☎ 7-0340
This shop organizes fishing trips for about $200 per day.

Scuba Diving and Snorkelling

Divers on Isla Mujeres congregate at Parque Nacional de El Garrafón. Although the coral reefs have been damaged by tourists, Hurricane Gilbert and disease, it is still possible to admire colourful fish. It is recommended to go early in the morning to avoid the crowds.

Experienced, licensed divers will not want to miss the **caves of the sleeping sharks**, northeast of the island. The caves were discovered by an island fisherman. For as yet unknown reasons, the sharks that inhabit these caves are plunged into a state of lethargy that renders them harmless. Many films have been shot at this spot, by Jacques Cousteau among others, and various theories have been proposed to explain this mysterious phenomenon.

Buzos de México
corner of Avenidas
Rueda Medina and Madero
☎7-0131
This outfitter is also called Mexico Divers, organizes various expeditions around the island *($15 for snorkelling and about $65 for scuba diving excursions)*, rents equipment, offers lessons, and also rents boats.

Bahía Dive Shop
Avenida Rueda Medina no. 166
near the port
☎7-0340
This dive shop also rents all of the necessary diving equipment, at rates comparable to those of Buzos de México.

Accommodations

There are about 25 hotels on the island, comprising a total of approximately 600 rooms. There are small, quiet, affordable hotels, and more luxurious, service-oriented hotels. Neither is accommodation limited to the city, as tourism industry

development has fostered the construction of increasing numbers of hotels along the west coast of the island, near the lagoon.

Belmar
$
≡
Av. Hidalgo no. 110
☎*7-0430*
⇌*7-0429*
This little hotel has only 11 rooms, but it is very pleasant. It is located in the heart of the city and can therefore be noisy at times. The rooms are comfortable and well appointed. The hotel also has a suite with a whirlpool bath, kitchenette and living room.

Francis y Arlene
$
≡, ℜ
Avenida Guerrero
☎*70310*
This friendly hotel has charming little rooms that are well-kept, well-equipped and economical.

Las Cabañas María del Mar
$ bkfst incl.
ℝ, ≡, ≈, ℜ
Av. Carlos Lazo no. 1
Playa Norte
☎*7-0179*
⇌*7-0156*
This establishment has 55 rooms that are decorated very attractively in typical Mexican fashion, with a hammock on every balcony in the new, modern section of this establishment. Since

the hotel is located diagonally across from Playa Norte, only one room has an ocean view. There is also a motorcycle rental counter on site.

Cristalmar
$$
≡, ⊗, K, ≈, ℜ
Paraíso Laguna Mar
☎/≠ *7-0007*
This hotel opens onto pretty Paraíso beach. Attractive and clean, its 38 large rooms are ornamented with local crafts.

Na-Balam
$$
≡, ≈, ℜ
Calle Zazil-Ha no. 118
Playa Norte
☎*7-0279*
≠*7-0446*
A lovely little hotel situated on Playa Norte, Na-Balam is divided into two sections: on one side, the balconies face the ocean, but the view is obstructed by luxuriant vegetation; on the other side, the rooms surround an interior courtyard. Rattan furniture and turquoise marble floors contribute to the pleasant ambiance of the rooms.

Las Perlas del Caribe
$$
≡, ≈, ℜ
Av. Madero, Playa Norte
☎*7-0120*
≠*7-0011*
This hotel encloses 91 medium sized rooms

with balconies. Those with city views are less expensive than those that open onto the ocean. Evenings at the hotel's restaurant-bar are animated by a live band.

Posada del Mar
$$
≡, ⊗, ≈, ℜ
Av. Rueda Medina no. 15A
☎*7-0044*
≠*7-0266*
This establishment has 40 spacious and well decorated rooms with balconies and rattan furniture. The recently added hotel bar attracts many patrons.

La Casa de los Sueños
$$$
≈, hw, pb
Carretera Garrafón
☎*70651*
≠*70708*
www.losuenos.com
By far one of the best establishments on the island, the inviting La Casa de los Sueños is a real little pearl of a bed and breakfast full of charm right near the Parque Nacional El Garrafón. La Casa is owned by a friendly woman from Québec who rents pleasant and charmingly decorated rooms with ocean views. Part of the hotel is used to display paintings and other works by Mexican artists. After a day at the beach, read a book by the pool

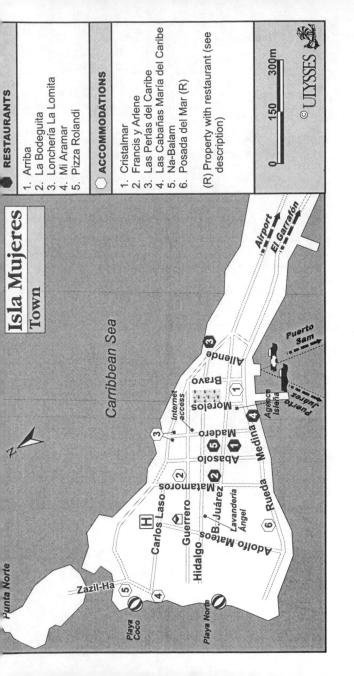

Isla Mujeres
Town

RESTAURANTS

1. Arriba
2. La Bodeguita
3. Lonchería La Lomita
4. Mi Aramar
5. Pizza Rolandi

ACCOMMODATIONS

1. Cristalmar
2. Francis y Arlene
3. Las Perlas del Caribe
4. Las Cabañas María del Caribe
5. Na-Balam
6. Posada del Mar (R)

(R) Property with restaurant (see description)

© ULYSSES

0   150   300m

Carribean Sea

Punta Norte

Playa Coco

Playa Norte

Zazil-Ha

Carlos Laso

Guerrero

Hidalgo

Adolfo Mateos

B. Juárez

Lavandería Ángel

Matamoros

Abasolo

Madero

Morelos

Bravo

Allende

Medina

Rueda

Internet access

Puerto Juárez

Agence Isleña

Puerto Sam

Airport

El Garrafón

and listen to the chirping of the birds mix with the tingling of the chimes while the sea breeze gently caresses your face. There are also two large, quiet dogs on the property called Franco and Maxime. La Casa de los Sueños is non smoking and for adults only.

 Maria's Kankin
$$$
hw, pb, ℜ
Carretera Garrafón
**mexicoweb.com/travel/kankineng.
html**

This hotel is a little oasis of tranquility next to the charming Casa de las Sueños. Though it is mostly known for its quality restaurant, the hotel has clean, well-equipped rooms of different sizes, some with kitchenettes.

Restaurants

While there are fewer than 15,000 residents on the whole island, quality restaurants are abundant due to the high tourist demand. As for dress codes, something thrown over a bathing suit and sandals will do.

Lonchería La Lomita
$
Av. Juárez 25B near Av. Allende

In this modest but pleasant decor, diners savour affordable seafood and fish of undeniable freshness. Dishes are accompanied, Mexican-style, by rice, black beans and tortillas. Breakfast is also served.

 **La Bodeguita**
$-$$$
Ave. Hidalgo 19A corner Matamoros

This cute little restaurant serves breakfast all day long. The continental breakfast *(28 pesos)* comes with free coffee which can be substituted by an espresso (very strong). Tapas, filet mignon, croissants and homemade cakes are also served here in a decor accentuated by colourful archways.

Miramar
$-$$$
Malecón

This restaurant is located near the pier where boats from the Zona Hotelera are docked next to fishing nets stretched out to the sun. Seafood, fish and tacos are on the menu.

Vegetarians

If you are vegetarian, don't worry about losing any weight during your trip to Mexico. However, if you are on a strict macrobiotic diet, you might have a harder time. If you do eat fish and seafood, you are in for some culinary delights!

Arriba
$$
Av. Hidalgo
between Madero and Abasolo
☎7-0458
Arriba offers small, simple and typical Mexican dishes. Meals are served on an upstairs terrace, shaded from the sun. "Happy Hour", between 5pm and 7pm, is a busy time.

María's Kan Kin
$$
near Parque Nacional El Garrafón in the southern part of the island
☎7-0015
The fare served here is a variation of French cuisine adapted for Yucatán specialties. Fish and seafood are served, as well as delicious desserts. From the terrace there is a pretty view of the ocean.

Pizza Rolandi
$$
Av. Hidalgo
between Madero and Abasolo
☎7-0430
This restaurant has another location in Cancún and also serves delicious wood-oven-cooked pizza. Also served are beautiful mixed salads, seafood, pasta and calzones. The Italian owner is also the chef at Casa Rolandi in Cancún. Coffee lovers can savour excellent espresso and cappuccino here.

Zazil-Ha
$$-$$$
Na-Balam hotel
☎7-0279
Yucatán specialties are the highlight at this small restaurant. The service is friendly and the ambiance relaxing. Savour a substantial breakfast in the morning or the catch of the day for supper. The tile floors, the walls decorated with several stone sculptures and the lovely colours add typical charm to this spot. We suggest that you dine on the terrasse which is close to the beach.

Entertainment

Come nightfall, Isla Mujeres offers enjoyable diversion in the few bars and restau-

Isla Mujeres

rants scattered over the island. Most of these establishments have a "happy hour", or a two-for-one special, between 5pm and 7pm. Music is omnipresent on the island, and, after having serenaded supping restaurant patrons, many local musicians entertain during evenings of dancing.

The **International Music Festival of Isla Mujeres** takes place annually during the last week of October. Over the several days of this event, groups of musicians and folk dancers from near and far perform at open-air concerts.

Cine Blanquita
Av. Morelos
between Guerrero and Hidalgo
This establishment, the only cinema in town, shows movies in English.

Ya Ya's
Av. Rueda Medina no.42
Playa Norte
At this restaurant-bar, there is dancing to the rhythm of reggae, rock and jazz until 2am or 3am.

La Peña
Av. Guerrero no. 5
☎7-0309
The sounds of Latin American and rock music and the enthusiasm of dancers reverberate on La Peña's terrace, which looks out over the sea.

Calypso Disco
Av. Rueda Medina
near the hotel Posada del Mar
At this nightclub, popular with locals, the reggae and funk beats are irresistible, despite the tiny size of the dance floor.

Buho's
Cabaña del Mar hotel
Playa Cocoteros
☎7-0086
Bubo's is a choice location for drinks on the patio before dinner. The music is not too loud and the ambiance is relaxing.

Shopping

All of the organized tour guides lead their groups through shops that proffer them commissions. These are not entirely uninteresting spots, but Mexican and Guatemalan crafts are available for much better prices elsewhere. Avenida Hidalgo is flanked by many small boutiques.

La Loma
Av. Guerrero no. 6
At La Loma, you will unearth terracotta masks; coral, silver, and leather jewellery; canvas and straw bags; and a whole assortment of hand-made goods. This is one of the largest stores on the island and

xico's craft markets are full of colourful merchandise for all tastes.
- *M. Daniels*

A beautiful beach on Laguna Nichu, strewn with *palapas* to re... under and sm... boats to sail ... to sea.
- *Tibor Bogna...*

The amazing ruins of Tulum stand at the edge of a cliff overlooking the turquoise-blue waters of the Caribbean Sea.
- *Morandi*

there are many bargains to be found here.

La Casa Isleña II
Av. Guerrero no. 3
☎7-0265
Forget about factory-made T-shirts: this boutique sells T-shirts that are hand painted by a gifted artist.

Casa del Arte Méxicana
Av. Hidalgo no. 6
This shop is worth visiting for stone sculptures created by a local artist. Hammocks, silver jewellery, batik clothing and leather goods are also sold.

Cozumel

Cozumel ★★★ is the biggest island in Mexico. Surrounded by turquoise waters and a spectacular string of coral reef, it is a scuba-diver's paradise.

Since the release of the documentary by marine explorer Jacques Cousteau in 1961, Cozumel has become a choice location, visited by thousands of scuba divers every year. Hundreds of cruise ships also make stop-overs here. The surrounding waters abound in countless aquatic species, colourful reefs and the remains of sunken Spanish galleons. In fact, more than 30% of visitors to Cozumel are scuba divers, or are aspiring to be! Other visitors can observe an extraordinary variety of migratory birds that spend a portion of the year here, visit the Parque Nacional y Jardines Botánicos Chankanaab, go shopping, go fishing, or simply relax on one of the magnificent beaches all around the island.

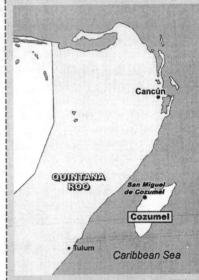

Located 19km from the coast, the island is flat and shaped like lobster claws. It's about 45km by 16km in size. The centre of Cozumel is overgrown with vegetation. Its periphery, though, is a continuous ring of white sand and limestone. Since the east coast of the island is exposed to high winds, tourist establishments and hotels are situated on the west coast. San Miguel, the only city on the island, with a population of about 50,000, is also on the west side.

Around the year 300, Cozumel was occupied by a Mayan tribe. It subsequently became an important port of commerce and ceremonial site. Women from the coast would come to Cozumel by pirogue (dugout canoe) to worship Ix-Chel, the goddess of fertility. There are more than 35 archaeological sites throughout the island but only a few are maintained. Cortez landed here in 1519 before he undertook the conquest of Mexican territory. He left two missionaries here to try to convert the population to Christianity; they were imprisoned. Cortez was preceded by Juan de Grijalva in 1518 who was seeking slaves.

The island's coves provided refuge to pirates, including the dreaded Jean Lafitte and Henry Morgan, who scoured the seas in the 17th and 18th centuries. These pirates sank countless merchant ships, the wrecks of which litter the ocean floor. In the 19th century, the economic activity of Cozumel centred around fishing, and Central American trade routes passed through here.

Cozumel's economic revival at the beginning of the century was prompted by the popularity of chewing gum in the United States. The island became a stopover on the import route from South America of *chicle*, an extract of the sapodilla tree and the base of chewing gum. This trade declined when a less expensive synthetic product was invented to replace chiclé. Later, the United States built an airforce base used by the Allies to pursue German submarines during the Second World War.

Finding Your Way Around

By Plane

Cozumel International Airport
about 3km northeast of San Miguel
☎20928
The airport has a bar-restaurant, souvenir shops and car-rental and tour counters.

AeroCozumel
☎23456

AeroCaribe
☎205503

These airlines make daily connections between Cancún and Cozumel (about 350 pesos one way). The flight takes 18min. A return trip from Cozumel to Playa del Carmen costs about 150 pesos. This flight takes 10min. For more details, contact **Mexicana** (☎20157). Mexicana also has frequent flights between Cozumel, Miami and San Francisco. Departure tax for international flights is $16.

From the airport you can take one of the frequent shuttles to San Miguel for a reasonable price. Taxis are also available at a fairly good price. This is the most common form of transport.

By Boat

There are around 20 crossings every day between Cozumel and Playa del Carmen *(from Playa to Cozumel: from 5am to 9pm, from Cozumel to Playa: from 4am to 8pm)*. It takes about 40min and costs 175 pesos return. The ferries dock at the local port of Cozumel, across from Benito Juárez Avenue in San Miguel. Be sure to bring along some motion-sickness medication and to eat only a light meal at least a half an hour before getting on the ferry. Since the sea is quite choppy, at least a third of passengers get seasick. On certain ferries you can sit outside on the deck. The following companies travel between these two cities. It is a good idea to confirm departures in advance.

Waterjet Service
Boats: Mexico I, Mexico II and Mexico III
☎21508

Aviomar
Hovercraft
☎20588

A car ferry crosses Cozumel and Puerto Morelos, a small village 36km south of Cancún. It also stops at San Miguel. The crossing takes

Cozumel

2.5hrs and you have to get there 3hrs in advance.

Canaco (*Cámara Nacional de Comercio - Servicios y Turismo de Cozumel*)
☎25014
The international port at Cozumel, a few kilometres south of Cancún, is specifically for cruise ships. Many dock here every day. The company *Canaco* regularly distributes the arrival schedule. This information is published in the regional newspaper *Novedades*.

By Car

Many hotels in Cozumel have car rental counters. Cars can also be rented at the airport and in San Miguel. A car ferry crosses once a day between Cozumel and Puerto Morelos but it's fairly complicated and expensive (see above). Puerto Morelos is 36km from Cozumel. The crossing takes 2.5hrs.

To reach various places on the island, you have to drive on very rough dirt roads. Insurance included in car rental does not cover damage incurred when not driving on Cozumel's paved road.

The island really has only one paved road which starts from the north point of the island, stretches along the west coast, and then curves around the south point and returns to San Miguel. A straight road crosses the island in the middle, from the east to the west coast (dangerous at night). When you arrive on Cozumel by boat you will be met by a crowd of people trying rent you a car or motorcycle. According to the car-rental agencies, it is better to make a reservation in advance from your country, which is less expensive and will save you time upon arrival. Ask for a written confirmation. In Cozumel, car-rentals cost at least $50 a day depending on the model. Renting a motorcycle for a day costs between $25 and $30, and a bicycle is around $10.

Here are a few businesses that rent cars, motorcycles and bicycles in Cozumel:

Aguila
☎20729
⇌23285

Budget
☎20903
⇌25177

Hertz
☎20151
⇌23955

If you are staying for several days it's probably better to get a long-term rental. The following company offers such rentals.

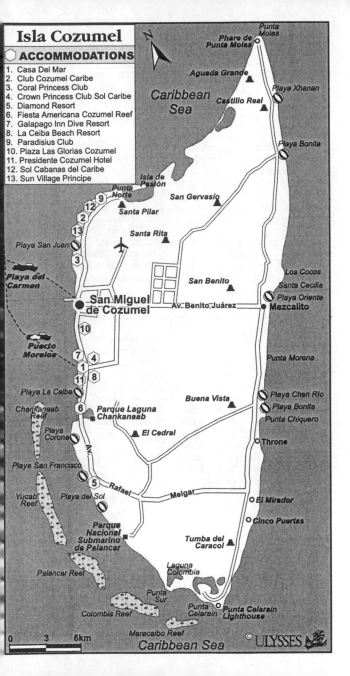

Isla Cozumel

⬭ ACCOMMODATIONS

1. Casa Del Mar
2. Club Cozumel Caribe
3. Coral Princess Club
4. Crown Princess Club Sol Caribe
5. Diamond Resort
6. Fiesta Americana Cozumel Reef
7. Galapago Inn Dive Resort
8. La Ceiba Beach Resort
9. Paradisius Club
10. Plaza Las Glorias Cozumel
11. Presidente Cozumel Hotel
12. Sol Cabanas del Caribe
13. Sun Village Principe

N

Caribbean Sea

Punta Molas
Phare de Punta Molas
Aguada Grande
Playa Xhanan
Castillo Real
Playa Bonita

Isla de Pasión
Punta Norte
Santa Pilar
San Gervasio
Santa Rita

Playa San Juan

Los Cocos
Santa Cecilia
San Benito
Playa Oriente
Mezcalito
Av. Benito Juárez

Playa del Carmen

San Miguel de Cozumel

Punta Morena

Puerto Morelos

Playa La Ceiba
Chankanaab Reef
Parque Laguna Chankanaab
Buena Vista
Playa Chen Rio
Playa Bonita
Punta Chiquero

Playa Corona
El Cedral
Throne

Playa San Francisco

Yucab Reef
Playa del Sol
Rafael
Melgar
El Mirador
Cinco Puertas

Parque Nacional Submarino de Palancar
Tumba del Caracol

Laguna Colombia

Palancar Reef

Punta Sur
Punta Celarain
Punta Celarain Lighthouse

Colombia Reef

Maracaibo Reef
Caribbean Sea

0 3 6km

© ULYSSES

Continental Car Rental
☎24525

By Motorcycle

Although this is a popular way to get around the island, accidents are very common since the roads are rough and traffic is heavy. Also, the roads are often not very wide leading to some close encounters between cars and motorcycles. Unless you are an experienced rider and are familiar with the road signs and the manner of driving in Mexico, you should take a taxi.

By Taxi

There are no taxis at the airport due to an arrangement between the taxi union and the bus union. Taxis can, however, take you to the airport. Since taxis don't have meters, the price depends on the distance travelled, the price of gas and your negotiating skills. Taxis are available 24 hours a day in Cozumel but there are additional costs between midnight and 6am.

Taxi station
Calle 2 Norte San Miguel
☎20041
In San Miguel there is a taxi station. At your hotel's reception desk they can inform you of current rates. Although they vary a lot, the

following prices (in pesos) may be helpful as an indication:

From San Miguel:

to the airport: *32*
to the cruise ship port: *50*
**to the northern
         hotel zone:** *34*
**to the southern
         hotel zone:** *117*
to the Palancar reef:*120*
to Celarain: *360*
to San Gervasio:*360*
to Parque Chankanaab: *70*
Tour of the island: *360*
Ruins and island tour: *480*

By Bus

At the airport, a *colectivo* takes travellers to either the northern or southern hotel zone for around $8. Because of an agreement between taxi drivers and bus drivers, there is no bus service between the two hotel zones.

Practical Information

Tourist Information

Be wary of tourist information booths close to the park. Their only goal is to sell time-sharing condominiums, and the tourist information they offer is not reliable.

Delegación estatal de Turismo
Edificio Plaza del Sol, San Miguel
☎*20972* or *20218*
Not always open.

Cozumel Hotel Association
Mon to Fri 8am to 7pm
☎*23132*
☎*22809*

Tour Companies

To go to Tulúm, Playa del Carmen, Cancún, Chichén Itzá, etc.:

Intermar Caribe
Calle 2 Norte no. 101B
☎*21535*

Apple Vacation
Corner Ave. 30 and Ave. 11
☎*24311*

Post Office

Mon to Fri 9am to 6pm, Sat 9am to noon
On Calle 7 Sur, at Av. Rafael Melgar
☎*20106*

Telephone

The area code for Cozumel is *987*. You can make long distance calls from telephone booths with a calling card.

Internet

Diamond Internet
Avenida 10 no. 200, between Calle 4 Norte and Calle 6 Norte
☎*21153*
service@dicoz.com
Diamond Internet belongs to the same owner as the Diamond Bakery. It offers six computers in air-conditioned premises at a price of $6 an hr or $3 for 15min.

Banks and Foreign Exchange Offices

Banks are open from 9am to 1:30pm from Monday to Friday. To change money it is better to arrive before 11am.

Atlántico
with automatic teller
Calle 1 Sur no. 11, San Miguel
☎*20142*

Banamex
Avenida 5 Sur, at Calle Adolfo Rosada Salas, San Miguel
☎*23411*

Serfin
Calle 1 Sur, between Avenidas 5 and 10, San Miguel
☎*20930*

Promotora Cambiaria del Centro
(foreign exchange office)
Mon to Sat 8am to 9pm
Av. 5A Sur, at Calle Salas

Cozumel

Health

Clinics and Hospitals

Most of the clinics in Cozumel are used to treating minor injuries associated with scuba diving because accidents happen frequently.

Cruz Roja (Red Cross) ☎*21058*

Hospital General
☎*203059*

Servicios de Securidad Subaquatica
subaquatic safety service
Avenida 5 Sur no. 21
☎*(98) 22387*
⇍*(98) 21848*
emergency: ☎*(98) 21430*
This clinic specializes in the pressure-related problems scuba divers can encounter. Open 24 hrs a day, it is financed almost entirely by a sort of "levy" imposed on diving excursions *($1/day)*.

Meditur
Offers the same services as the above clinic
Calle 2 Norte, between Avenidas 5 and 10
☎*23070*

Clinica Cozumel
☎*23545*
⇍*24070*
Affiliated with the South Miami Hospital, this clinic is open 24 hrs a day and provides service in English.

Pharmacies

In San Miguel there are three Canto pharmacies, and four Joaquín pharmacies. The following two are centrally located pharmacies:

Farmacia Canto
Avenida Pedro Joaquin Coldwell no. 498, at Avenida 5 Sur, San Miguel
☎*22589*

Farmacia Joaquín
Avenida Benito Juárez, beside the Parque Central, San Miguel
☎*20125*

Safety

Police
☎*20092*

Fire
☎*20800*

Publications

In many shops and hotels you can get the Blue Guide *(Guía Azul)*, a free English publication that comes out three times a year. It contains a lot of advertising but may be useful.

Gas Station

The only gas station on the island is in San Miguel, at the corner of Benito Juárez Avenue and Avenida 30. It

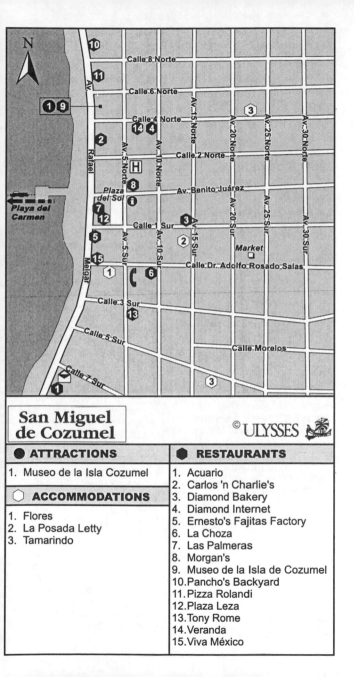

San Miguel de Cozumel

© ULYSSES

● ATTRACTIONS

1. Museo de la Isla Cozumel

⬠ ACCOMMODATIONS

1. Flores
2. La Posada Letty
3. Tamarindo

⬡ RESTAURANTS

1. Acuario
2. Carlos 'n Charlie's
3. Diamond Bakery
4. Diamond Internet
5. Ernesto's Fajitas Factory
6. La Choza
7. Las Palmeras
8. Morgan's
9. Museo de la Isla de Cozumel
10. Pancho's Backyard
11. Pizza Rolandi
12. Plaza Leza
13. Tony Rome
14. Veranda
15. Viva México

is open every day from 7am to midnight. Avoid going there around 3pm because that is when the staff changes shifts and there is a long wait.

Photoshops

Foto Omega
Plaza Orbi, Avenida 3 Sur no. 27, at Avenida Rafael Melgar
One-hour service.

Exploring

San Miguel

This small city is the heart of the island, and the grid-system of streets makes it is easy to find your way around. The action centres around the **Plaza del Sol**, the main park of the city. From approximately 8pm to 10pm on Sunday nights the mariachi bands can be heard, and all the locals gather together to celebrate. Although the selection of craft and t-shirt shops, cafés and jewellery shops is very tourist-oriented in this region, the city has kept its Mexican spirit. Most of the island's restaurants are found in this area, and many shops line the *malecón* (seaside promenade).

The **Museo de la Isla de Cozumel** ★★ *($3; every day 9am to 5pm; Av. Rafael Melgar, between Calles 4 and 6, ☎221434)*, located in the centre of San Miguel, was moved into a stylish hotel dating from the early 1900s. This little museum offers insight into the anthropological and cultural history of Cozumel. There are interesting artifacts like a statue of the goddess Ix-Chel, stone snake-heads, and an enormous Olmeca jade head. It is possible to take photographs although lighting may not be sufficient. Short slide shows present the flora and fauna, the reefs and the aquatic species of the island. The museum visit takes 1hr. In conjunction with certain government agencies, the museum organizes biologist-led night excursions from May to September to observe the giant sea turtles laying their eggs on the isolated beaches of the island. The museum also serves as a cultural centre offering many activities including Mayan language courses, craft demonstrations and theatrical productions. The museum's restaurant, on the top floor, offers a panoramic view of the Caribbean Sea.

The South of the Island

At the south end of the island, the road opens onto the **Faro Celarain** ★ *(about $1)*. This gleaming white lighthouse borders the Tumba del Caracol ruins which formerly served as a landmark for sailors. The lighthouse was constructed in 1901 by Felix Garcia Aguilar who lived in the little adjoining building for over 50 years. Today, his son, Primo Garcia Valdés, takes care of the lighthouse and a little seafood restaurant on the ground floor (open Sundays). It's worth the trouble to climb the 130 steps to the top; there you will discover a spectacular panoramic view of the region. The lighthouse is difficult to access being 4km from the main road at the end of a small rocky dirt road.

The North of the Island

Although the **Faro Punta Molas** ★, at the north end of the island, is difficult to reach, it's worth the trip. It is a secluded spot where the beach is lovely. The road leading here is only passable with an all-terrain vehicle.

The Ruins

The island's nine ruins demonstrate Cozumel's importance as a ceremonial site and centre of commerce. Most of the remains are small low square buildings.

Since the semi-destruction of El Cedral (see below), **San Gervasio** ★ *($3.50; every day 7am to 5pm)* has become the most important group of ruins on the island. It is thought that San Gervasio was inhabited by Mayans from the year AD 300 to approximately 1500. It was, at that time, the capital of the island. There is a group of small sanctuaries and temples that were erected to honour Ix-Chel, the Mayan goddess of fertility. Each of the ruins has an accompanying plaque with text in Mayan, English and Spanish. Overall, San Gervasio consists of stone structures, lintels and columns, all scattered around a large area, and a few groups of less important ruins that disappear in the forest. At the entrance to the site, where you purchase your ticket, there are craft shops and a snack bar. To reach San Gervasio, take the road that traverses the island eastward from San Miguel. A sign will indicate which junction to take, then you will have to

Cozumel

drive about 10km north. San Gervasio receives an average of about 285 visitors every day.

South of San Francisco beach, a 3.5km-long paved road, leads inland to **El Cedral** ★, the oldest construction on the island. Before Hurricane Roxanne (1995), traces of old painted Mayan frescoes could still be seen here. This site site has suffered over the years. In 1518, the Spanish practically reduced it to nothing. Then, during the Second World War, the Americans levelled it to make room for a landing strip. From May 1 to 3, an annual celebration with music, dancing, bullfights and competitions is held at El Cedral.

The **Tumba del Caracol** ★ ruins at the south end of the island get their name from a temple that has a square base with a snail-shaped (in Spanish: *caracol*) dome on it. Today it is half demolished. It is thought that this site was constructed in homage to the wind or to the Mayan god *Kukulcán*. On the west side of the temple, over the door, traces of red paint can still be seen.

On the northeast coast of the island is **Castillo Real**, a small group of ruins that includes

a tower, the remains of a pyramid, and a square temple which is cracked in the middle. You will also notice colour frescoes on the inside. To get to the ruins from the dirt road you have to cover about 30m of difficult terrain on foot.

Parks and Beaches

Parks

Ten kilometres south of San Miguel you will find **Parque Nacional Chankanaab** ★★ (*$8; every day 8am to 4:30pm; Carretera Sur Km 9*), one of the most attractive sites of the island. It contains a large **botanical garden**. The Chankanaab lagoon is a natural aquarium supplied with sea water from underground tunnels. Approximately 50 species of fish, crustaceans and corals can be observed here but scuba diving is not permitted. A winding path leads you through the botanical garden, with its 350 types of plants and tropical trees from 22 different countries. An interesting museum describes the life of the Mayas. From the neighbouring beach you can swim in the calm lagoon. Snorkellers can explore the fascinating caverns and tunnels in the limestone. The 320m-wide Chankanaab coral reef attracts many scuba divers with its countless colourful species. You have to dive to a depth of between 2 and 18m to examine the sights: the coral, a bronze statue of Christ, a statue of the Virgin Mary, cannons, ancient anchors and a sunken ship. Scuba-diving equipment can be rented or bought on site. At the entrance to the site, there are change rooms, beach huts, a snack bar, a bar-restaurant and gift shops. Many lounge chairs and *palapas* (straw parasols) are available to tourists.

Coral Reefs

As earlier mentioned, Cozumel is renowned for the great quantity and tremendous beauty of its coral reefs. Rumour has it that 1,500 scuba divers visit the island every day.

The **Palancar reef**, easily the most spectacular for its size and fabulous schools of fish, alone draws thousands of swimmers every year. Chankanaab park is the ideal place to learn how to scuba dive. There are even stairs you can go down leading to the submerged bronze statue of Christ.

The **Yucab reef**, reserved for intermediate divers, is perfect for underwater photography of species that stay immobile to avoid the current.

The **Santa Rosa and Colombia reefs**, famous for their immense size, are worth more than one visit. The DC-3 airplane that rests at the bottom of the Ceiba reef attracts not only frog-people... but also filmmakers! Sea horses have chosen it as their home.

Finally, the **El Paso del Cedral reef** allows novices to visit a cavern and encounter big hungry fish that don't like tourists who come empty-handed...

Cozumel

West-Coast Beaches

Playa San Juan

This beach lines the whole northern hotel zone of San Miguel and ends at Punta Norte. It is a quiet beach where you can find all sorts of diving equipment, as well as certified instructors. Windsurfing is recommended here. There are many bars and snack bars.

Playa San Francisco

This beach is 5km long and is considered one of the most appealing on the island. Many conveniences (bar, restaurant, change rooms, boutiques, lounge chairs and *palapas*, diving-equipment rental, volleyball net) are provided. Underwater wonders can be found in the calm waters close to shore. On Sundays, this beach is particularly popular with locals. Also on Sundays, many local musicians come here to play.

Playa Escondida

Located 19km south of San Miguel, this beach is graced with clear tranquil water. From the main road, there is a sign indicating the dirt road which leads here.

Playa del Sol

Just south of Playa San Francisco, this beach is a popular day-trip destination. All the amenities are available: a bar-restaurant, changing rooms and lockers, gift shops and an equipment-rental counter for snorkelling and scuba diving. Horseback riding outings are also organized.

Playa La Ceiba

Beyond the abundance of corals and sponges in the waters off this calm beach are the remains of a Convair airplane. It is 7.7m down, 140m from the water's edge. It was deliberately sunk for the Mexican film *Survive II*.

East-Coast Beaches

Playa Oriente

This beach is slightly north of the road that traverses the island, at the end of the paved road. The water here is among the choppiest of all the island's beaches, and only experienced surfers should take on the waves here. There is a restaurant.

Playa Chiquero

Tucked in a crescent-shaped cove, this is one of the most charming beaches on the east coast of the island. It is protected from waves by a reef and is ideal for swimming and surfing. A seafood restaurant named Playa Bonita is located here.

Playa Chen Río

This beach is near the middle of the east side of the island, about 5km north of Punta Chiqueros. The clear, relatively calm waters are suitable for surfing. There is parking, a restaurant and a bar.

Outdoor Activities

Fishing

Beach Clubs

Beach clubs combine the practical and the pleasant, serving as both restaurant and sports facility. The most popular sport at Cozumel being, you guessed it, scuba diving.

Playa Sol
10am to 5pm
south route near El Cedral
☎*21935*
Well known among hungry divers ready to head off to discover Palancar, this beach club offers an outdoor restaurant, a souvenir shop, changing rooms and even a relaxing little zoo with alligators, parrots and rabbits.

Playa Corona
1km south of Chankanaab park

Sponsored by the beer of the same name, the offers diving, deep-sea fishing, refreshments and meals at its restaurant. What makes this site interesting is its proximity to underwater flora and fauna making observation very easy.

Club Nautico de Cozumel
Zona Hotelera Norte Km 1.6
☎*20118* or *21135*
This club has organized a world-class fishing tournament in April or May of each year since the 1970s.

Antonio Gonzalez Fernandez
This sports-fishing tournament, which takes place in November from the San Miguel quay, usually has about 30 participants. In 1996, the winner pulled in an impressive 54kg blue marlin and a 6kg red snapper.

Semarnap
Secretaria del Medio Ambiante, Recursos Naturales y Pesca
Bulevar Kukulkan
☎*830474* or *830601*

Based in Cancún, this governmental organization responsible for natural resources and fishing can supply information regarding upcoming events.

The **Caleta Marina** quay, located two steps away from the Presidente hotel, is a good spot for fishing excursions throughout the year.

Cozumel

Horseback Riding

It's very pleasant to discover the region on horseback. A 4hr tour costs about $60 and usually includes a guide, transport to the hotel and refreshments.

The following organization offers such excursions:

Rancho Buenavista
departures from Mon to Sat
☎*21537* or *24374*

Scuba Diving

Of course coral reefs are a fantastic sight to see while exploring the sea's depths but coral grows very slowly. Avoid touching it as this causes damage to the coral and you may injure yourself.

Businesses offering scuba-diving services with a guide, equipment and transportation to diving sites abound in Cozumel. Large hotels can also arrange for all necessary outfitting. The cost of a diving excursion may depend on various factors: lessons for beginners, distance to diving sites, excursion-cruise with a meal on a boat, etc. For example,

it may cost about $60 for a day of scuba diving with a trained guide and two oxygen tanks. On the island you will find many advertising pamphlets and diving magazines which offer an exhaustive list of diving centres. Here are a few specialized businesses in Cozumel:

Pasqual's Scuba Center
Av. Rosado Salas, at Calle 5
☎*25454*
There are no diving mysteries left for the owners of Pasqual's, who have acquired 45 years of experience between them. Pasqual and Ernesto's speed boat gets you to the site and has everything necessary on board for a trouble-free excursion.

Aldora Divers
☎*24048*
www.aldora.com
dave@Aldora.com
Aldora Divers has established a significant presence in cyberspace with their internet web site. Aldora attracts divers from around the world. Until the time of their visit, clients use the web site to maintain a friendly relationship with those who work there. After returning home, divers can visit the Aldora web site to give an assessment of their expeditions.

**Sea Urchin Dive
Shop and Travel**
☎*24517*
This diving centre organizes
diving trips around
Cozumel.

Dive Paradise
Av. Rafael Melgar no. 601
☎*21007*
≈*21061*
Dive Paradise has an im-
pressive team of 58 instructors.

Yucatech
Avenida 15, near Calle A. Salas
☎*25659*
In addition to organizing
diving days, Yuchatech can
preserve your adventure on
video.

TTC Diving
Playa San Juan, Club Cozumel Caribe
Hotel
☎*24476*
TTC Diving has been established in Cozumel since
1969.

Deep Blue
Corner Ave. 10 and A.R. Salas
☎/≈*25653*
deepblue@cozumel.com
Deep Blue organizes scuba-
diving excursions at the
beginners and advanced
levels.

It is also possible to take
PADI-certification (recognized internationally)
courses. For an advanced
course, the price is around
$700. These courses are
spread out over a number of

sessions. You can also take
shorter courses on the ba-
sics.

Cruises

Nautilus IV
around $35 US
Zona Hotelera Sur Km 1.7
☎*20831*
This glass-bottomed boat is
much like the one in
Cancún's hotel district (see
p 109). It offers cruises
complete with spectacular
views of the region's
subaquatic flora and fauna.
The semi-submersible is
15m long and air condi-
tioned. It is stationed across
from the Fiesta Inn
Cozumel. Departures are at
10am, noon and 2pm. The
cost includes refreshments
and a guide to provide
explanations.

El Zorro
$50 US
☎*20522*
You can get close to the
sea and the wind aboard El
Zorro's 13m catamaran
by relaxing in the boom
netting. On board the
catamaran there are
drinks, meals,
snorkelling equip-
ment and guides.
Everything is
included in the
price.

Cozumel

**Fury
Catamarans**
$40 US
Zona hotelera Sur Km 4, near the Casa
del Mar hotel
☎25145
Fury Catamarans offers the
same type of activities except that the trip also leads
to a private beach where
there are other activities
(volleyball, kayaking, etc.).
On Tuesdays and Thursdays,
Fury Catamarans go to the
Palancar reef.

Capitania de Puerto Cozumel
Av. Rafael Melgar no. 601
☎22409
If you have your own boat
or rent one, it is recom-
mended that you contact the
Capitania de Puerto
Cozumel, or the office of the
Cozumel harbour master,
before you leave to find out
weather conditions and to
get information for problem-
free navigating.

Accommodations

With respect to lodgings, the
island is divided into three
areas: San Miguel, the hotel
zone north of San Miguel
along the waterfront (Zona
Hotelera Norte), and the
hotel zone south of San
Miguel (Zona Hotelera Sur).
The northern zone has the
most luxurious hotels on the
island. The most recent ho-

tels, however, are found in
the southern zone as it is
developing more rapidly.
The southern zone is also
conveniently located close
to Parque Chankanaab,
Cozumel's main attraction.

La Posada Letty
$
Avenida 14, corner Calle 1
La Posada Letty rents simple, economical rooms that
are a bit worn but have
humming fans.

🌴Tamarindo
$
bkfst
Calle 4 Norte no. 421
☎/≈23614
tamarindo@cozumel.com.mx
Run by a friendly French-
man and his Mexican wife,
the bed and breakfast, is a
good choice in the centre
of San Miguel. This charming establishment is a 5min
walk from the central park
and the ocean. There are
three simple rooms, which
are quite big, clean, comfortable and decorated in
the most genuine Mexican
style. The Tamarindo has
an attractive shaded courtyard where you can relax
in a hammock. Guests can
use the communal kitchen,
which has an unlimited
supply of purified water.
Daycare service is available
upon request. The owner is
in the process of building
another property, and the
work should be completed
in the next few months.

Casa del Mar
$$

≡, ≈, ℜ

Zona Hotelera Sur Km 4

☎*21900*

⇌*21855*

casamar@cozumel.rce.com

The 106 rooms of the Casa del Mar are attractively decorated with local crafts. The rooms overlook either the ocean or the pool. The hotel also has eight *cabañas*, which are a bit more expensive but up to four people can stay in them. The Casa del Mar has a dive shop, a car-rental counter, two restaurants, two bars and a travel agency.

Club Cozumel Caribe
$$$

⊗, ≡, ≈, ℜ

Playa San Juan Km 4.5

☎*20100* or *1-800-327-2254*

⇌*20288*

The Club Cozumel Caribe makes life easy for its occupants. This is the hotel that initiated the all-inclusive package in Cozumel. Even though its beach is small, it is excellent for scuba diving. The rooms are large, decorated in modern fashion and have air conditioning and telephones. Most of them have a view of the sea and a balcony. The hotel has 260 rooms in a 10-storey tower that was added to the original three-story building. The pool is medium in size. There is a dive shop, a tennis court and a shopping promenade.

 ## La Ceiba
$$$

◷, ≡, ℝ, ≈, ℜ

Carratera de Chankanaab Km 4.5

☎*20379, 20815* or

800-777-5873

⇌*20065*

La Ceiba lodges almost exclusively scuba divers, curious to see the ruins of the airplane in the nearby waters. The hotel is located about three kilometres south of San Miguel, close to the cruise ship docks. The 113 rooms are inviting, with beige tiling and solid wood furniture. They all have an ocean view and a mini-bar. The building is a simple highrise but the gardens are pretty, and from the beach there is open access to an underwater diving site, with all the necessary diving equipment supplied by the hotel. There is also a large square pool with a swim-up bar and a whirlpool.

Crown Princess Club Sol Caribe Cozumel
$$$

≈, ≡, ℝ, ℜ

Playa Paraíso Km 3.5, Zona Hotelera Sur

☎*20388*

⇌*21301*

cpczm@cozumel.czm.com.mx

Crown Princess Club Sol Caribe Cozumel is a 350-room, nine-storey hotel. The beach, across the street, is accessible by a tunnel. The hotel has an impressive lobby with a

Cozumel

large thatched roof. Across from the beach is the arabesque-shaped pool and the refreshing shade of some large trees. The rooms, decorated in pastels, are equipped with wicker furniture, a marble bathroom, a telephone, a minibar and a small balcony. The hotel has a complete dive shop, two lit tennis courts and a private beach.

🦑 Allegro Resort

Hotelera Sur Km 16.5
☎ *23433*
📠 *24508*
www.allegroresort.com
At the edge of Playa San Francisco, close to the Palancar reef, is the Allegro Resort, an all-inclusive hotel with 300 rooms in two Polynesian style two-storey pavilions. The rooms are bright, quite big and austerely decorated. They all have air conditioning. The hotel has two pools, two bars, a dining room and four lit tennis courts. Bicycles and motorcycles can be rented here. A small boat takes hotel guests to the Palancar reef and the hotel supplies all the necessary equipment for scuba diving and snorkelling. Every night the hotel organizes an event based on a theme (tropical dance, performance by a hypnotist, disco night, karaoke, cabaret, Mexican folklore, etc.).

Paradisus Club
$$$
≡, ≈, ☉, ℜ
Zone Hotelera Norte Km 3.8
☎ *20412*
📠 *21599*
Previously known as the Meliá Mayan Cozumel, the is a luxurious hotel surrounded by tall trees. There are 200 rooms richly decorated in Mexican style, all of which offer a private balcony and a view of the ocean. Some of them have whirlpools. The hotel has a very good restaurant, two pools and two tennis courts. Fishing, diving, surfing and horseback riding are some of the activities organized at the Paradisus. All drinks and meals are included in the price of the room.

Sol Cabañas del Caribe
$$$
≡, ≈, ℜ
Carretera Costera Norte Km 5
☎ *20017* or *1-800-336-3542*
📠 *21599*
paradisu@cozumel.czm.com.mx
The intimate and peaceful Sol Cabañas del Caribe is close to a beach that is perfect for sailing and diving. There are 50 rooms and nine private *cabañas* close to the beach, as well as a restaurant. All the necessary equipment for snorkelling, scuba diving, fishing and other aquatic sports is supplied. Musicians provide evening entertainment at the small lounge-bar.

Sun Village Principe
$$$

⊗, ≡, ≈, ℜ

Calle San Juan Km 3.5

☎*20144*

⇒*20016*

dzavala@cozumel.czm.com.mx

The Sun Village Principe hotel has 97 comfortable rooms on three floors. They all have a telephone and a view of the sea. Only a few have private balconies. The decor is simple, modern and colourful. The biggest pool is bordered on one side by an outdoor restaurant-bar covered with a great *palapa* roof. There is another, smaller pool and a wading pool for kids.

Plaza Las Glorias
$$$

≡, ≈

Av. Rafael Melgar Km 1.5

☎*22000*

⇒*21937*

You can almost touch the water from the Plaza Las Glorias, a Mexican-style hotel that has 170 large, well-decorated rooms, each with a private balcony and a view of the ocean. There are two bars, two restaurants, a dive shop and boutiques. You can rent a moped here. Local bands play here almost every night.

Fiesta Americana Cozumel Reef
$$$-$$$$

bkfst; ≡, ≈, ℜ

Carretera de Chankanaab Km 7.5

☎*22622*

⇒*22154*

azubieta@fiestamericana.com.mx

Formerly the flagship of the Holiday Inn chain, the Fiesta Americana Cozumel Reef is a 228-room hotel facing a very attractive beach. It is located close to the Chankanaab lagoon. The spacious rooms all have balconies and a view of the sea. They are charmingly decorated with wood and rattan furniture and colourful walls. As well as a large pool, this hotel has two restaurants, two tennis courts, a sailing and windsurfing school, a bar on the beach, a souvenir shop and a dive shop.

Galapago Inn
$$$-$$$$

≡, ℝ, ≈, ℜ

Carretera de Chankanaab, Km 1.5

☎*20663*

Galapago Inn is a three-storey establishment that attracts a lot of scuba divers because of its extensive facilities (school, equipment, boats and dock). A number of diving packages are available depending on the season. Located 1.5km south of San Miguel, across from the Fiesta Inn, this Mexican-style hotel has 50

Cozumel

rooms. The rooms have tile floors, are clean and modestly furnished and all have a balcony, a fridge and a bathroom with a shower stall. The beach is pleasant and lined with hammocks.

Coral Princess Club
$$$$

Zona Hotelera Norte Km 2.5
☎ *22911*
⇋ *22800*
coralprin@cozumel.finred.com.mx

Located on a small beach north of the city, the Coral Princess Club has 139 suites. The suites are comprised of either a bedroom and living room, or one or two bedrooms with a kitchen and a living room. The decor is plain and modern in style, with white wicker furniture and colourful bedspreads. All the rooms have a view of the ocean and a telephone. Among other amenities, they offer a restaurant, a pool, a travel agency and a dive shop.

Presidente Cozumel
$$$$$

ℝ, ≡, ≈, ℜ

Carretera de Chankanaab Km 6.5
☎ *20322*
⇋ *21360*
cozumel@interconti.com.mx

Located away from the commotion, the Coral Princess Club is situated close to a beach that is excellent for diving and is surrounded by greenery. The lobby is mod-

ern and covered with a thatched roof. The 253 large, comfortable and luxuriously decorated rooms all have a private balcony. The rooms are divided among small one- to four-storey buildings. Most of the rooms have a view of the sea. The hotel has a big square pool, two excellent restaurants (Caribeño and Arecife), two bars, a billiard room, everything required for scuba diving, a car and motorcycle rental counter and two lit tennis courts. Interesting bit of trivia: this beautiful hotel was the setting of the film *Against All Odds*, starring Rachel Ward, Jeff Bridges and James Woods.

Restaurants

In general, it is much less expensive to eat at one of the many restaurants in San Miguel than at the hotels. Nevertheless, certain hotels have highly recommended restaurants. Cozumel's cuisine is similar to Cancún's: typically Mexican dishes as well as French, Italian and American food. Large chains such as Dairy Queen, Subway and Kentucky Fried Chicken have arrived in Cozumel over the last few years.

Diamond Bakery
$
Avenida 15
Small, modern and air-conditioned (!), Diamond Bakery makes croissants, cookies, cakes and ice-cream. Good view of the street corner from its panoramic windows. Friendly service.

Diamond Internet
10 Avenida no. 200, between Calle 4 Norte and Calle 6 Norte
☎*21153*
service@dicoz.com
Belonging to the same owner as the Diamond Bakery (see above), the Diamond Internet is air conditioned and has six computers that cost $6 for one hour of use or $3 for 15 min.

La Choza
$-$$
8am to 11pm
Av. Rosada Salas no. 200
☎*20958*
With its *palapa* roof and tasty little dishes, La Choza is one of the best Mexican restaurants on the island. The country's specialties (*pibil* chicken, *sopa de lima*, *guacamole*, etc.) can be savoured here at very reasonable prices. La Choza is a favourite among local residents. The ambiance is relaxing and the terrace is always nice and breezy. Economical breakfasts.

Ernesto's Fajitas Factory
$-$$
Avenida Rafael Melgar
Ernesto's Fajitas Factory not only serves fajitas, but the usual assortment of tacos, quesadillas and burritos, as well as some vegetarian dishes. Breakfast costs only $3.

Restaurante del Museo
$-$$$
9am to 5pm
Av. Rafael Melgar between Calles 4 and 6
☎*221434*
Before visiting the Museo de la Isla de Cozumel (see p 172), have something to eat at the Restaurante del Museo which serves delicious Mexican food. The breakfasts are big and there is a pretty view of the sea.

Acuario
$$-$$$
Av. Rafael Melgar at Calle 11
☎*21097*
Acuario means aquarium in Spanish. The dining area is surrounded by aquariums full of fish. The plates, too, are full of fish since this restaurant specializes in fresh fish and seafood; you will eat well here.

Carlos 'n Charlie's
$$-$$$
Av. Rafael Melgar no. 11
☎*20191*
Like the one in Cancún, this restaurant-bar is somewhat of a zoo, with its blaring rock music, constantly

Cozumel

flowing beer, a ping-pong table and busy decor. They serve generous portions of ribs, grilled steak and chicken. Facing the sea, one block north of the port, Carlos 'n Charlie's is easily recognizable by its red exterior.

Morgan's
$$-$$$

Ave. Benito Juárez, corner Calle 5

☎20584

Morgan's is named after the notorious pirate who once scoured the Atlantic and looted Spanish galleons. Today his picture is on the popular brand-name bottle of rum called Captain Morgan's. Steak and seafood dishes are served here. The elegant decor and discrete service will make your evening an enjoyable one.

Pancho's Backyard
$$-$$$

Avenida Rafael Melgar, between Calle 8 Norte and Calle 10 Norte

Pancho's Backyard is aptly named, because it is literally located in the "backyard" of the Cinco Soles souvenir shop, and there is no sign to indicate that it is. Once past the sliding doors, you will be immersed in a buccolic interior courtyard, a tranquil spot in which to eat and relax. The white-stucco walls and red-tiled roof evoke the colonial style. Marimba shows liven things up for diners while they

savour the classics of Mexican cuisine.

Pizza Rolandi
$$-$$$

Av. Rafael Melgar between Calles 8 and 10

☎20946

Cozumel has its own Pizza Rolandi, just like in Cancún. Here too they serve mostly pizza cooked in a wood-burning oven, but also seafood and steaks. This is one to remember.

Tony Rome
$$-$$$

Avenida 5 between Calle Salas and Calle 3 Sur

☎20131

Tony Rome's large dining room looks like a Mexican sugar shack. The patrons don't seem to care about the decor, but rather about stuffing themselves with the very simple but filling spare ribs and grilled chicken. All kinds of shows are put on at night, whereas karaoke is organized on some nights for patrons who aren't afraid of losing their inhibitions

Veranda
$$-$$$

Calle 4 Norte, between Ave. 5 Norte and Ave. 10 Norte

☎24132

This restaurant's facade does in fact look a lot like a veranda. The decor is simple, the food is excellent, and the staff is very friendly. When the sun sets over the ocean, the terrasse becomes the ideal spot for a romantic dinner. The restaurant serves all kinds of fish and seafood dishes.

Entertainment

Neptuno
Corner Av. Rafael Melgar and Calle 11
☎21537
If you still have energy after a long day at the beach or underwater, head to Neptuno. With videos, laser lights and booming music, it's *the* nightclub for young people in Cozumel.

Scaramouche
Calle Salas, at Calle 11 Sur
☎20791
At Scaramouche, the mood is the same as Neptuno's. It has a very large dance floor and usually fills up only on weekends.

Planet Hollywood
Near Scaramouche
☎25271
Planet Hollywood opened in November of 1996. The building is particularly unusual with its facade in the shape of giant pink and purple sunglasses.

Joe's Lobster
Av. 10 Sur no. 21 between Calles A. Salas and 3 Sur
☎23275
To hear reggae and salsa music, the best place in the city is definitely Joe's Lobster. Musiciens perform on weekends.

Hard Rock Cafe
Av. Rafael Melgar, near Benito Juárez
☎25271
As with all the other locations, Cozumel's appeals to fans of loud popular rock music. The staff takes it upon themselves to liven up customers that are too relaxed.

The Greenhouse Cigar Bar
Calle 2 Norte, between Avenida 5 Norte and Avenida Rafael Melgar
☎20541
For aromatic cigars, head to The Greenhouse Cigar Bar. The ambiance, though a bit stiff, is enhanced by the wood paneling. Cold beer and other kinds of alcoholic beverages are served here.

Scruffy Murphy's Irish Pub
Avenida R. Salas, between Calle 10 and Calle 15
A pub with Celtic charm, Scruffy Murphy's serves none other than *Guiness* to quench your thirst. The pub is a popular meeting place for tourists who come to talk about their travels over a good, cold beer. The menu offers simple, salty food, but in generous portions.

Cozumel

Shopping

In Cozumel, many stores and offices close between 1pm and 4pm or even 5pm. Stores on Rafael Melgar Avenue, however, stay open during the high season for the flood of tourists who arrive every day by boat.

As in Cancún, the good buys in Cozumel are crafts, hammocks, silver jewellery and cigars. Do not buy anything made of black coral even if they say it is *the* specialty of the island, because this species is threatened with extinction. Take the time to discover the shops in San Miguel rather than just wandering near the port where prices are more expensive and the area is less interesting. There are dozens of craft boutiques close to the park. Payment is accepted in pesos and in US dollars. Credit cards aren't accepted everywhere, and when they are, there is a surcharge.

San Francisco de Asis
Av. 65 between Calles 25 and 27
In Cozumel there are large markets that sell everything: oven-fresh bread, clothing, crafts, cosmetics – and alcohol that is significantly less expensive than at the duty-free shop in the port district! San Francisco de Asis is one of the best markets in Cozumel.

La Retranca
Calle 11 at Av. 30
A market in the same style as San Francisco de Asis, la Retranca is open 24 hrs a day.

Mercado Municipal
7am to 1pm
Av. Salas between Av. 20 and Av. 25
The municipal outdoor market is alive with the hustle and bustle of *Cozumeleños*.

Los Cinco Soles
Avenida Rafael Melgar, between Calle 8 Norte and Calle 10 Norte
Located in front of Pancho's Backyard (see p 186), this shop is an absolute must for Mexican crafts. There is also a small café inside.

Prococo
Av. Rafael Melgar no. 99
☎*21875*
You can find everything at Prococo, including food, alcohol, jewellery, and a large selection of hand-made objects that make lovely gifts.

Van Cleef & Arpels
Av. Rafael Melgar no. 54
☎*21443*
This jewellery store sells original, fine-quality gold and silver creations at top prices.

From Cancún to Tulúm

Geographically speaking, what is known as the "Tulúm corridor" begins in Puerto Morelos and ends south of the Tulúm ruins.

The Sian Ka'an biosphere reserve, where thousands of animal and plant species cohabit, is just a few kilometres south of Tulúm.

This part of Mexico, which overlooks the Caribbean Sea, has become a much-frequented tourist destination. Cancún and Cozumel are, of course, exceedingly popular, but the Tulúm corridor, with its series of beaches, caves, charming small towns and Mayan ruins, is becoming increasingly accessible to tourists, and not just for day trips. Its natural beauty and magnificent landscapes attract visitors from Cancún in search of a little more authenticity. There are fewer restaurants, bars and boutiques, but the region has much to offer nevertheless.

Paradoxically, this long-unrecognized region, owes its popularity and recent renown to Cancún's success as a seaside resort, drawing thousands of visitors to the area. During the 1980s, day excursions from Cancún to the ruins of Tulúm and to the enchanting diving site at Xel-Há revealed what would become the region's claim to fame. The tourist craze in Cancún opened up this new opportunity for travellers seeking more intimate settings. Tourist infrastructure began to take shape in the Tulúm corridor during the early 1990s, following the opening of the first major hotels, and, though no official statistics exist, it is estimated that the region now boasts over 3,000 rooms.

Finding Your Way Around

By Car

Puerto Morelos

Gas Stations

There is a gas station in the heart of the village of Puerto Morelos (*Carretera Cancún-Tulúm, one street north of Parque Central*). Because there are few others along the way, drivers would do well to fill up before resuming the trip along the Tulúm corridor.

Tres Rios

Tres Rios is located about 10min north of Playa del Carmen.

Playa del Carmen

It takes 45min to drive from Cancún to Playa del Carmen along the coast.

Car Rental Agency

Budget
Continental Plaza Hotel
☎*730100*

Playacar

Car Rental Agencies

Hertz
7am to 9pm
Plaza Marina, Playacar
☎*730703*

Tulúm

From Cancún, if you wish to visit the entire length of the Tulúm corridor, it is preferable to rent a car or, better yet, an all-terrain vehicle, because you will have to contend with many bumpy roads. It is possible to take a bus from Cancún to any of the villages along the coast, but making your way from village to village in this manner will prove long

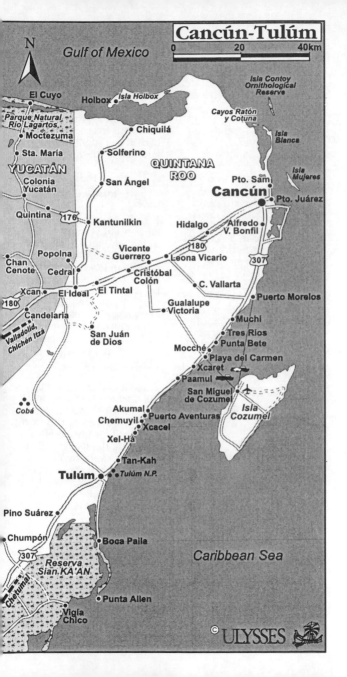

and arduous. You can also visit the various parts of the region by taxi, but fares are high.

Route 307 is a recently re-surfaced and very well-maintained four-lane highway (on which no speed limit is respected) that runs the length of the Tulúm corridor. But don't drive too fast because the police use radars to control speeding. Roadwork was still in progress at press time. The villages by the sea are, on average, two kilometres from Route 307 along narrow roads in very poor condition. If you opt to rent a car to explore the region, an all-terrain vehicle would be a judicious choice.

Cobá

Just south of the ruins of Tulúm, turn right and drive 47 km to the ruins of Cobá. Look out for the speed bumps as they are not indicated.

Reserva de la Biosfera de Sian Ka'an

The Carreterra Tulúm-Boca Paila, a bumpy and dusty road south of the Tulum ruins, goes right to the entrance of the Sian Ka'an reserve and continues to the small village of Punta Allen.

The reserve is about 16km south of Tulum. A military outpost is located just after the entrance to the reserve. Tourists are rarely stopped here, but make sure to have the proper identification on you just in case.

Boca Paila and Punta Allen

If you are going by car, it takes a little over four hours to get to Punta Allen from Cancún. The Cancún-Tulúm road is in good condition, but becomes a rocky and bumpy dirt road south of the Tulúm ruins. During the rainy season, this road is often closed.

By Plane

Travellers can reach Playa del Carmen by plane from Cancún or Cozumel. Situated just south of the town, the small airport receives domestic flights. Travellers must get there two hours ahead of time. From Playa del Carmen, there are two flights a week to Chichén Itzá and Cozumel.

Aerocozumel
☎730350

Aerosaab
☎730804

Expert astronomers, the Mayas studied the stars
from this observatory known as "El Caracol". - *Tibor Bognar*

Market stalls full of fresh peppers, a common ingredient in Mexican cuis[i]
- *M. Daniels*

Trees grow on this small temple of Chichén Itzá.
- *A. Cozzi*

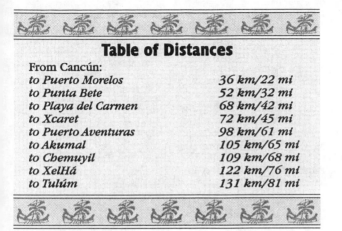

Table of Distances

From Cancún:
to *Puerto Morelos*	*36 km/22 mi*
to *Punta Bete*	*52 km/32 mi*
to *Playa del Carmen*	*68 km/42 mi*
to *Xcaret*	*72 km/45 mi*
to *Puerto Aventuras*	*98 km/61 mi*
to *Akumal*	*105 km/65 mi*
to *Chemuyil*	*109 km/68 mi*
to *XelHá*	*122 km/76 mi*
to *Tulúm*	*131 km/81 mi*

By Bus

Tres Rios

Take one of the many buses going to Cancún and ask the driver to let you off at the entrance to the reserve. The trip costs around 10 pesos.

Playa del Carmen

Many busses run regularly between Cancún and Playa del Carment. The fare is $2 and the trip takes one hour.

Tulúm

Buses travel from Playa del Carmen to Cancún every half hour. The trip lasts one hour and costs 20 pesos. The two bus companies that serve the Cancún-Playa del Carmen route are Interplaya and Playa Express. There are departures for Chichén Itzá on first-class buses at 7:30am and 12:45pm. There are also many departures throughout the day for Tulúm and Xcaret. The bus station in Playa del Carmen is on Avenida 5, at Avenida Juárez.

Auto transportes de Oriente
☎730109

The Cobá Ruins

Buses run between Playa del Carmen and Cobá, with a stop in Tulúm. The trip takes 2hrs and 15min and costs a little over $3.

From Cancún to Tulúm

Reserva de la Biosfera
de Sian Ka'an

There are no buses going
directly to the Sian Ka'an
reserve.

Boca Paila and
Punta Allen

No buses run between
Cancún and Boca Paila or
Punta Allen. Buses only go
to the village of Tulúm.

By Boat

There are about 25 cross-
ings in both directions every
day between Playa del
Carmen and Cozumel,
aboard modern ferries. The
first departure is at 5am, the
last at 9pm, and the rest at
approximately 2hr intervals.
Schedules tend to vary,
however. The Playa del
Carmen port is at the southern extremity of the city.
Tickets are obtained at the
port entrance *(approx.
175 pesos return)*. The crossing takes between 35 and
45min. According to statistics, close to 30% of passengers suffer from seasickness.
Eat lightly at least half an
hour before departure, and
bring plastic bags!

By Taxi

There is a taxi stand in
Playa del Carmen at the
corner of the pedestrian
mall and Avenida Juárez.
From Playa del Carmen to
Xcaret, the fare is around
120 pesos. Taxis can accommodate up to five people.
Having the exact fare is
preferable, since drivers
never have change. As well,
contrary to popular belief,
they do appreciate tips.

Tres Rios

A taxi from Playa del
Carmen to Tres Rios costs
around 100 pesos.

Boca Paila and
Punta Allen

From Tulúm, you can take a
taxi to Boca Paila or Punta
Allen.

Practical
Information

Playa del Carmen

Tourist Office

Playa Info
Avenida 5, between Calles 10 and 12
☎*761344*
Maps and brochures are
available at this small tourist
booth.

Doctor

Dr. Victor Macias
Avenida 35, between Calles 2 and 4
☎730493
☎744760 (cellular phone)

Pharmacy

Pharmacy Melodia
Calle 6, just east of Avenida 5
or
Avenida 5 at the corner of the street
that leads to the pier

Banks and Exchange Offices

Bancomer
Avenida Juárez, five houses west of
Avenida 5
open 9am to 1pm
Bancomer exchanges foreign money until noon. Visitors can also obtain cash advances on Visa or MasterCard credit cards here.

There are many Casa del Cambio on Avenida 5.

Post Office

Mon to Fri 8am to 5pm
Sat 9am to 1pm
Avenida Juárez, at Avenida 20

Tour Companies

Centro Bilingue Travels
Avenida 5, next to the bakery
☎730558

This company organizes trips to Chichén Itzá and Sian Ka'an

Tropical Island
Avenida 15, at Calle 1 Sur
☎451265

La Bamba
Avenida 5, between Avenida Juárez and Calle 2 Norte

Exploring

Near Puerto Morelos

The **Dr. Alfredo Barrera Marin** ★ *(40 pesos; Mon to Sat 9am to 5pm; Hwy. 307, Km 38, 1km south of Puerto Morelos)* is actually a nature trail that allows visitors to discover the region's ecological wealth. In addition to the plants, trees and flowers of the region, visitors can see monkeys, iguanas and an interesting little Mayan temple. The garden also boasts a lovely collection of orchids.

A stone's throw from the aquarium is **Crococún** ★★ *(90 pesos; every day 8am to 6:30pm; Hwy. 307, Km 30)*, a large crocodile farm where visitors can observe "Moreletti" crocodiles of all ages and sizes – well screened behind a metal barrier. Guides sometimes open the cages and allow visitors to touch the animals. Lucky visitors also get to see parrots and snakes. This site comprises a little boutique and a restaurant, as well. The journey by bus from Cancún to Puerto Morelos takes half an hour. The driver makes a special stop in Crococún upon request.

The **Instituto de Ciencia del Mar ★** *(in plain view on Avenida Niños Héroes, ☎810219)* in Puerto Morelos opened its doors in 1984. Among other reasons, it was created to carry out scientific research in order to contribute to the development and knowledge of the oceans and continental waters of Mexico. Coral reefs, marine sediment, coral fossils and more are studied here.

Puerto Morelos

Thirty-six kilometres south of Cancún, Puerto Morelos is a small fishing village from which car ferries leave for Cozumel. Imported products meant for Cancún and Cozumel are transported in freighters, which pass by Puerto Morelos, the second largest port in the region next to Puerto Juárez, situated a few kilometres north of Cancún. Tourist development here, though not as intense as in Playa del Carmen, is well under way. The beach is beautiful and the city lies only a half hour by car from Cancún. While hotels and condominiums may not be springing up like mushrooms, they are growing at a rapid rate nevertheless. A coral reef just off the coast is ideal for scuba diving and snorkelling. Puerto Morelos is a quiet town where life is simple and people prove to be very gracious.

Although Puerto Morelos is a quiet village, there have been reports of rental-car thefts. As a security measure, try to park your car where you can keep an eye on it, do not leave any valuable items in it and always make sure the doors are properly locked.

Visitors en route to Cozumel by car from Puerto Morelos can expect at least a two hour's wait. The crossing takes between 2.5 to 4hrs, and it is far from cheap: 250 pesos per car and 50 pesos per person. The first car-ferry departure for Cozumel is usually at 6am, but schedules change constantly. For accurate departure times, call ☎720827.

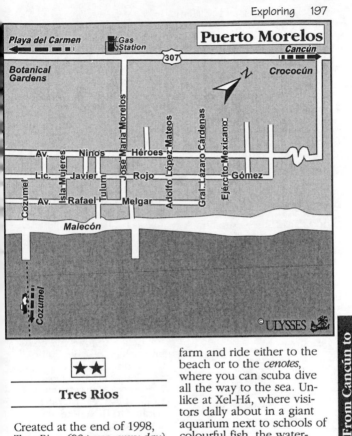

Puerto Morelos

Playa del Carmen · Gas Station · 307 · *Cancún*

Botanical Gardens · Crococún

José María Morelos · Adolfo López Mateos · Gral. Lázaro Cárdenas · Ejército Mexicano

Av. · Ninos · Héroes

Lic. · Javier · Rojo · Gómez

Isla Mujeres · Tulum

Av. · Rafael · Melgar

Cozumel

Malecón

Cozumel

© ULYSSES

★★

Tres Rios

Created at the end of 1998, Tres Rios *(90 pesos; every day)* is located only 15min north of Playa del Carmen by bus, right after Punta Bete. This private ecological reserve covers 150ha and is named for three waterways that empty into the ocean and whose source is three *cenotes* (natural pools) on the reserve. After paying the entrance fee, you can take one of the many bicycles parked next to the ostrich farm and ride either to the beach or to the *cenotes*, where you can scuba dive all the way to the sea. Unlike at Xel-Há, where visitors dally about in a giant aquarium next to schools of colourful fish, the waterways at Tres Rios are surrounded by luxurious vegetation, are more isolated and less frequented. You can also kayak down the waterways which wind through forests and mangroves. Horses can also be rented to gallop on the beach. Finally, for $45, scuba divers can't miss the deep-sea wreck not far offshore. The reserve also has a restaurant and a souvenir shop. Towels (*$2*) and lockers (*$2*) can also be rented.

Punta Bete

Punta Bete can be reached via a bumpy 3km road. This quiet spot's camping sites and beautiful 3km-long beach and lack of tourist facilities make it a popular off-the-beaten-track destination. It is also ideal for swimming and diving. Several families live here from the meagre income derived from a now-decimated coconut plantation. Punta Bete has some simple restaurants and hotels as well as *palapas* on the beach.

★★

Playa del Carmen

In Mayan times, this place was known as *Xaman Ha* (Mayan word meaning "Waters of the North"). Today, locals and regular visitors alike simply call it "Playa". The liveliest and most touristy city between Cancún and Chetumal, Playa del Carmen has approximately 17,000 residents. Because of its geographic location, the town is the ideal place from which

to begin a tour of the region. Several boats make daily crossings to Cozumel. Cruise ships frequently drop anchor in front of the city; their twinkling lights sparkling on the horizon at night are a beautiful sight. Playa del Carmen is mainly frequented by hikers, archaeology enthusiasts and those who love roaming the outdoors and basking in pleasurable idleness.

On Playa del Carmen's main street, Avenida 5, there is a succession of restaurants, bars and shops, testifying to the pronounced tourist development experienced by this region.

Avenida 5 follows the coastline behind a series of hotels and restaurants. A pedestrian mall, it makes driving on cross streets difficult. In Playa, streets running parallel to the shore are *avenidas* (avenues), and those that are perpendicular are *calles* (streets). The city's roads are all very poorly paved, so motorists should make a point of driving slowly. There is a gas station at the corner of Avenida Juárez and Avenida 40.

Time quickly goes by and changes everything in its course. The first time we visited Playa del Carmen, eight years ago, it was nothing more than a quaint little fishing village with ramshackle huts, dusty, pothole-strewn roads lined with several small, homey, unpretentious restaurants. Sometimes a hen would come out of nowhere and roam through the little village cackling while her owner ran after her to the laughter of children. An old couple sat on a wooden bench holding hands under a shady tree while the flies buzzed over a dog and cat quietly sleeping with their fists closed. In the late afternoon, a fisherman came home with the catch of the day slung over his shoulder. The beach was devoid of hotels (and of cigarette butts), and you could dip your toes in the water or sling a hammock between two palms and enjoy the *farniente* without being disturbed by single soul. Playa del Carmen is definitely not what it used to be and is rapidly changing to meet the needs of tourists who flock here year-round. Hotels, restaurants, travel agencies and boutiques are springing up everywhere. Avenida 5, once a bumpy road full of potholes, is now the town's main road. Between Calle 6 and Calle 1, this

road is a pedestrian street closed to traffic and lined with a succession of outdoor cafés, hotels, restaurants, bars and stores with their vendors standing outside yelling "Amigo, cheaper for you, come inside." But don't worry, Playa del Carmen is not like Cancún with its sickeningly rich luxury establishments, except for the chic district of Playacar. The beach is as splendid as ever, sunbathing in the nude is still permitted and the sun continues to shine on visitors with its dazzling rays.

Playacar

This major tourist project is presently taking shape south of downtown Playa del Carmen, on the other side of the airport. The 354ha development is constantly developing and comprises an 18-hole golf course, a tennis centre, several hotels, an arts centre and a shopping mall. All of the major hotel chains are represented here and are all-inclusive.

Visitors must enter the Playacar complex in order to admire the three post-classical Mayan ruins at the site. The first group of ruins is approximately 300m from the entrance, to the right, easily visible from the road. It consists of a small raised structure whose façade is guarded by a row of stone columns. The two other groups are a few metres away along the same road, and seem very interesting as well.

The **Aviario Xaman-Ha** ★ *(every day 9am to 5pm; Paseo Xaman-Ha, Fracc.,* ☎/≈ *730593)* is an ornithological reserve for endangered bird species that are found in the Yucatán and elsewhere in Mexico: pink flamingos, toucans, pelicans, ibis, herons, parrots, cormorants and storks, as well as certain species of wild duck. The site is divided into six sections, according to groups of birds. Researchers are studying the breeding habits of about thirty different species in this reserve.

The **Playacar golf course** (☎ *730624*) is laid out over a vast undulating expanse of greenery. Designed by Robert von Hagge, it is rated one of the best in the country and often hosts international tournaments.

Xcaret

The history of Xcaret (pronounced Ch-ca-ret) begins around the year 600, when it was a Mayan ceremonial centre, a market and the principal gateway to Cozumel. Francisco de Montejo Sr., who at the time was preoccupied with the conquest of the Yucatán, lost several men here during the course of a battle in 1528. This enchanting site once comprised a subterranean river, Mayan ruins and a cenote. Today, these are supplemented by restaurants, shops, a marina and neighbouring hotels.

Xcaret (a Mayan word meaning "little bay") is now a 40-ha property where visitors can dive, sail, horseback ride, swim with dolphins, or just meditate. The site also comprises a museum, a small zoo, an aquarium, a botanical garden and a reconstruction of a Mayan village. Every night, the *"Xcaret de Noche"* show, a big historical musical production, is presented here. There is so much to do in Xcaret that visitors can easily spend the whole day here.

The popular new watersport in Xcaret is called "snuba". This activity, a cross between scuba diving and snorkelling, involves breathing through a long tube attached to an oxygen tank. So, with the help of an experienced diver, you can snuba down to the ocean floor and explore the fascinating underwater world.

Every day, buses shuttle back and forth between Cancún and Xcaret, leaving from the head office of the private enterprise that runs the site, in Cancún, at 9am, 10am and 11am *(next to the Fiesta Americana Coral Beach hotel, ☎830743, ≈ 833324).*

Food, beverages, radios and sun lotion are prohibited in Xcaret. The only accepted lotion is the 100%-natural *Xcaret* lotion.

The site is open from April to October, every day from 8:30am to 10pm. From November to March, it is open every day from 8:30am to 10:30pm.

Admission fee: *$30*
Renting a locker: *$2*
Renting a towel: *$3*
Horseback riding: *$30/hr*
Swimming with dolphins: *$65*

★

Paamul

Paamul, a well-sheltered little beach, tucked away in a bay, may not seem that heavenly at first glance because of the seashells and pieces of coral that litter it and make walking barefoot on it dangerous. Those who love Paamul mainly come to scuba dive, for the sea is crystal-clear here and a great variety of tropical fish can be observed in its waters.

Every July and August, giant turtles arrive during the night to nest on the beach. Visitors must take particular care not to touch the eggs or shine any lights in their direction so as not to frighten the turtles, who already see half their offspring devoured by predators.

★

Akumal

Akumal is a 15km-long crescent beach bordered by the ocean on one side and a long row of palm trees on the other. There is a resort here as well as a small residential district. Akumal (Mayan word meaning turtle) was once part of a large

From Cancún to Tulúm

coconut plantation. The site was first developed in 1958 by divers who were exploring the submerged wreckage of a Spanish galleon. This group founded CEDAM, an international association of divers, which dedicates its efforts to protecting the environment. Akumal's magnificent beaches are sheltered from the open sea by barrier reefs, which divers from the world over have been coming to observe and explore for many years. The quiet bay, measuring approximately 500m in length, is ideal for sailing, surfing and snorkelling. Its quiet serenity is its other major draw. Development has been carried out in harmony with nature so that you still get the impression of being in a wide open space. Akumal also boasts a few good seaside restaurants and bars.

The **Yal-ku lagoon** (like Xel-Há, only smaller) is situated just north of Akumal, beyond the crescent-shaped bay. This spot is hard to reach and doesn't get many visitors, but those who take the trouble will be amply rewarded for their pains. Sun lotion is forbidden here. There is a nominal admission fee to gain access to the lagoon.

Founded in 1991, the **Planetary Coral Reef Foundation** (PCRF) (☎ *743484*), aims to heighten divers' awareness of the fragility of coral reefs and the marine ecosystem. The PCRF works with Akumal's ecological centre, dedicated to the preservation of the environment, to develop a database on the state of Akumal's reef and set up a garbage recycling program.

Puerto Aventuras

Puerto Aventuras, 20km south of Playa del Carmen, is undergoing rapid expansion. Formerly deserted, this bay is now the setting of an ambitious, luxury hotel complex, opened in 1987 (see p 221), that extends over 365ha. An additional 600ha are currently under development. Its main attractions are a marina and an 18-hole golf course. Puerto Aventuras comprises private bungalows, condominiums, several hotels, boutiques and restaurants. Public access to the complex is limited and authorization must be obtained to enter. The "time-share" formula is very popular here.

In 1741, the Spanish galleon *El Matancero* struck the reefs near Akumal. The **Pablo Bush Romero museum of submarine archaeology** ★ *(voluntary* *donation; everyday 10am to 1pm and 2pm to 6pm; ☎735129)* exhibits various objects recovered from the wreck such as belt buckles, cannons, coins, pistols and terracotta vases from Mayan ruins in the area.

Xpu-Há

Idyllic Xpu-há beach, which is now becoming overrun by hotels, is hidden 3km south of Puerto Aventuras. For the moment, however, it remains a quiet place where scuba diving and snorkelling are readily enjoyed.

Katenah

Before reaching Akumal, you will come across the long-deserted Kantenah beach, where two large hotel complexes now stand (see p 222).

Chemuyil

Chemuyil's white-sand beach is magnificent. Scuba diving in its crystalline, turquoise waters is a real pleasure. Though several palm trees were ravaged by the violent hurricanes that hit the coast over the last few years, a few still stand near the shore, supplying a

bit of welcome shade. Chemuyil boasts a small restaurant, a camping site, a few hotels and a scuba-diving shop. The Marco Polo is a fine seafood restaurant.

Xcacel

Beachside and palm-shaded camping sites can be found in Xcacel. It is a lovely spot, but wearing shoes here is essential, for this beach is covered in shells and coral; insect repellent is also a must. There is a restaurant and a small cenote here. Bird-watching enthusiasts will enjoy the parrots and *mot-mot* birds (named for their cry) who inhabit the region. The best time to spot these small creatures is early in the morning. Xcacel's calm and crystal-clear waters are ideal for water sports. A little path leads to Chemuyil and Xel-Há from here.

Xel-Há

Xel-Há deserves two stars, but we'll give it three for scuba diving. In fact, Xel-Há is really only worth visiting if, and only if, you like scuba diving. Large schools of fish, coloured blue, yellow and orange like parrots, offer a spectacular underwater show. And for

From Cancún to Tulúm

$90 more, you can swim with dolphins; these adorable marine mammals will bring smiles to the young and old alike.

Known as the biggest "natural aquarium" in the world, Xel-Há (pronounced Chel-Ha) consists of 4ha of exotic lagoons, coves and creeks naturally furrowed into the crumbly limestone, characteristic of the region. Certain creeks, however, have been encouraged by human intervention. Large stretches of calm, crystal-clear water teem with multicoloured fish. Xel-Há is a paradise for experienced divers, but is also suitable for first-timers. Land-lubbers can admire the marine flora and fauna from the promenade overhanging the shores, as the water is so clear. There are showers and boutiques as well as a seafood restaurant on site. Diving gear can also be rented here.

The site is open every day from 8am to 5pm. Admission fee for adults is $19, $11.40 for children under 12, and free for chiildren under 5 years of age. It is forbidden to enter the site with food or beverages. It is also forbidden to use sun lotion here, for this product contains ingredients harmful to the underwater fauna. Changing rooms and lockers are available for a fee, as is diving gear.

Tan-Kah

The archaeological site of Tan-Kah lies 9km south of Xel-Há and contains no less than 45 ancient Mayan structures in the depths of the forest. Excavations are presently in progress to unearth the temples buried under vegetation.

Tulúm

The archaeological city of Tulúm (Mayan word meaning "wall") was inhabited between around 900 and 1540, that is at the time of the decline of Mayan civilization. These temples and buildings, much smaller than those of Chichén Itzá, testify to strong Toltècan and Mayan influences. It is the only Mayan port city uncovered to this day, and one of the rare ceremonial centres still in use in the 16th century when the Spanish arrived. While on a naval expedition, which skirted the Yucatán coast in 1518, Juan de Grijalva was very impressed by this majestic city set atop a 12m-high cliff. The walls of Tulúm's temples were then painted in bright, contrasting colours, few traces of which remain today. This legendary fortified Mayan city marks the southern extremity of the Tulúm corridor.

Tulúm was originally inhabited by a few hundred people. It was also a major market, particularly in later years, and was linked by paths paved with white stones known as *sacbeob* to several neighbouring cities, Cobá and Xel-Há among them. Though Tulúm was abandoned in the 16th century, it served as a refuge for Mayans from Chan Santa Cruz (now renamed Felipe Carillo Puerto) during the armed conflict between the Spanish and the Amerindians: the caste war. Most of the inhabitants of the village of Tulúm (just south of the actual archeological site) are, in fact, direct descendants of this proud and independent people.

In 1993, the government launched a massive restoration and conservation program of the Tulúm ruins, thus acknowledging their historical significance. It is impossible, however, to differentiate between what was restored and what is still standing on its own.

Many tourists staying in Cancún or Cozumel discover Tulúm through one of the numerous guided bus tours organized by almost all tour companies in the region. On the coast, it is the most popular excursion, often combined with a trip to Xel-Há. Tulúm receives approximately two million visitors a year. One can therefore imagine how crowded the place can get, particularly at the height of the tourist season. The most pleasant time of day to visit Tulúm is in the late afternoon, when tourists have left and the heat of the sun has abated. The tour of the ruins lasts about two hours.

At the entrance to the site are a noisy outdoor souvenir market, arts and crafts boutiques, a museum and a few snack bars. Unfortunately, shoppers do get assailed by a barrage of aggressive salespeople. Behind the entrance, visitors can sometimes see *Voladores* at work. It is a very impressive sight, combining acrobatics and music. Behind the parking lot, a dirt road leads to the Sian Ka'an reserve, an ecotourism Mecca in Mexico. The village of Tulúm, approximately 4km south of El Crucero (the fork that leads to the ruins), is also worthy of interest. The village has a post office and a hotel, but no bank.

The Tulúm Ruins

In order to preserve the ruins of Tulúm, most of the more interesting attractions are closed to the public as too many tourists were visiting them daily. Due to this restriction, it is no longer possible to go inside the main attraction, El Castillo. Therefore, the structures can only be observed from the outside. But the beauty of the place makes up for this. Tulúm was built on a cliff overlooking the ocean and surrounded by magnificent countryside. Remember to bring your bathing suit to take a refreshing dip in the sea or in the creek where boats used to dock. Don't venture to far out too sea because the surf can be quite strong.

To reach the site, you must take the El Crucero fork, 1km from the ruins, where the hotels and boutiques are concentrated. You will come across a Pemex gas station on Highway 307, a little farther south of this junction.

From Monday to Saturday, the admission fee for adults is 25 pesos and free for children 12 and under. Admission is free on Sundays. Renting a locker, located at the entrance to the site, costs 18 pesos and renting a video camera costs 30 pesos. The entrance, which was once near the ruins, now gives out on the parking lot *($1)*, right next to Highway 307, which obliges visitors to cover about 500m on foot or by mini-train *($1 return)*. A guide can be hired at the site's entrance.

Visitors enter the ruins through a narrow passage in the stone wall surrounding the city. The first building you will come upon is the Temple of the Frescoes. When facing the ocean, El Castillo is visible from the highest point. The Temple of the Diving God is right next to it. A few other structures of lesser importance are scattered throughout the grounds.

The Temple of the Frescoes

This two-story temple is composed of a large base, with four stone columns along one of its sides. Visitors cannot enter the temple, but can discern the painted frescoes inside quite well nevertheless; these represent the universe as the Mayans perceived it. Drawings made by the Mayas by dipping their hands in red dye can be seen on the outside of the temple.

El Castillo

Perched on the edge of a cliff, this temple is unfortu-

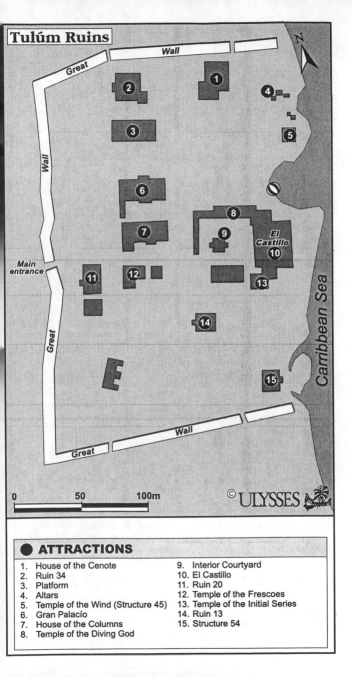

Tulúm Ruins

Great Wall

N

Wall

Great Wall

Main entrance

E

El Castillo

Carribbean Sea

Great Wall

0   50   100m

© ULYSSES

● ATTRACTIONS

1. House of the Cenote
2. Ruin 34
3. Platform
4. Altars
5. Temple of the Wind (Structure 45)
6. Gran Palacío
7. House of the Columns
8. Temple of the Diving God
9. Interior Courtyard
10. El Castillo
11. Ruin 20
12. Temple of the Frescoes
13. Temple of the Initial Series
14. Ruin 13
15. Structure 54

nately closed to visitors. Its entrance is flanked by two columns representing serpents and a diving god.

The Temple of the Diving God

Visitors enter this two story-structure through a small door surmounted by a figure carved out of the rock representing the "diving god", that is to say a winged human form whose feet point toward the sky and whose head points toward the ground. Whether this figure represents a bee or the setting sun is unknown.

Cobá

Cobá is a picturesque little village on Lago Cobá, right near the ruins of the same name. The village has almost no tourist facilities.

Silent witnesses to the timeless beauty of the glorious Mayan empire, gone forever but not forgotten, the ruins of Cobá *(about $3 or 25 pesos; every day 8am to 5pm)* are 47km west of Tulúm in luxuriant vegetation under a blazing sun. According to archeologists, only a small percentage of the ruins is visible, and if the funds were available to restore the whole site, Cobá would be one of the largest Mayan cities ever discovered. It is believed that Cobá was at its peak be-

tween AD 800 and 1000, with a population of about 50,000, and rivaled the splendid city of Tikal, Guatemala in prestige. But unlike the ruins of Chichén-Itzá and Tulúm, which are a mix of Mayan and Toltec architecture, Cobá is 100% Mayan and its architecture is very similar to the Peten style of the Tikal ruins. The Cobá ruins, however, do not (yet) posess the splendour of Tikal, Chichén-Itzá or Palenque. Few structures have been uncovered and those that have been are very far away from each other, so we strongly suggest that you wear a hat, bring a bottle of water and insect repellent to visit the ruins. If you want to get more than a quick look at the ruins and to learn more about the site's architecture, it is best to hire a guide at the entrance to the site.

The first group of ruins, called the Cobá group, is about 100m from the entrance on your right. The second largest pyramid (22 m) of the site, called **Iglesia**, is located here. There is also a small but relatively well-restored, *juego de pelota* (ball court) near the pyramid.

A little further is a second group of ruins called **Las Pinturas** because of the colourful frescos on its facade.

Just after Las Pinturas is **Xaybe**, which means "at the crossroads" in the Mayan language. The circular ruins are about 12m high and on three levels. It seems that these ruins stood in the middle of four Mayan roads and were used strategically as a watchtower and an astronomical observatory.

The site's main attraction, **Nohoch Mul**, is located about 1km from the entrance and at 42m high, is the tallest pyramid in the Yucatan. There are 120 stairs going up to the top of the pyramid. A cord is used as a ramp to help visitors with vertigo get back down. Next to the pyramid is a 4m-high, 4-ton **stele** inscribed with hieroglyphs that have recently been de-coded and, it seems, bear the date November 30, 780.

Numerous *sacbeos* (Mayan routes) criss-cross the region, contributing to the theory that Cobá was an important place in the Mayan empire. To avoid getting lost, stay on the marked path, but briefly take one of the many *sacbeos* that cross it. The *sacbeos* pass some scattered, partially emerged Mayan ruins that are shrouded in mystery in the middle of exuberant vegetation. These ruins possess a definite charm and looking at them, it is not hard to believe that these vestiges of a rich era gone by were once, long ago, even more spectacular than what you see now.

Reserva de la Biosfera de Sian Ka'an

In the Mayan language, Sian Ka'an *(donations appreciated; every day 8am to 5pm)* means "the place where the sky was born". This reserve covers 1.3 million acres of land along the coast, south of Tulúm. The Sian Ka'an reserve is made up of tropical forests, *cenotes*, savannahs, dunes, lagoons, and 100m of coral reef. There are also many small Mayan ruins scattered about. This fascinating mix of luxuriant vegetation, both on land and in the ocean, serves as a natural habitat for a very diverse fauna and flora. For example, the reserve contains 300 species of birds fluttering about at their fancy. Among the most popular are the toucan, the ara and the pink flamingo.

Listen to the wind gently caress the leaves of the trees and rustle their

From Cancún to Tulúm

branches where a flock of colourful birds sometimes perches. Though the larger animals tend to flee at the slightest hint of human presence, you may be able to see a puma or a jaguar swiftly leaping through the green foliage, monkeys chasing each other from branch to branch, crocodiles slowly gliding on the water after their prey in the dissipating morning mist, or sea turtles frolicking about in the lagoons.

Though it might be more interesting to travel without any itinerary or time constraints, it is not such a bad idea to go with a travel agency. In fact, the best way to visit the reserve is with **Amigos de Sian Ka'an** (*AP 770, Cancún, CP 77500, Quintana Roo, Mexico, www.Cancun.com/siankaan*), an organization whose goal is to promote and protect the reserve's splendid natural environment. The excursion leaves from the Ana y José hotel (see p 223) and lasts 6hrs. Half of the excursion is by boat. It costs $48 per person if you get to Boca Paila in your own vehicle, otherwise it costs $10 more from the Ana y José hotel with transporta-

Ton provided by the organizati

The Cabañas Ana y José hotel also organizes tours of the reserve.

Boca Paila and Punta Allen

Boca Paila and Punta Allen are two picturesque villages whose main activities are fishing and tourism. They are located on a small peninsula in the Reserva de la Biosfera de Sian Ka'an. Here, electricity is supplied by generators and there are hardly any tourist facilities.

Boca Paila is bordered by a pretty white-sand beach on one side and by a bay full of fish called Bahía de la Ascención on the other. Most tourists come here to fish. The **Casa Blanca** (*www.casablancafishing.com*) is a hotel made up of *cabañas* that are very clean, covered with palm-thatched roofs and have private bathrooms as well as a terrace looking out to sea. The hotel offers guided fishing trips with professional guides who will show you the best places to fish. Some of the fish swimming in the area include the bonefish, tarpon and snapper. Visitors can also go sea kayaking, scuba diving or just lounge on the beach with a good book.

Founded in the middle of the 20th century for lobster fishing, the quaint little village of Punta Allen is located on the Bahía de la Ascención and has a population of 1,000. Punta Allen is also home to the Bahía del Espíritu Santo, which, at 120,00 ha, is the second-largest lobster reserve in Mexico. Tourist facilities are few, but the small restaurants serve the catch of the day. The beaches are long and a bit rocky. The hotels offer spartan comfort and camping is permitted.

Outdoor Activities

Scuba Diving and Snorkelling

Two hundred metres from the shores of Puerto Morelos is a coral reef much prized by divers. Since March 1997, it has been protected by Mexico's department of the environment. It is the longest reef in the northern hemisphere. Numerous ships have run aground in the area since the beginnings of Spanish colonization, including a Spanish galleon that attracts many divers. The Bahía Maya Village hotel (see p 213) rents out diving gear and also organizes excursions to Puerto Morelos and to the very beautiful Dos Ojos cenote *(90 km inland)*. This centre also offers day or half-day deep-sea fishing expeditions.

Punta Bete

Buccaneer's Landing
in the Posada del Capitan Lafitte hotel
☎99-230485
This is a full-service dive shop. All the necessary diving and snorkelling gear can be rented here. Horseback riding excursions are also organized.

Playa del Carmen

Several enterprises rent snorkelling or scuba diving gear and organize excursions. Here are a few:

Seafari Adventures
Avenida 5, between Calle 2 Norte and Avenida Juárez
☎730901

Costa del Mar Dive Shop
On the beach
next to the Blue Parrot hotel

Shangri-La Dive Shop
Shangri-La Caribe hotel

Yax Ha Dive Shop
On the beach
between Calles 10 and 12

Phocea Caribe
Avenida 5, between Calles 12 and 14
☎/≈731024
This outfitter offers one-day
introductory diving courses
as well as longer, more
extensive courses.

Puerto Aventuras

Golf, deep-sea fishing,
scuba diving, snorkelling,
sailing and kayaking are all
possible here. One kilo-
metre south of the complex
is the **Azul Cenote** *(entrance
on Highway 307)*, where
visitors can swim in clear
and refreshing water.

Mike Madden's CEDAM
Dive Center
Club de Playa hotel
☎722233
This outfitter offers diving
certification courses, rents
all the necessary equipment
and organizes excursions to
neighbouring cenotes. Mike
Madden is a world-famous
expert diver who has ex-
plored many cenotes in the
region.

Dive Center Akumal
On the beach
☎/≈59025
*www.akumaldivecenter
.com*

Horseback Riding

Punta Bete

Rancho Loma Bonita
Route 397, Km 49
before Punta Bete
☎875465
This ranch has been offering visitors the chance to
ride through wild jungle or
along kilometres of beach
for over 25 years now. You
can even play polo on don-
keys while armed with a
broom! Twice a day, a bus
shuttles back and forth between Cancún and the
ranch. Rates, which vary
according to the activity,
include accident insurance.
There is also a restaurant
here.

Accommodations

Puerto Morelos

Hacienda Morelos
$
⊗, ≈
on the beach near Quay 8
☎/≈710015
This hotel has 15 rooms
with large beds. The rooms
are spacious and charmingly
decorated in Mexican style.

The swimming pool is surrounded by *palapas*. Slightly raised, it offers a lovely view of the sea.

Posada Amor
$
⊗, ℜ
Ave. Xavier Rojo Gómez
☎*710033*
≈*710178*
This establishment has 18 small, simple and comfortable rooms decorated in Mexican style, distributed throughout dwellings that surround a small, shaded interior courtyard. Some rooms have a private bathroom with a shower. It is also possible to rent a *cabaña* for four people.

Rancho Libertad
$ bkfst incl.
⊗
south of the port
☎*710181*
≈*710182*
This property is run by Americans. The main building houses a large, ground-level room that is covered in sand, where guests can play checkers, gaze at the stars through a telescope, strum the guitar or play the drum. A well-equipped communal kitchen is open to all. The 12 rooms have ceiling fans and some have beds suspended from ropes. Or, if guests prefer, there are hammocks. The hotel's beach is very lovely. Turning in early and sleeping

late are *de rigueur* here. Guests can also rent a kayak for 21 pesos an hour, a bicycle for 50 pesos a day and snorkelling gear for 60 pesos a day.

Caribbean Reef Resort
$$
⊗, ≡, ≈, ℜ
☎*710191*
This is a modern, very comfortable hotel. Its 21 spacious rooms offer a lovely view of the ocean. The hotel comprises a swimming pool, a tennis court, a bar-restaurant and a dive shop. The management organizes scuba diving excursions as well.

Bahía Maya Village
$$$ bkfst incl.
⊗, ≡, ℝ, ≈, ℜ
on the beach
☎*871776*
≈*843849*
The Bahía Maya Village has 100 rooms and each one has a minibar and a fan. Some have air conditioning. This hotel consists of two buildings surrounded by gardens. The swimming pool is large and surrounded by *palapas*, hammocks and deckchairs. The hotel boasts an Italian restaurant, a nightclub, a boutique, a diving centre and a car-rental counter.

From Cancún to Tulúm

Punta Bete

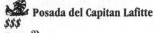 **Posada del Capitan Lafitte**
$$$
⊗, ≈, ℜ
☎*99-230485*
This establishment is an institution in Punta Bete. Its 40 units distributed throughout a series of thatch-roofed cottages, each comprise a bedroom and a terrace with a view of the ocean. A few of the units have two bedrooms. The bathrooms are only equipped with showers, however. Toward the end of the day, mariachis perform near the pool. The Posada rents horses and organizes scuba-diving excursions.

Playa del Carmen

Most of the hotels in Playa del Carmen are located on the beach, just a few steps away from the ocean. Some of them rent *cabañas*. The pricier and more comfortable ones are situated at the northern and southern extremities of the city.

Camping La Ruina
facing the sea
This property has about 30 rooms; prices are a bit high and the level of comfort varies from room to room. The best rooms are above the hotel restaurant, facing the sea. Behind the restaurant is a sandy courtyard with a luxuriant vegetation where campers can pitch their tent for a small fee. There is also a Mayan ruin on site, adding to the campground's relaxing and exotic atmosphere.

Mom's
$ bkfst incl.
≈, ℜ, ⊗, ≡
Avenida 30, at Calle 4
☎/≈*730315*
moms@caribe.net.mx
Built somewhat like a hacienda with a central courtyard and a small swimming pool, Mom's is rather secluded. It is situated about five minutes' walking distance from the pedestrian street. The 16 rooms are clean, comfortable, large and cool, with private bathrooms. Some offer air conditioning. The proprietor has a very interesting library and will be delighted to lend you a few books, which you can peruse on the terrace upstairs.

Pelicano Inn
$ bkfst incl.
⊗, ℜ
on the beach, at Calle 6
☎*730997*
☎*1-800-538-6802*
≈*730998*
This is a new 36-room hotel, surrounded by a tropical garden. The rooms have either two queen-size beds or one king-size bed. At breakfast, guests serve themselves from the buffet

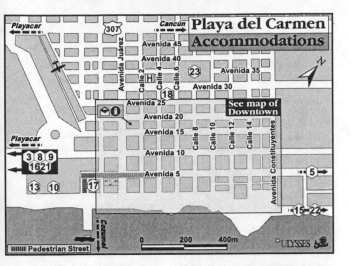

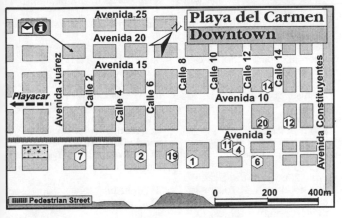

ACCOMMODATIONS

1. Albatros
2. Alejari
3. Allegro
4. Baal Nah Kah
5. Balcones del Caribe
6. Blue Parrott Inn
7. Camping y Cabañas La Ruina
8. Caribbean Villages
9. Club Royal Maeva Playacar
10. Continental Plaza
11. Copacabana
12. El Tucán
13. Fisherman's Village
14. La Tortuga
15. Las Palapas
16. Mayan Paradise
17. Molcas
18. Mom's
19. Pelícano Inn
20. Quinta Mija
21. Royal Hideway Resort and Spa
22. Shangri La Caribe
23. Villa Deportiva Juvenil

table. The hotel has a fishing and dive shop.

Villa Deportiva Juvenil
$
Avenida 30, at Calle 8
Undoubtedly one of the least expensive places to stay in Playra del Carmen, this is a youth hostel for all, with 200 beds distributed throughout 10 dormitories and five *cabañas*. The latter, equipped with fans and private showers, can accommodate three or four people. By sharing the cost of these modest dwellings with a few other people, you can pay even less than you would for a bed in the dormitory. Men and women sleep in separate dormitories and *cabañas*, which are all relatively clean. Ideal for no-fuss travellers.

Albatros
$-$$ bkfst incl.
≡, ⊗, ℜ
On the beach, at Calle 8
☎730933
Only 20m from the beach, this hotel with 31 rooms is composed of beige, thatch-roofed cottages. Every room has a private balcony with a hammock. They are painted white and soberly decorated with ceramic-tiled floors. Coffee and croissants are served in the morning. The hotel organizes scuba diving excursions and rents all the necessary diving gear.

Balcones del Caribe
$$
⊗, ≡, ≈, K, ℜ
Calle 34
between Avenida 5 and Avenida 10
☎730830
This all-inclusive hotel has 72 two-bedroom suites. Each is pleasantly decorated and equipped with a kitchenette, a dining room and air conditioning. They are distributed throughout two modern, four-story buildings. The Balcones also has a tennis court and a car-rental counter. There is a ferry going to the beach.

Blue Parrot Inn
$$
⊗, ≡, ℜ
On the beach, at Calle 12
☎730083
Very popular because of the many services it offers, the Blue Parrot organizes a variety of water activities (kayaking, scuba diving, snorkelling, fishing, etc.). Every one of its 50 rooms is air conditioned.

El Tucán
$$
≈
Ave. Norte, N° 5A
between Calles 14 and 16
☎730417
≈730668
The El Tucán has 65 rooms that are clean and comfortable but somewhat small. There is, however, a small refreshing private garden with waterfalls and a small

cenote next to the hotel near the reception.

Alejari
$$-$$$
hw, pb, ℜ
On the beach corner Calle 6
☎30374
≈30005
This small, seaside, family hotel attracts visitors for its clean rooms, smiling service and prices that won't dig too deep into your budget.

Baal Nah Kah
$$-$$$
pb, hw
Calle 12, corner Avenida 5
☎30110
≈30050
marino@pya.com.mx
Comfort and a warm welcome await at Baal Nah Kah, a cute little bed and breakfast. Up to six rooms are available for rent, and though each is a different size, all are charmingly decorated in a simplistic but refined Mexican style. Two rooms have balconies, but all visitors can use the kitchen. The beach is a 30-second walk away, and the service is friendly.

Copacabana
$$-$$$
pb, hw
Avenida 5
between Calle 10 and Calle 12
☎30218
Next to the restaurant 100% Natural (see p 228), the Copacabana is very

close to the beach and has pretty rooms that are clean, colourful and laid out around an interior courtyard. There is also an outdoor whirlpool bath to relax in after a day at the beach. The hotel also rents bicycles and organizes scuba-diving and deep-sea fishing excursions.

La Tortuga
$$-$$$
pb, hw, ≈, ℜ
Avenida 10, corner Calle 14
☎/≈31484
hotel_la_tortuga@bigfoot.com
Open since 1997, La Tortuga is located only two streets away from the beach, but far enough from the bustle of Avenida 5. The rooms are quiet and well-decorated. All the suites are equipped with whirlpool baths. Good value for your money.

Molcas
$$$
Calle 1, corner Avenida 5
☎30070
≈30315
molcas@qrooltelmex.net.mx
Molcas has managed to adapt to the recent hotel boom and still looks good after all these years. Located two steps away from the pier for boats going to Cozumel, this establishment has simple, clean and modern rooms.

Las Palapas
$$$ bkfst and dinner incl.
≈, ℜ
Route 307, Km 292
☎730610
☎1-800-433-0885
≈730458
palapas@playadelcarmen.com
With a total of 55 rooms,
Las Palapas is located ap-
proximately 2km north of
Playa del Carmen, on the
beach. The hotel's propietor
is German. The rooms con-
sist of circular, one- or two-
story bungalows with
thatched roofs. Each has a
bathroom, fans, double
beds and a balcony. Break-
fast and dinner are included
in the price of the room.
The complex boasts a bou-
tique and two restaurants; it
also organizes excursions.

Quinta Mija
$$$-$$$$
pb, hw, ℜ, ≈
Avenida 5, corner Calle 14
☎301111
quinta@playadelcarmen.com
A short distance from the
frenzy south of Avenida 5,
but only 1.5 blocks from the
ocean is the charming
Quinta Mija. The simple,
pleasant and quiet rooms
surround a bucolic interior
courtyard and come with
kitchenettes. The pool is
good for a dip after a long
day visiting the nearby ruins
under the blazing Yucatán
sun, or after tanning your-
self on the hotel's terrasse
where there is an excellent

view of the ocean. The ho-
tel also has several comput-
ers with Internet access; of
course, this costs extra.

Shangri-La Caribe
$$$$
pb, hw, ℜ, ≈
About 2 km north of downtown
P.O. Box 2664, Evergreen Colorado
☎1-800-538-6802
info@turqreef.com
The Shangri-La Caribe is a
little bit far from downtown
Playa del Carmen and right
next to Las Palapas. This
chic hotel is just the place
to get away from it all and
has everything to make
your stay as pleasant as
possible. The spacious
cabañas have comfortable
beds and balconies with
hammocks slung between
palm trees, two steps away
from a calm, sandy beach.
The services and facilities
include a car-rental office,
taxi service, scuba-diving
shop, professional massage
service, two pool tables, a
ping-pong table, two excel-
lent restaurants (see p 228)
and a fresh-water pool. Im-
peccable service with a
smile.

Playacar

Caribbean Village
$$$
⊗, ≡, ≈, ℜ
☎730506
≈730348
This all-inclusive hotel
complex is located near the

Playacar golf course and contains 300 large, modern and comfortable rooms with two large beds, a television and a telephone. There are two swimming pools and three tennis courts in the gardens surrounding the hotel. The establishment also has a car-rental counter and a dive shop. The cost of the room includes a daily round of golf *(golf cart $15)*.

Continental Plaza Playacar
$$$

⊗, ≡, ≈, ℜ

☎730100

The 188 rooms and 16 suites at this hotel each contain a television and private balcony, and are decorated in Mexican fashion. The hotel faces one of the loveliest beaches in the area, and is within walking distance of downtown Playa del Carmen. This hotel has a car-rental counter, tennis courts and a dive shop. Guests can enjoy a host of activities, including water-skiing and sailing. It is the only hotel in Playacar that is not all-inclusive.

Fishermen's Village
$$$

Bahía del Espíritu Santo #9

☎/⇆31390

reserv@mail.fishermen.com.mx

The Fishermen's Village is located next to the Continental Plaza and offers the "all-inclusive formula". All the rooms are comfortable and have a lovely view of the ocean. The pool is the perfect place to relax after taking a dip in the ocean or before the evening buffet is served.

Allegro
$$$-$$$$

pb, hw, ℜ, ≈

www.allegrpresort.com

Formerly known as the Diamond Resort, the Allegro is also an all-inclusive hotel. Its 300 rooms are impeccably furnished with palm-thatched roofs and slope gently down toward the ocean. In front of each room is a hammock where guests can read or casually observe the different kinds of birds flying about. This hotel is ideal for romantic couples or families. Children can play in the game room or swim in the kiddie pool. There is another pool for adults who just want to lounge about and mind their own business. The beach is clean and quiet.

Club Royal Maeva Playacar
$$$$

≡, ⊗, ≈, ℜ

☎731150

⇆731154

This is a large, 300-room, all-inclusive complex with a modern decor in quintessentially Mexican colours; most have a view of the ocean. Guests can enjoy a host of sports activities here, and there are two holiday camps for children 2 to 4 and 4 to 12 years old.

From Cancún to Tulúm

This hotel is the third of its kind in Mexico; the first and second of this chain's establishments are in Huatulco and Manzanillo.

Mayan Paradise
$$$$
hw, pb, ℜ, ≈
☎*31400*
📠*31424*

This is another big hotel complex that offers the "all-inclusive formula". The air-conditioned rooms are located inside colourful buildings that are attached together all the way to the pool. In this luxury hotel where every demand is met, guests will find everything they need, so that they don't have to leave the property. The beach is calm and the pool is almost right next to it.

Royal Hideway Resort and Spa
$$$$
≈, ℜ
Lote Hotelero 6
☎*35400*
📠*34506*
☎*305-262-5909* (US)
📠*262-8789* (US)
☎*416-593-3787* (CAN)
📠*204-1939* (CAN)

If money is no object and you want to immerse yourself in absolute luxury, the Royal Hideway is a sparkling grand hotel with a somewhat pompous decor. The Royal Hideaway offers a unique all-inclusive package: unlike other hotels that prefer quantity to quality, it offers a more personalized service and is the only all-inclusive hotel in Cancún that belongs to the Preferred Hotels and Resorts Worldwide. The moment you arrive, you will be greeted with a glass of champagne. Freshly cut flowers adorn the rooms along with a basket of fresh fruit. The rooms are in small colonial-style villas where a concierge takes care of your dinner reservations and your every desire. Each room is equipped with a VCR, a stereo system with a selection of CDs, as well as a modem hookup for portable computers. The bathrooms are made of marble. There is also a 220-seat theatre where guests can dine while watching folk shows. A pool, bar, gym, travel agency, tennis court, health club and the usual services and water sports are offered at this high-class establishment.

Paamul

Paamul
$ bkfst incl.
⊗, ℜ
☎*743240*

This modest hotel is run by a friendly Mexican family. The establishment is plain, but guests eat well here. This same family also runs the only camp site in Paamul, situated quite close to the hotel *(30 pesos, includ-*

ing shower and toilets). Guests will find a dive shop and a laundromat at the hotel.

Akumal

Club Akumal Caribe & Villas Maya
$$
≈. ⊗, *K*, ℜ
☎722532
This large complex offers different types of accommodations, ranging from large, fully equipped *cabañas* to one- or two-bedroom condominiums to small hotel rooms. There are tennis and basketball courts, but scuba diving is the activity of choice, what with the complex's two dive shops.

Club Oasis Akumal
$$$
⊘, ⊗, ≈, ℜ
☎722828
⊷735051
The 120 large rooms of the Club Oasis all have a large balcony with a view of the ocean or the gardens, and most offer air conditioning. This U-shaped hotel is on a very lovely beach. Its architecture is quintessentially Mexican. Club Oasis has a tennis court, a travel agency, a car rental counter and a diving club, the *Oasis*, run by CEDAM

Hacienda la Tortuga
$$$
⊗, ≡, *K*, ≈, ℜ
10 minutes' walk from the Club Akumal Caribe
☎722421
This is a small hotel situated on the beach; it encompasses nine condominiums, each of which has one or two rooms, a kitchenette and a sizeable bathroom.

Puerto Aventuras

Club de Playa
$$$
⊗, ≡, ≈, ⊘
On the beach, close to the marina
☎/⊷735100
Club de Playa comprises 300 spacious rooms, with balconies and a magnificent view of the ocean. Guests can play for free at the Puerto Aventuras golf course. The hotel also has a dive shop.

Club Oasis Puerto Aventuras
$$$$
≈, ≡, ⊗, *K*, ℜ
At the northern end of the beach
☎735050
⊷735051
The Club Oasis Puerto Aventuras houses 275 rooms, some of which have a whirlpool bath and a kitchenette. This hotel has adopted the "all-inclusive" formula and organizes numerous activities for its guests. Transportation to the marina is also included in the price of the room.

Continental Plaza
$$$$
K, ⊗, ≈, ≡, ℜ
Right near the marina
☎*735133*
⇌*735134*

The 60 rooms of the Continental Plaza are decorated in the shades of blue and peach so dear to Mexicans, and open out on large balconies overlooking the sea. Most rooms have a kitchenette. The hotel rents bicycles and cars, and provides transportation to the beach, only a few minutes away.

Kantenah

El Dorado Resort
$$$$$
⊗, ≡, ≈, ℜ
☎*98-843242*
⇌*846952*

The El Dorado Resort occupies a large part of the Kantenah beach. This complex consists of 135 large suites with marble floors and satellite televisions. The hotel also boasts two swimming pools, two restaurants, three bars and vast gardens. All meals and sports activities are included in the above-mentioned rate.

Robinson Club Tulúm
$$$$$
⊗, ≈, ≡, ⊙, ℜ
☎*811010*

A little farther south, the Robinson Club offers 300 lovely rooms decorated in pastel shades. Despite its

name, this hotel is several kilometres north of Tulúm.

Tulúm

There are a few hotels at the El Crucero junction, but these are not close to the ocean. South of the ruins, on a dirt road that leads to Boca Paila, a series of *cabañas* is spread out on a long stretch of beach, bordered by palm trees. Most offer simple comfort and something to eat. Some of these *cabañas* do not even have running water, while others are quite suitable. The Tulúm-Boca-Paila road is bumpy, dusty and runs along the beach south of the Tulúm ruins until the Sian Ka'an reserve.

Acuario
$
≈, ⊗, ℜ
El Crucero
☎*844856*

Opened in 1990, the Acuario has 27 large and comfortable rooms with colour televisions and private bathrooms, something of a luxury south of Tulúm. Buses to Playa del Carmen leave from this hotel's parking lot.

Cabañas Don Armando
$
sb, ℜ
On the beach
just south of the Tulúm ruins

This establishment is very popular with globetrotters without much cash. The rooms are spartan but are perfectly ideal for those looking for a hut on the beach. Women can also go topless on the beach. When the sun goes down, everyone goes to the bar for a pitcher of sangria and a good time.

Cabañas Santa Fe
$
ℜ
600 m south of the ruins
The Cabañas Samta Fe are essentially small rooms measuring approximately 3m² where you can either have a bed (60 pesos) or sling a hammock (30 pesos). For 12 pesos, you can pitch your tent near this lively spot. Most of the guests are divers and students. Good local cuisine is offered here and, at night, musicians perform at the bar-restaurant.

El Paraíso
$
ℜ
Approximately 1.5km from the ruins
☎721717
By continuing south, travellers will come across the El Paraíso hotel. The rooms each include two large beds and a private bathroom. The hotel boasts a very satisfactory restaurant and the beach is magnificent. There is no electricity after 10pm,

but management provides candles.

Piedra Escondida
$$
pb, ℜ
Carretera-Boca Paila, km 3.5
☎/≈12217
The Piedra Escondida has simple *cabañas* with tiled floors that lead to a balcony strung with a hammock that will take the shape of your body the moment you lay in it. There is no electricity during the day, but each room has a lamp that lights up between 8pm and 11pm. Smiling staff.

Cabañas Ana y José
$$-$$$
pb, hw, ℜ, ≈
Carretera Tulúm Bocapaila, km 7
☎806022
≈806021
www.tulumresorts.com
This charming establishment has 15 rooms two steps away from the beach, but only five have ocean views and are obviously more expensive. However, all the rooms are charming, ultra-clean, decorated in a Mexican style and have mosquito screens. The pool is pleasantly located in the middle of a peaceful garden. There is also a car-rental office, and you can pick up your car either at the airport or at the hotel. Free parking for guests.

From Cancún to Tulúm

Tropical Padus
$$-$$$
pb, ℜ
Carretera Tulúm-Boca Paila km 9
☎ *987-68088*
⇌ *12092*
www.secom.net/troppicalpadus
Run by a friendly Italian couple, the Tropical Padus is primarily known its quality restaurant Da Orazio (see p 231), but the establishment also rents clean, comfortable and spacious *cabañas*. It is also possible to rent fishing, scuba-diving or snorkelling equipment. There is also private parking for guests.

Maya Tulum
$$$
sb, pb, ℜ
Carretera Tulum-Boca Paila, km 7
www.mayantulum.com
maya@mayantulum.com
Formerly known as the Oslo Tulum, the Maya Tulum attracts visitors seeking relaxation since yoga and meditation sessions are given on the beach. The establishment is located two steps away from the beach, near the Sian Ka'an reserve, and rents 31 *cabañas* spread out in the middle of a lush palm grove. Some *cabañas* have splendid sea views, while others are a little bit removed from the beach. The beds are covered with mosquito netting to protect guests from menacing mosquitos and other blood-sucking insects. There is no electricity in the rooms. The atmosphere is rather soothing and restful.

Cobá

El Bocadito
$
sb, ℜ
☎ *63738*
Right next to the bus stop, the El Bocadito rents rooms with the basic comforts but perfect for adventurers who want to stay as close as possible to the Cobá ruins.

Club Med
$$$
pb, hw, ≈, ℜ
on Lago Coba
☎/⇌ *42087*
Obviously in a higher price category, Club Med is suitable for those with a bigger budget who also want to be close to the Cobá ruins. The main building is on the lake and the entire property was built exactly like the Club Med near the Chichén-Itzá ruins. The 40 rooms are clean and surround an interior courtyard where the pool is located. The hotel also has a pool room with a small library that guests can use after spending a day at the ruins.

The bas-reliefs on this well-preserved entrance to a temple add to the impression that this is a sacred place. - *A. Legault*

The imposing pyramid of Chichén Itzá stands out against the deep-blue sky, almost touching it.
- *Sappa*

During Christmas and other holidays, colourful paper flowers are used as decoration to brighten up festivities.
- *M. Daniels*

Restaurants

Puerto Morelos

Cafe de la Plaza
$
Plaza Morelos
This establishment is located inside a simply decorated space that can barely fit five tables. Healthy, homemade food is served in a casual and bohemian ambiance.

Kab Meyah
Calle Tulum, south of Plaza Morelos
This establishment is both a handicraft shop and an Internet café. It costs 25 pesos to surf the Net.

Pelicanos
$-$$
Ave. Rafael Melgar, by the ocean
☎710014
Here, fresh fish, seafood and Yucatec specialties are served in a warm and inviting ambiance and at very good prices.

Posada Amor
$$
Ave. Xavier Rojo Gómez
☎710033
Delicious, hearty breakfasts are served at the restaurant of the Posada Amor hotel (see p 213). There is even real maple syrup to go with the pancakes! On Sundays, very generous buffets featuring Mexican and North American dishes are served.

Punta Bete

Frederiko Hotel
$-$$$
On the beach
Right next to Su Amigo Pancho (see below), the restaurant of this hotel also offers a menu similar to its neighbour.

Su Amigo Pancho
$-$$$
On the beach
Popular with globetrotters, this is a small, unpretentious restaurant. The menu features fish and seafood and can change according to the catch of the day.

Playa del Carmen

Atomic Internet Cafe
$
Calle 8, corner Avenida 5
This Internet café has a modern decor and is air-conditioned. People come here to sip a frothy cappuccino and have a bite to eat while sending E-mail to faraway friends. It costs 1.5 pesos per min to surf the Net or 200 pesos for 200 min.

Cyberia Internet Cafe
$
Calle 4, corner Avenida 15 north

Internet addicts get together at the Cyberia Internet Cafe to surf the Web or read their E-mail from friends back home. The place is not air conditioned, but the fans and a cold beer should keep you cool. Free films are also presented starting at 5pm. It costs 1 peso per min to surf the Net.

 Sasta
$

Avenida 5
between Calle 12 and Calle 14
Sasta, a charming, lively little café with a colonial-style facade, is run by a dynamic American from Minnesota who decided to keep some of Mexico's quality coffee within the country. She can often be seen grinding, roasting and preparing the coffee behind the counter. Tourists sit on the terrasse drinking strong espresso or quenching their thirst with a *granité* (coffee shake) while observing the passersby through the smoked-glass windows.

Andale
$-$$

Avenida 5
between Calle 6 and Calle 8
Refreshing ice-cream, crispy pizzas, strong coffee and smiling service await at Andale. This small restaurant has a terrasse used as a sort of lookout station to watch the activity on the main street of Playa del Carmen.

Sabor
$-$$

Avenida 5, at Calle 4
Sabor is very popular for its salads, tofu burgers, sandwiches and delectable desserts. It is the favourite haunt of vegetarians in Playa del Carmen.

Bistro
$-$$$

Calle 2, corner Ave. 10
A little off busy Avenida 5, the charming little Bistro is run by a French-Canadian couple. All the classics of French cuisine are served: filet mignon, *quiche lorraine*, *salade nicoise*, chocolate mousse, etc.

Da Gabi
$-$$$

Avenida 5, at Calle 12
This popular Italian restaurant offers fish and seafood dishes, fresh pasta and, to top off your meal, a very good espresso. The dining room is large, well-decorated and ventilated by ceiling fans.

Karen's Grill & Pizza
$-$$$

Avenida 5
between Calle 2 and Calle 4
Pizza and hamburgers share the menu with traditional Mexican dishes at Karen's Grill & Pizza. The ambiance become quite festive when South American folk music shows liven up *muy caliente* evenings.

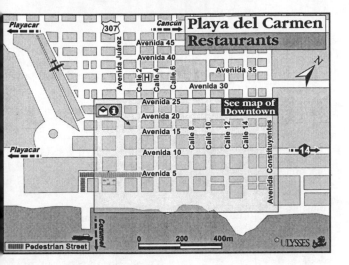

Playa del Carmen Restaurants

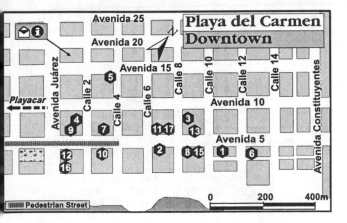

Playa del Carmen Downtown

RESTAURANTS

1. 100% Natural
2. Andale
3. Atomic Internet Cafe
4. Bistro
5. Cyberia Internet Cafe
6. Da Gabi
7. Karen's Grill & Pizza
8. La Parilla
9. La Choza
10. Lazy Lizard
11. Limones
12. Máscaras
13. Media Luna
14. Sangri La Caribe
15. Sasta
16. Tarraya
17. Zulu Lounge

Lazy Lizard
$-$$$
Avenida 5,
between Calle 2 and Calle 4
Lazy Lizard's shady, attractive terrace attracts many tourists who come to satisfy their appetite with homemade pasta, juicy hamburgers, grilled shrimp or Mexican specialities. Most decide to linger like lazy lizards in the sun, washing down their meal with a cold beer.

100% Natural
$-$$$
Avenida 5
between Calle 10 and Calle 12
For good, healthy Mexican cuisine, 100% Natural is located in the Copacabana hotel (see p 217), more specifically in a splendid interior courtyard shaded by tall trees and covered with a thatched roof. An excellent assortment of fruit juices is served, as well as light meals for those who are careful about what they eat.

Máscaras
$$
Ave. Juárez, facing the park ☎730194
At the Máscaras bar-restaurant, guests can enjoy delicious pizzas baked in a wood-burning oven (the three-cheese pizza is out-

standing). Salsa bands play every night as early as 7pm.

La Choza
$$-$$$
Ave. 5, at Calle 2
☎730327
La Choza serves good little authentic Mexican dishes in a friendly and cheerful ambiance.

Media Luna
$$-$$$
Avenida 5
between Calle 12 and Calle 14
Diagonally across from the Sasta café (see further above), the Media Luna serves copious breakfasts and a reasonably priced *table d'hôte* menu. At night, the restaurant is illuminated by candles in wall recesses, giving it a pleasant, romantic ambiance. There are some vegetarian dishes on the menu, but we suggest the marvelously prepared filet of fish.

Shangri-La
$$-$$$
2 km north of Playa del Carmen on the beach
It is very surprising that the restaurant of the Shangri-La hotel is not one of the more popular restaurants of the region. Sure it might be a little expensive, but the quality of the food is unparalleled. The menu changes according to the whim of the chef who successfully mixes Mexican and classic

international cuisine. Clearly, his goal is to tantalize your tastebuds! Every Sunday night, a lavish Mexican buffet is served and entertainment is provided by mariachis. The restaurant is airy, and the service is impeccable and discrete.

Zulu Lounge
$$-$$$
Avenida 5
between Calle 6 and Calle 8
Zulu Lounge is a bar-restaurant whose African motifs provide an eclectic atmosphere to the dining room. The chef prepares Thai food with Mexican influences for a casual, bohemian clientele. There are also several pool tables where you can distract yourself, engage in conversation, or simply enjoy a cocktail or a cold beer.

La Parilla
$$-$$$$
Ave. 5, at Calle 8
☎730687
Like Cancún, Playa del Carmen has a branch of this restaurant where pizzas baked in a wood-burning oven, seafood as well as Mexican and Italian specialties are served. The restaurant prepares breakfast, lunch and dinner. Every night, around 7pm, musicians come by and play for the enjoyment of diners.

Akumal

Dining in Akumal proves to be a pleasant experience. There are few restaurants, but those that are here offer variety and, especially, a warm ambiance and an enchanting setting. Local and foreign cuisine can be enjoyed here.

Near the city's main entrance, is the **Super Chomak** store. Adjacent to this market, a little snack bar sells good little tacos for a pittance.

Buena Vida
$-$$
On the beach road, north of Akumal
This bar-restaurant offers a lovely view of the bay. Guests can lazily sip a cocktail here with their toes in the sand. Its breakfasts will not disappoint.

La Lunita
$-$$
Hacienda Las Tortugas
Patrons can sit inside or out on the beach at La Lurita. Here, they can enjoy contemporary and creative Mexican dishes, a great variety of desserts and good coffee. The restaurant is open every day for lunch and dinner, and for breakfast during the winter months.

From Cancún to Tulúm

Lol-ha
$-$$$
Playa Akumal
This popular restaurant
serves fresh fish, seafood
and tacos for dinner. It is a
lively and very colourful
place. It is also open for
huge breakfasts, but closes
for lunch.

Que Onda
$$
Near the Yal-ku lagoon
Que Onda is an Italian restaurant that serves fresh
home-made pasta. It has a
good selection of Italian
wines, a lounge bar, a
lovely terrace and a pool
that is illuminated at night.

Puerto Aventuras

For a good meal at a low
price, there is a **small market**
facing Club de Playa. You
can enjoy delicious tacos
while comfortably seated at
one of six tables inside. You
can also wash this meal
down with a local beer.
Every night, on the little
island across from the market, people can witness the
amazing sight of the birds
returning to their nests.

Cafe Ole International
$
A few minutes walking distance from
the Club de Playa hotel
This restaurant offers rea-
sonably-priced Mexican
specialties, topped off by

good coffee. The fixed-price
menu is the best bet here.

Papaya Republic
$-$$
Behind the golf course
The dining room, tables and
chairs here have been re-
placed by the sand! Sur-
rounded by palm trees, this
restaurant serves appetizing
fish and seafood dishes in a
relaxed ambiance.

Carlos 'n Charlie's
$$
Inside the shopping centre
That's right, the links of this
chain have reached all the
way to Puerto Aventuras.
Generous portions of grilled
meats and Tex-Mex food
are served here.

Tulúm

At the entrance to the
Tulúm ruins, there are a
handful of **snack bars** where
you can have something to
eat for under 20 pesos.

 Christina
$-$$
El Crucero
☎*844856*
The restaurant inside the
Acuario hotel (see p 222)
offers typically Mexican
dishes, prepared with care.
Copious breakfasts.

Maya Tulum
$-$$
Carretera Tulum-Boca Paila, km 7
www.mayantulum.com
maya@maytulum.com
This is a vegetarian restaurant, but since the sea is right nearby, fish and seafood, including lobster, are available on the menu.

Cabañas Ana y José
$$-$$$
7 km south of the ruins
☎*712004*
The restaurant of this hotel is a feet-in-the-sand kind of place that comes highly recommended.

 ## Da Orazio
$$-$$$
Carretera Tulum Boca Paila, km 9
☎*987-62088*
www.secom.net/tropicalpadus
If you are craving homemade pasta and other well-prepared Italian dishes, head to this charming restaurant inside the Tropical Padus hotel (see p 224). The owner is also the chef and concocts delectable culinary creations that will literally melt in your mouth and satisfy your taste for exoticism.

Entertainment

Playa del Carmen

Bars and Nightclubs

Beer Bucket
Avenida 5
between Calle 10 and Calle 12
The Beer Bucket is a small but friendly place that serves the cheapest beer in town. The beer is served in an ice-bucket containing five bottles for about 35 pesos. Come here especially if you like *Corona*. This open-air bar with mellow music is perfect for conversing while watching the passersby on Avenida 5. There are few seats, so get there early.

Cabalooa Sports Bar
Avenida 5, corner Calle 16
Sportsfans can watch their favourite games at the Cabalooa Sports Bar located on the second floor of the Mosquito Blue hotel. Games are broadcast on a giant screen hooked up to a satellite antenna. If you are not interested in watching a match, or there is no more room at the Beer Bucket (see above), you can always take in the night-time entertainment on the third floor.

From Cancún to Tulúm

Capitán Tutix
On the beach, corner Calle 4
Friday nights after 11pm, when other bars are closing their doors, locals get together with fun-seeking tourists to party at Capitán Tutix. The bar looks sort of like the hull of a ship and the dance floor fills up when the musicians start to play. There are tables and chairs stuck in the sand outside where you can drink a beer on the beach while listening to American pop music. The bar is frequented by local performers and artists providing guests with an alternative form of entertainment.

Karen's Grill & Pizza
Avenida 5
between Calle 2 and Calle 4
This is a restaurant with a large dance floor where Latin folk musicians perform at night.

Pez Vela
Avenida 5, corner Calle 2
Pez Vela advertizes what you're in for right at its door: food, drinks and rock'-n'roll. Come nightfall, amateur bands burn down the house with old rock classics

La Raya
On the beach, next to Capitán Tutix
For those of you who want to get away from the Latin beat, La Raya is a bar that plays mostly techno music. Since the bar is next to Capitán Tutix, the entrance is by the beach through an intimate terrace that leads inside a dark room with an atmo sphere created by artificial fog. If you can put up with the smoke, go upstairs to the second floor, which is usually empty. The future of this bar is bleak because techno does not seem to be catching on very well with tourists in Playa del Carmen.

La Tequilaría
Avenida 5
between Calle 4 and Calle 6
Look for the flag flying the Mexican standard and you will be right in front of the lovely orange facade of La Tequilaría. Four small tables and as many chairs are set up on the terrasse, where passersby can stop and have a drink and a bit of conversation. Or, if you can't deal with the heat, go inside and sit upstairs in front of the open window and quench your thirst with one of the 269 different kinds of tequila or several kinds of mescal. At night, guitar-playing mariachis serenade tourists.

Shopping

Puerto Morelos

Kab Meyah
Calle Tulúm, Plaza Morelos
☎/≈*710164*
The boutique of this Internet café features local arts and crafts.
Hand-painted terracotta vases, finely-chased silver bracelets and lovely drawings are made and sold here. You can see the artists at work in the back of the shop.

Playa del Carmen

The dozens of boutiques all along pedestrian Avenida 5 sell *huipils*, hand-woven wool blankets, terracotta vases and masks as well as a variety of *objets d'art*. Playa del Carmen also has good beachwear and dive shops.

Mexican Amber
Avenida 5
between Calles 4 and 6
☎*730446*
This boutique stocks beautiful amber jewellery.

Galería Arte y Vida
Avenida 10
between Calles 10 and 12
This gallery sells paintings with hand-made frames. A variety of *objets d'art*, illustrations and everyday objects such as lamps and teapots, made in the region, are also found here. The boutique is set back from Avenida 10, on a small road.

Fuente
50m from the port
facing Cicsa Money Exchange
This jewellery store sells hand-made silver bracelets, rings and earrings. To ensure that a silver piece is authentic, check to see if it bears the inscription "925".

From Cancún to Chichén Itzá

Chichén Itzá, the most visited archaeological site in the Yucatán Peninsula, lies in the heart of the forest, where the only water holes to be found are a few dispersed cenotes and the trees, though numerous, are somewhat stunted.

Major restorations have resulted in the revitalization of the temples and ruins, which were once overgrown by vegetation. From Cancún, the site may be reached by car or bus, on a smooth road, or even by plane. Making the journey by car, however, allows travellers to discover a few places very much worth visiting, such as Valladolid and the caves of Balancanché.

Valladolid is the Yucatán's second largest city, with over 70,000 inhabitants. It was founded in 1543 by Francisco de Montejo, on the very site of the present-day Zací Mayan ceremonial centre. Its layout and its houses are those of a classic colonial city. From the onset of the class war in 1847, Valladolid was attacked by Mayans in revolt, and a sizable portion of its residents of Spanish descent sought refuge in Mérida. Those who stayed were virtually all slaughtered. Valladolid also suffered a great deal during the Revolution.

Today, Valladolid is a quiet city. Young people leave the city in droves to move to tourist centres where they are almost sure to find work. Valladolid's central park also serves as a market. The city is renowned for its sausages, which can be savoured in several little restaurants around the park.

The Balancanché caves, once a place of pilgrimage for Mayans and Toltecs, are a few kilometres from Valladolid and deserve a visit. To tour the Balanchanché Caves, take the stairs going underground. A tape plays as you descend to the humid depths of the caves, creating a somewhat fake mystical atmosphere. The tour is unfortunately not guided but a cave employee who follows groups of visitors tries to answer their questions. A bottle of water would be a good thing to bring unless you have the endurance of a camel.

The village of Pisté is something of a commercial extension of Chichén Itzá. The village boasts arts and crafts boutiques, restaurants, hotels, a campsite, a Pemex petrol station and a bank.

Finding Your Way Around

By Car

From Cancún, Highway 180 passes straight through Valladolid and Balancanché, before reaching Chichén Itzá and the small village of Pisté. The trip to Valladolid takes approximately two hours. Once in the city, the central park serves as an orientation point, as the city's main attractions are situated around it.

If you are renting a car to get to the fabulous ruins of Chichén Itzá, there are some additional expenditures involved. There are two toll booths en route: the first costs 120 pesos, and the second, which is located closer to the ruins, costs 30. Don't forget to double these amounts because you will have to pay again on the way back. Parking costs around 10 pesos and visiting the ruins costs 70. Finally, you will need extra pesos for food and gas.

Highway 180 used to run right by Chichén Itzá, but was diverted for conservation purposes. Arriving from Cancún, you will have to take the turnoff approximately 2km south of the entrance to the archaeological site. Follow the road signs from there.

By Plane

Aerocaribe
☎842000
This airline offers same-day return flights from Cancún to Chichén Itzá for 120 pesos. The flight takes about 20min; there are approximately three return flights per day. The airport is located close to the taxi stand from which drivers take travellers to the ruins.

By Bus

Valadolid Bustop
Calle 37, close to the park.
From 6am to 9pm, buses leave the Cancún station every hour for Valladolid. The trip costs 20 pesos.

From the Cancún terminal, first and second-class buses leave every hour during the day for Chichén Itzá. The trip costs about 30 pesos, and, depending on the type of bus, can take from two to three hours. The last night bus from Chichén Itzá to Cancún leaves at 11pm. Check the schedule because it is often subject to change.

Practical Information

Valladolid

Post office
Mon-Fri 8am to 6pm
Sat 9am to 1pm
Calle 40 no. 195A
on the east side of the park
right next to a bank.

Paulina Silva
4 pesos/hour
Calle 44, between Calles 39 and 41
Located right across the street from the Maria Guadalupe hotel in

Valladolid, the shop rents bicycles by the hour or for the day.

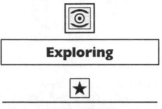

Exploring

★

Valladolid

The city of Valladolid is divided into straight, intersecting streets bearing numbers rather than names. The central park is bordered by Calles 39, 40, 41 and 42. It is ringed by a large church, the post office, a bank and several hotels. A map is nonetheless essential for exploring the neighbourhood.

Valladolid was the scene of the bloody "Caste War" (see p 24), a dark page in Mexico's history.

By the beginning of the 19th century, the Spanish had already gained control of the Yucatan Peninsula and carried out a repressive regime against the Mayas, reducing them to servitude. The Mayas tried several times to rebel, but without success. The peninsula's social and economic situation remained the same for years to come, and the Mayas continued to suffer under the Spanish. By 1847 they had had enough, and suddenly the winds of revolt blew all over the Yucatán Peninsula, unifying the Mayas into one strong army. Sick of the inhumane treatment they suffered from the conquistadors, they turned their anger on the Spaniards and everything to do with colonization by and massacring every white inhabitant of Valladolid and destroying the village. Overwhelmed by their attackers and unable to defend themselves, the few Spanish survivors of the region fled to the nearest refuge, the town of Mérida. But the sword of Damocles hung over their heads, for they were not safe for long. The Mayas quietly followed them and laid siege to Mérida. Then, against all odds, as the Spanish, at the point of breaking, were preparing to receive the final blow from the Mayas that would have destroyed them, the impossible happened – the Mayas suddenly retreated. According to the Mayan calendar, it was time to plant corn. Unfortunately, their harvest was cut short by the Spanish, who unleashed a terrible and merciless revenge.

Today, whereas Cancún has been artificially recreated with a *zona hotelera* full of hotels and restaurants for surf- and sun-seeking tourists, Valladolid has pre

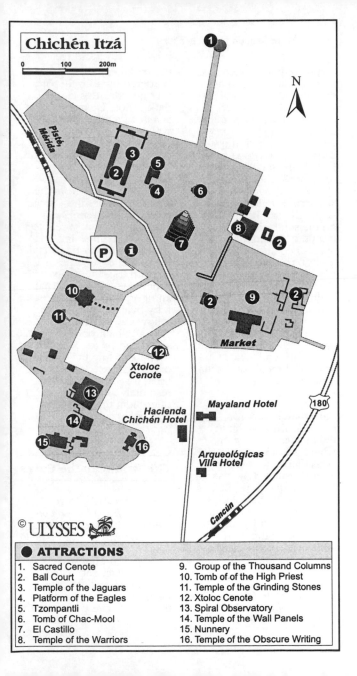

Chichén Itzá

0   100   200m

N

Pisté, Mérida

P

i

Xtoloc Cenote

Market

Mayaland Hotel

180

Hacienda Chichén Hotel

Arqueológicas Villa Hotel

Cancún

© ULYSSES

● ATTRACTIONS

1. Sacred Cenote
2. Ball Court
3. Temple of the Jaguars
4. Platform of the Eagles
5. Tzompantli
6. Tomb of Chac-Mool
7. El Castillo
8. Temple of the Warriors
9. Group of the Thousand Columns
10. Tomb of of the High Priest
11. Temple of the Grinding Stones
12. Xtoloc Cenote
13. Spiral Observatory
14. Temple of the Wall Panels
15. Nunnery
16. Temple of the Obscure Writing

served certain elements of its past, making it an authentic and picturesque colonial village. For all these reasons, many tourists decide to stay here for several days and visit the surrounding attractions which include the fabulous Mayan ruins of Chichén-Itza.

San Gervasio cathedral ★, facing the San Roque park on the south side, dates from the beginnings of Spanish colonization. If you visit Chichén Itzá on a guided tour starting from Cancún, you will have only 5min to visit the cathedral and admire the Mayan artwork that adorns its entrance hall. This sight is literally overrun by busloads of tourists, and, since tourists attract merchants selling trinkets, it can get quite hectic.

Valladolid in fact has several colonial-style churches, the most interesting of which is **San Bernardino de Siena church** ★, situated approximately 1.5km south of San Roque park. Built in 1522, it is the oldest Christian church in the Yucatán. It was pillaged by Amerindians during the class war and again in 1910, at the very beginning of the Revolution.

The **Zací cenote** *(8 pesos; 8am to 8pm; Calle 36, between Calles 37 and 39)* is right in the middle of the city and bordered by a lovely park on one side. This large, dark cenote is covered by a layer of greenish scum, which makes swimming here unthinkable, but it is very impressive nonetheless.

Seven kilometres from the central park lies the **Dzitnup cenote** ★ *(10 pesos; 7am to 6pm)*, a very lovely cenote where you can swim. It is accessible by car or by taxi. A taxi will cost 35 pesos for a return trip; the driver will wait for you for about half an hour. You can also reach it by bike *(20min)*. By car, follow Calle 39 for about 5km at which point you will see a sign by the side of the road indicating the direction of the cenote. On the spot itself, a swarm of children resolutely await tourists to offer them their services and wares.

The Balancanché Caves

The Balancanché caves *(40 pesos, free admission on Sundays, 30 pesos to rent a video camera; everyday 9am to 4pm)* are situated approximately 4km north-east of Chichén Itzá, and may be visited only with the services of a guide. Expeditions leave every hour; tours are offered in English and Spanish and last 35min. These caves were a place of pilgrimage for Mayans and Toltecs, and inside them visitors can admire numerous vases and other Mayan pottery fashioned centuries ago. A short distance away is a subterranean water table teeming with fish. The caves are not easy to explore, however, for they are filled with stalactites and stalagmites. It is sometimes even necessary to crawl through narrow passages. Visitors must be in good shape and have good walking shoes to avoid sprains. Near the entrance to the site, son-et-lumière shows relate the history of the Mayans. Travellers can reach Balancanché from Chichén Itzá by taxi or by bus.

★★★

Chichén Itzá

Travellers to the Yucatán Peninsula cannot in good conscience fail to visit the large archaeological town of Chichén Itzá. Covering close to 8km², numerous temples and buildings bear witness to a bygone era: the golden age of the Mayan civilization.

Chichén Itzá has been ranked a World Heritage Site by UNESCO. It is one of the best-restored sites on the peninsula, as well as one of the biggest, even though some of its buildings remain buried beneath a thick blanket of earth and vegetation.

Chichén Itzá ("Place of the Well of the Itzá") is a very popular spot; there are simply hordes of people here during the day. The best time to discover the charms of this ancient city is early in the morning, before the intense heat of midday and, above all, before the tour buses arrive *(toward 11am)*. Getting here early will also give you greater freedom to admire the sumptuous Castillo, the large ball court or the Group of the Thousand Columns. If you're passing through during the spring or autumn equinox (March 21st and September 21st, respectively), you can observe the descent of the serpent (see box).

The Chichén Itzá site is open everyday from 8am to 5pm; admission costs 75 pesos *(except Sundays, when admission is free)*. At the entrance to the site, there are a restaurant *($-$$)*, a free cinema, a small museum that recounts the history of the site, a book shop and many souvenir shops. There are also a free check room *(8am to 5pm)*, bathrooms and a large parking lot *(10 pesos for the day)*.

From Cancún to
Chichén Itzá

The Serpent's Descent

During the spring and autumn equinoxes (March 21st and September 21st), the shadow cast by the sun forms a sinuous shape resembling a serpent slowly slithering its way down one of the corners of El Castillo. This phenomenon lasts approximately 15 min. The rays of the sun gliding over the steps create the illusion that an animal is actually in the process of moving. Moreover, there is an enormous stone serpent head with gaping mouth at the foot of each of the four corners of the temple, which leads one to believe that, if the phenomenon were merely a coincidence, the Mayans knew full well how to exploit it and turn it into a dramatic event. Because the Mayans were keen observers of the stars and sky, it would hardly be surprising if the temple plans were, in fact, conceived with the particular intention of creating this effect.

Those who prefer to use a guide will have to keep up a quick pace. Video cameras may be rented for 30 pesos.

A son et lumière is presented every night in Chichén Itzá *(in English at 9pm for $5, or in Spanish at 5pm)*. Major events, such as tenor Luciano Pavarotti's performance in December 1996, are sometimes organized. Because the site is mostly out in the open, a hat or a cap, sunscreen lotion, bottled water and sunglasses are essential. Good walking shoes are also a must.

History

Archaeologists agree that the construction of Chichén Itzá began at the end of the classical period, between AD 500 and 900. Presumably, Mayan tribes erected the first monuments at the site, which was then known as *Uucil-Abna*, and then Chichén Itzá was virtually abandoned until the 11th century, although doubts

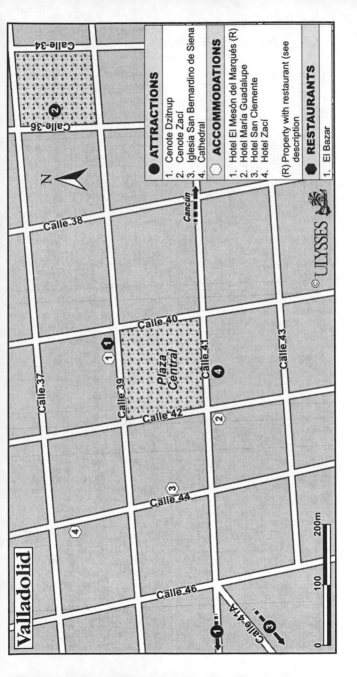

Valladolid

● ATTRACTIONS
1. Cenote Dzitnup
2. Cenote Zací
3. Iglesia San Bernardino de Siena
4. Cathedral

⬡ ACCOMMODATIONS
1. Hotel El Mesón del Marqués (R)
2. Hotel María Guadalupe
3. Hotel San Clemente
4. Hotel Zací

(R) Property with restaurant (see description)

● RESTAURANTS
1. El Bazar

© ULYSSES

N

Calle 34
Calle 36
Calle 37
Calle 38
Calle 39
Calle 40
Calle 41
Calle 42
Calle 43
Calle 44
Calle 46
Calle 41A

Plaza Central

Cancún

200m
100

persist about this. In 964, Mayan Itzás from Guatemala settled in this area, giving the city its present name: Chichén Itzá, "Place of the Well of the Itzá". The Itzás were then joined by the Toltecs, whose arrival is placed at the end of the 10th century. It has, in fact, been noted that a major Toltec influence began in this period, attested to by architectural ornaments like serpent heads. Does this mean the Toltecs ruled over the Mayas, or did the two civilizations coexist in peace? Mayan art, in any case, experienced an unparalleled revival during the 200 years of this "fusion".

According to Mayan accounts, from the year 1224 onwards, Chichén Itzá was gradually abandoned in favour of Mayapán. In 1533, the Spaniard Francisco de Montejo, busy conquering the Yucatán Peninsula, discovered the site, which was still serving the Mayas as a place of pilgrimage, and established a small colony there. The American John Lloyd Stephens undertook research there from 1841 to 1842, along with Frederick Catherwood, who created wonderful illustrations of the temples, by then in ruins and almost entirely covered in vegetation. Stephens gave an account of his adventures in a travelogue entitled *Incidents of Travel in Yucatán*, which created quite a sensation at the time.

Popul Vul

The *Popul Vul* was the Mayan bible. It is an incredible reference tool on the Mayan civilization because it contains their customs, beliefs, traditions and knowledge. When the Spanish took control of the Yucatán Peninsula, Catholic priests, who wanted to propagate the Christian faith and convert the pagan Amerindians, burnt copies of the *Popul Vul* before startled and helpless Mayans. Only four copies of the book survived the autodafé and continue to be studied by specialists who have unravelled some of the mysteries left by this brilliant civilization which is gone forever.

Over the course of the 19th century, several archaeologists took an interest in Chichén Itzá. An American consul named Edward Thompson put together a research team from 1905 to 1907 to inventory the treasures that lay hidden in the city. Divers discovered that the Sacred Cenote contained human bones as well as a great number of valuables – undoubtedly sacrificial offerings to the gods. Thompson acquired the entire site in 1885 and took numerous objects out of the country, objects that remain in the museum at Harvard University to this day.

In the years that followed, many restoration efforts, lead by the Mexico's institute of anthropology and history (INAH) among others, have made Chichén Itzá what it is today: one of Mexico's most interesting archaeological sites.

The site consists of two parts: the North Group and the South Group. The North Group chiefly contains Toltec elements such as the statue of the god Chac-Mool, "the red jaguar", whose stomach is turned toward the sky and resembles a flat table. South of the site, in the forest, lies a cluster of ruins known as Ancient Chichén. Some of these ruins are not open to the public in order to better preserve them.

The North Group

El Castillo
(Temple of Kukulkán)
Situated more or less in the middle of the site, this temple dominates the others because of its height (30m). El Castillo, a pyramidal temple, combines elements of Mayan and Toltec cultures and displays several cosmological symbols. The Mayas intimately linked the study of stars and mathematics with religion. As such, El Castillo comprises 365 steps on each of its four sides (corresponding to the number of days in the solar year), 52 paving stones (the number of years in a Mayan century) and 18 terraces (the months of the sacred year).

Several brave tourists scale El Castillo for the stunning view its summit offers of the surrounding area. This is no easy task, however, for the steps are at a 45° angle. Moreover, the descent is harder than the ascent.

El Castillo harbours a smaller, older temple, reached by a narrow flight of steps. The entrance to this staircase is at the base of the temple, on the north side.

The Temple of Warriors
(*Templo de los Guerreros*)
Surmounted by a statue of Chac-Mool and two serpent-shaped columns, this temple could be an imitation of the morning star temple in Tula, only bigger. It is an imposing structure, surmounting a tiered platform, surrounded by stone columns. There is also an older warrior temple of more modest size inside.

The Group of the Thousand Columns
(*Grupo de las Mil Columnas*)
CLOSED
Precisely aligned the length of the Temple of Warriors, these imposing stone columns, whose original role remains unknown, seem to go on forever. Some are half-crumbled.

The Tomb of Chac-Mool
("Platform of Venus")
CLOSED
North of El Castillo, on the road that leads to the Sacred Cenote, stands a square structure, decorated with numerous sculpted low reliefs and serpent heads. Visitors can reach this temple's summit by climbing one of the staircases going up each of its four sides.

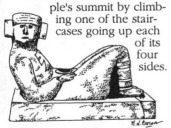

There, a large platform may have served as a place for sacred dances.

The Sacred Cenote
(*Cenote Sagrado*)
From the Tomb of Chac-Mool, a 300m-long path surrounded by towering trees leads to the Sacred Cenote. Virtually perfectly round, this natural well, measures 55m in diametre and 25m in depth and holds greenish, opaque water. Victims of all ages were thrown into the cenote during sacrificial ceremonies, undoubtedly from a small temple whose ruins overhang the well. The "fortunate elects" were offered to the gods in the hopes of putting an end to periods of drought. About 50 skeletons (mostly men and children), and gold, copper, jade and obsidian artifacts as well as rubber dolls have been brought to the surface in searches of the cenote. There is a little snack bar nearby where visitors can enjoy refreshments.

Tzompantli
(Platform of the Skulls)
A large square platform, this structure served as the base of a wall on which the skulls of sacrificed victims were lined up. The stone low relief is adorned with carved skulls, full-face or in profile, each one unique. Warriors giving battle are also depicted.

The House of Eagles
(*Casa de los Aguilas*)
Close to Tzompantli is a platform known as "house of eagles" because its walls are adorned with images of eagles clutching human hearts in their talons. The stairs are flanked by stone serpents on either side.

The Ball Court
(*Juego de Pelota*)
At the northwestern extremity of the site extends the largest pelota field ever discovered. Measuring 145m by 37m, the field is lined on either side by two 8m-high stone walls. Both these walls have a stone circle

Juego de pelota

The *juego de pelota* or the *pok-ta-pok*, was first practised by the Olmecs and later by the Mayas. This game was a cross between *fútbol* and rugby, where all kinds of shots were permitted, and had a religious significance. Nobody knows exactly how many players were in the game or exactly what the rules were, but we know that matches were played on fields that had a particular shape and various dimensions. Two long stone walls bordered the field, in the middle of which was a huge stone ring. The opponents wore protective gear on their knees and hips and without using their hands

or legs, had to pass around a ball, probably made of rubber and about 10cm in diametre, without dropping it until someone scored by throwing it through the ring. Clearly, the games were long and difficult. And the outcome of the game? During the Mayan period, it is believed that the winner was allowed to offer sacrifices to the gods. Another explanation is that after the despotic and war-like Toltecs were integrated into Mayan empire, the game took on a whole new meaning. Sometimes the losers were decapitated, and sometimes the winners were sacrificed to the gods.

through which players were to toss a rubber ball. The ball, symbolizing the sun, had to stay off the ground at all times. The way sound reverberates inside the playing field is impressive. Adjacent to the field's southeast wall, the Temple of Jaguars (*Templo de los Tigres*) is adorned with many friezes depicting jaguars. A jaguar statue also faces the House of Eagles, and two serpent-shaped columns frame the entrance.

The South Group

The Tomb of the High Priest
(*Tumba del Gran Sacerdote*)
At the South Group's entrance, along the road that once linked Mérida to Puerto Juárez, stands this 10m-high pyramid. Skeletons and precious artifacts have been discovered inside.

The House of the Snail
(*Caracol*)
CLOSED
To the left of this building stands a round, two-storied structure, which undoubtedly served as an observatory. Narrow windows, which only let the sun in for a few seconds twice a year, doubtlessly enabled the Mayan priests to measure time.

The Nunnery
(*Edificio de las Monjas*)
Continuing south, visitors reach this building whose richly adorned façade depicts the Mayan god Chac.

The Church
(*Iglesia*)
Right next door, this small building in the Puuc architectural style presents a façade of geometric motifs and animals, notably the four bearers of the sky as they are represented in Mayan mythology: a crab, a snail, an armadillo and a tortoise.

In this same area, the following attractions should be highlighted: the **Temple of the Sculptured Panels** (*Templo de los Tableros*), the **Temple of the Obscure Writing**, the **Temple of the Window Lintels**, the **Temple of Grinding Stones**, another **small ball court** and the **Xtoloc Cenote**, which presumably served as a water reservoir.

Accommodations

Valladolid

Maria Guadalupe
$

⊗

Calle 44 no. 188, between Calles 39 and 41

☎862068

Visitors can find inexpensive lodging at this simple and clean establishment near the park. Rooms with private showers and ceiling fans are available for slightly higher rates.

Maria de la Luz
$

⊗, ≈, ℜ

Calle 42 no. 195, close to Calle 39

☎562071

This hotel's 33 rooms all have air conditioning and televisions. The rooms are bright and attractively decorated. The hotel is built around a swimming pool and a little garden.

San Clemente
$

⊗, ≡, ≈, ℜ

Calle 42 no. 206, corner of Calle 41

☎562208

This establishment has 64 rooms that are decent and comfortable.

Zací
$

⊗, ≡, ≈

Calle 44 no. 191

between Calles 37 and 39

☎562167

The rooms here surround a pool and a refreshing little garden.

El Mesón del Marqués
$-$$

≡, ≈, ℜ

Calle 39 no. 203, north of the park

☎562073

This is Valladolid's most beautiful hotel. Its 26 colonial-style rooms are comfortable but the decor lacks pizazz. This hotel, originally a real hacienda, surrounds a very lovely garden. Behind the hotel, a more modern building comprises rooms with air conditioning.

Chichén Itzá

Hacienda Chichén
$$

≡, ≈, ℜ

Carretera Mérida-Cancún Km 120

☎98-510129

Built in the 17th century, this property is located on an old agave plantation. The explorers John Lloyd Stephens and Frederick Catherwood stayed here during the first archaeological digs in the Yucatán, around 1840. It later belonged to the American consul Edward Thompson, while he studied Chichén Itzá. It is now a picturesque inn with 18 rooms, a delightful garden and a large swimming pool. Simply decorated in the colonial style, the rooms all boast verandas and private bathrooms. The lobby and the outbuildings are full of artifacts and Mayan arts and crafts. The hacienda also rents cottages comprised of two simply furnished rooms, featuring exposed ceiling beams. The hacienda is open from November to April.

🦐 Mayaland
$$ bkfst
⊗, ≈, ℜ
Carretera Mérida-Cancún Km 120
☎*98-872450*
↝*99-642335*
Quite close to the ruins, this a modern complex is built around a main building with a colonial-style architecture. The hotel has 65 rooms surrounded by lush vegetation. The Mayaland offers all the amenities of a luxury hotel, notably four restaurants, four bars and a swimming pool. Guests can stay in thatched-roofed cottages or colonial-style rooms in the main building.

Villas Arqueológicas
$$
≈, ℜ
100 m east of the Mayaland
☎*98-562830*
This property has white-stucco walls with a red-tile roof. Each of its small rooms contains twin beds

and a bathroom with shower facilities. The hotel itself has a library well-stocked with books on Mayan culture, as well as a restaurant and a pool surrounded by gardens. Though the establishment is affiliated with Club Med, it is possible to simply rent a room for a night or two.

Pisté

Dolores Alba
$ bkfst
⊗, ≡
Carretera Pisté-Cancún Km 122
☎*99-285650*
This is a "budget" hotel with 28 rooms that are modest but clean and comfortable. Not all of the rooms are air-conditioned, so visitors must ask for this amenity if they want it. The hotel also offers free transportation to the ruins.

Pirámide Inn
$
≈, ℜ
☎*98-562462*
This property consists of two buildings housing 44 modern rooms with white walls and floors. The hotel boasts a garden, a swimming pool, a tennis court and a good restaurant. Guests can also pitch tents on a small campsite adjacent to the hotel. Campers have access to the pool, and hot water showers have been installed for their use

(about 60 pesos for two people).
The hotel is situated at the
eastern extremity of Pisté,
near the ruins.

Misión Chichén
$-$$
≡, ≈, ℜ
☎98-562671
Located 2km from the ruins
of Chichén Itzá, in the village of Pisté, the Misión
Chichén offers comfortable
rooms. It is a little set back
from the main road, and its
front stairs are framed by
two feathered serpents.

Restaurants

Valladolid

El Bazar
Corner of Calles 39 and 40
just north of the park
right across from the church.
Very good Yucatán meals
can be had at any of a
dozen canteens near the
park for next to nothing. El
Bazar, as it is called, is an
island of small open counters that serve breakfast,
lunch and dinner. You can
enjoy a main dish, soup and
a beer for about 35 pesos.

Maria de la Luz
$-$$
Calle 42 no. 195 , near Calle 39
At this hotel's restaurant,
you can savour a large
sandwich for about
20 pesos. A hot dish of fish
or chicken comes to about
20 pesos. This restaurant is
very popular with tourists,
who eat in the open air
facing a lovely park.

El Mesón del Marquez
$-$$$
Calle 39, north of the zocalo
☎562073
The restaurant of this hotel
(see p 249) has two dining
rooms: one outside, in the
bucolic interior courtyard,
and another inside which is
air-conditioned and thus
sheltered from the ever-
present humidity.
The menu focuses on Mexi-
can dishes but also offers
some more "touristy" ones.

Chichén Itzá

There is a small cafeteria (***$***)
as well as an air-condi-
tioned restaurant (***$$***) at the
archaeological site. The
latter serves simple, decent
food. Another option is to
go to one of the restaurants
described above, or to head
for Pisté, a small village
1km from Chichén Itzá.

Hacienda Chichén
$$
Carretera Mérida-Cancún
This restaurant serves delicious Yucatán specialties at very reasonable prices.

Mayaland
$$-$$$
Carretera Mérida-Cancún, km 120
At this hotel, there are four restaurants that serve different specialties. The food is rather expensive, but patrons can admire the hotel's beautiful gardens.

Villas Arqueológicas
$$$
100 m east of the Mayaland
This hotel houses a very elegantly decorated restaurant offering French and Mexican cuisine. Whether for lunch or dinner, the fixed-price meal is a better choice than the more expensive *à la carte* menu.

Pisté

Route 180 passes a multitude of small restaurants that have fixed-price menus and serve local dishes.

In Pisté itself, facing the Misión Chichén hotel, is the **Sayil** restaurant, where diners eat very well for under 30 pesos.

Visitors can enjoy the buffet in the comfortable, air conditioned dining room of the **Xaybe** restaurant, right near Sayil. The food is quite good and it is all you can eat at lunch time for about 45 pesos. The dinner buffet is slightly more expensive.

Glossary

GREETINGS

Goodbye	*adiós, hasta luego*
Good afternoon and good evening	*buenas tardes*
Hi (casual)	*hola*
Good morning	*buenos días*
Good night	*buenas noches*
Thank-you	*gracias*
Please	*por favor*
You are welcome	*de nada*
Excuse me	*perdone/a*
My name is...	*mi nombre es...*
What is your name?	*¿cómo se llama usted?*
no/yes	*no/sí*
Do you speak English?	*¿habla usted inglés?*
Slower, please	*más despacio, por favor*
I am sorry, I don't speak Spanish	*Lo siento, no hablo español*
How are you?	*¿qué tal?*
I am fine	*estoy bien*
I am American (male/female)	*Soy estadounidense*
I am Australian	*Soy autraliano/a*
I am Belgian	*Soy belga*
I am British (male/female)	*Soy británico/a*
I am Canadian	*Soy canadiense*
I am German (male/female)	*Soy alemán/a*
I am Italian (male/female)	*Soy italiano/a*
I am Swiss	*Soy suizo*
I am a tourist	*Soy turista*
single (m/f)	*soltero/a*
divorced (m/f)	*divorciado/a*
married (m/f)	*casado/a*
friend (m/f)	*amigo/a*
child (m/f)	*niño/a*
husband, wife	*esposo/a*
mother, father	*madre, padre*
brother, sister	*hermano/a*
widower widow	*viudo/a*
I am hungry	*tengo hambre*
I am ill	*estoy enfermo/a*
I am thirsty	*tengo sed*

DIRECTIONS

beside	*al lado de*
to the right	*a la derecha*

to the left	*a la izquierda*
here, there	*aquí, allí*
into, inside	*dentro*
outside	*fuera*
behind	*detrás*
in front of	*delante*
between	*entre*
far from	*lejos de*
Where is ... ?	*¿dónde está ... ?*
To get to ...?	*¿para ir a...?*
near	*cerca de*
straight ahead	*todo recto*

MONEY

money	*dinero / plata*
credit card	*tarjeta de crédito*
exchange	*cambio*
traveller's cheque	*cheque de viaje*
I don't have any money	*no tengo dinero*
The bill, please	*la cuenta, por favor*
receipt	*recibo*

SHOPPING

store	*tienda*
market	*mercado*
open, closed	*abierto/a, cerrado/a*
How much is this?	*¿cuánto es?*
to buy, to sell	*comprar, vender*
the customer	*el / la cliente*
salesman	*vendedor*
saleswoman	*vendedora*
I need...	*necesito...*
I would like...	*yo quisiera...*
batteries	*pilas*
blouse	*blusa*
cameras	*cámaras*
cosmetics and perfumes	*cosméticos y perfumes*
cotton	*algodón*
dress jacket	*saco*
eyeglasses	*lentes, gafas*
fabric	*tela*
film	*película*
gifts	*regalos*
gold	*oro*
handbag	*bolsa*
hat	*sombrero*
jewellery	*joyería*
leather	*cuero, piel*
local crafts	*artesanía*

magazines	*revistas*
newpapers	*periódicos*
pants	*pantalones*
records, cassettes	*discos, casetas*
sandals	*sandalias*
shirt	*camisa*
shoes	*zapatos*
silver	*plata*
skirt	*falda*
sun screen products	*productos solares*
T-shirt	*camiseta*
watch	*reloj*
wool	*lana*

MISCELLANEOUS

a little	*poco*
a lot	*mucho*
good (m/f)	*bueno/a*
bad (m/f)	*malo/a*
beautiful (m/f)	*hermoso/a*
pretty (m/f)	*bonito/a*
ugly	*feo*
big	*grande*
tall (m/f)	*alto/a*
small (m/f)	*pequeño/a*
short (length) (m/f)	*corto/a*
short (person) (m/f)	*bajo/a*
cold (m/f)	*frío/a*
hot	*caliente*
dark (m/f)	*oscuro/a*
light (colour)	*claro*
do not touch	*no tocar*
expensive (m/f)	*caro/a*
cheap (m/f)	*barato/a*
fat (m/f)	*gordo/a*
slim, skinny (m/f)	*delgado/a*
heavy (m/f)	*pesado/a*
light (weight) (m/f)	*ligero/a*
less	*menos*
more	*más*
narrow (m/f)	*estrecho/a*
wide (m/f)	*ancho/a*
new (m/f)	*nuevo/a*
old (m/f)	*viejo/a*
nothing	*nada*
something (m/f)	*algo/a*
quickly	*rápidamente*
slowly (m/f)	*despacio/a*
What is this?	*¿qué es esto?*
when?	*¿cuando?*
where?	*¿dónde?*

TIME

in the afternoon, early evening	*por la tarde*
at night	*por la noche*
in the daytime	*por el día*
in the morning	*por la mañana*
minute	*minuto*
month	*mes*
ever	*jamás*
never	*nunca*
now	*ahora*
today	*hoy*
yesterday	*ayer*
tomorrow	*mañana*
What time is it?	*¿qué hora es?*
hour	*hora*
week	*semana*
year	*año*
Sunday	*domingo*
Monday	*lunes*
Tuesday	*martes*
Wednesday	*miércoles*
Thursday	*jueves*
Friday	*viernes*
Saturday	*sábado*
January	*enero*
February	*febrero*
March	*marzo*
April	*abril*
May	*mayo*
June	*junio*
July	*julio*
August	*agosto*
September	*septiembre*
October	*octubre*
November	*noviembre*
December	*diciembre*

WEATHER

It is cold	*hace frío*
It is warm	*hace calor*
It is very hot	*hace mucho calor*
sun	*sol*
It is sunny	*hace sol*
It is cloudy	*está nublado*
rain	*lluvia*
It is raining	*está lloviendo*
wind	*viento*
It is windy	*hay viento*
snow	*nieve*
damp	*húmedo*

dry	*seco*
storm	*tormenta*
hurricane	*huracán*

COMMUNICATION

air mail	*correos aéreo*
collect call	*llamada por cobrar*
dial the number	*marcar el número*
area code, country code	*código*
envelope	*sobre*
long distance	*larga distancia*
post office	*correo*
rate	*tarifa*
stamps	*estampillas*
telegram	*telegrama*
telephone book	*un guía telefónica*
wait for the tone	*esperar la señal*

ACTIVITIES

beach	*playa*
museum or gallery	*museo*
scuba diving	*buceo*
to swim	*bañarse*
to walk around	*pasear*
hiking	*caminata*
trail	*pista, sendero*
cycling	*ciclismo*
fishing	*pesca*

TRANSPORTATION

arrival, departure	*llegada, salida*
on time	*a tiempo*
cancelled (m/f)	*anulado/a*
one way ticket	*ida*
return	*regreso*
round trip	*ida y vuelta*
schedule	*horario*
baggage	*equipajes*
north, south	*norte, sur*
east, west	*este, oeste*
avenue	*avenida*
street	*calle*
highway	*carretera*
expressway	*autopista*
airplane	*avión*
airport	*aeropuerto*
bicycle	*bicicleta*
boat	*barco*

bus	*bus*
bus stop	*parada*
bus terminal	*terminal*
train	*tren*
train crossing	*crucero ferrocarril*
station	*estación*
neighbourhood	*barrio*
collective taxi	*colectivo*
corner	*esquina*
express	*rápido*
safe	*seguro/a*
be careful	*cuidado*
car	*coche, carro*
To rent a car	*alquilar un auto*
gas	*gasolina*
gas station	*gasolinera*
no parking	*no estacionar*
no passing	*no adelantar*
parking	*parqueo*
pedestrian	*peaton*
road closed, no through traffic	*no hay paso*
slow down	*reduzca velocidad*
speed limit	*velocidad permitida*
stop	*alto*
stop! (an order)	*pare*
traffic light	*semáforo*

ACCOMMODATION

cabin, bungalow	*cabaña*
accommodation	*alojamiento*
double, for two people	*doble*
single, for one person	*sencillo*
high season	*temporada alta*
low season	*temporada baja*
bed	*cama*
floor (first, second...)	*piso*
main floor	*planta baja*
manager	*gerente, jefe*
double bed	*cama matrimonial*
cot	*camita*
bathroom	*baños*
with private bathroom	*con baño privado*
hot water	*agua caliente*
breakfast	*desayuno*
elevator	*ascensor*
air conditioning	*aire acondicionado*
fan	*ventilador, abanico*
pool	*piscina, alberca*
room	*habitación*

NUMBERS

1	*uno*	30	*treinta*
2	*dos*	31	*treinta y uno*
3	*tres*	32	*treinta y dos*
4	*cuatro*	40	*cuarenta*
5	*cinco*	50	*cincuenta*
6	*seis*	60	*sesenta*
7	*siete*	70	*setenta*
8	*ocho*	80	*ochenta*
9	*nueve*	90	*noventa*
10	*diez*	100	*cien*
11	*once*	101	*ciento uno*
12	*doce*	102	*ciento dos*
13	*trece*	200	*doscientos*
14	*catorce*	300	*trescientos*
15	*quince*	400	*quatrocientoa*
16	*dieciséis*	500	*quinientos*
17	*diecisiete*	600	*seiscientos*
18	*dieciocho*	700	*sietecientos*
19	*diecinueve*	800	*ochocientos*
20	*veinte*	900	*novecientos*
21	*veintiuno*	1,000	*mil*
22	*veintidós*	1,100	*mil cien*
23	*veintitrés*	1,200	*mil doscientos*
24	*veinticuatro*	2000	*dos mil*
25	*veinticinco*	3000	*tres mil*
26	*veintiséis*	10,000	*diez mil*
27	*veintisiete*	100,000	*cien mil*
28	*veintiocho*	1,000,000	*un millón*
29	*veintinueve*		

Index

Index

Order Form

ULYSSES TRAVEL GUIDES

☐ Atlantic Canada . . .	$24.95 CAN $17.95 US	☐ Lisbon	$18.95 CAN $13.95 US
☐ Bahamas	$24.95 CAN $17.95 US	☐ Louisiana	$29.95 CAN $21.95 US
☐ Beaches of Maine . .	$12.95 CAN $9.95 US	☐ Martinique	$24.95 CAN $17.95 US
☐ Bed & Breakfasts . . in Québec	$13.95 CAN $10.95 US	☐ Montréal	$19.95 CAN $14.95 US
☐ Belize	$16.95 CAN $12.95 US	☐ New Orleans	$17.95 CAN $12.95 US
☐ Calgary	$17.95 CAN $12.95 US	☐ New York City	$19.95 CAN $14.95 US
☐ Canada	$29.95 CAN $21.95 US	☐ Nicaragua	$24.95 CAN $16.95 US
☐ Chicago	$19.95 CAN $14.95 US	☐ Ontario	$27.95 CAN $19.95US
☐ Chile	$27.95 CAN $17.95 US	☐ Ottawa	$17.95 CAN $12.95 US
☐ Colombia	$29.95 CAN $21.95 US	☐ Panamá	$24.95 CAN $17.95 US
☐ Costa Rica	$27.95 CAN $19.95 US	☐ Peru	$27.95 CAN $19.95 US
☐ Cuba	$24.95 CAN $17.95 US	☐ Portugal	$24.95 CAN $16.95 US
☐ Dominican . . . . Republic	$24.95 CAN $17.95 US	☐ Provence - . . . . Côte d'Azur	$29.95 CAN $21.95US
☐ Ecuador and . . . . . Galapagos Islands	$24.95 CAN $17.95 US	☐ Québec	$29.95 CAN $21.95 US
☐ El Salvador	$22.95 CAN $14.95 US	☐ Québec and . . . . . Ontario with Via	$9.95 CAN $7.95 US
☐ Guadeloupe	$24.95 CAN $17.95 US	☐ Toronto	$18.95 CAN $13.95 US
☐ Guatemala	$24.95 CAN $17.95 US	☐ Vancouver	$17.95 CAN $12.95 US
☐ Honduras	$24.95 CAN $17.95 US	☐ Washington D.C. . .	$18.95 CAN $13.95 US
☐ Jamaica	$24.95 CAN $17.95 US	☐ Western Canada . . .	$29.95 CAN $21.95 US

ULYSSES DUE SOUTH

☐ Acapulco	$14.95 CAN $9.95 US	☐ Cancun Cozumel . .	$17.95 CAN $12.95 US
☐ Belize	$16.95 CAN $12.95 US	☐ Puerto Vallarta	$14.95 CAN $9.95 US
☐ Cartagena . . . . (Colombia)	$12.95 CAN $9.95 US	☐ St. Martin and . . . . . St. Barts	$16.95 CAN $12.95 US

ULYSSES TRAVEL JOURNAL

☐ Ulysses Travel . . . . Journal (Blue, Red, Green, Yellow, Sextant)	$9.95 CAN $7.95 US	☐ Ulysses Travel . . . . Journal 80 Days	$14.95 CAN $9.95 US

ULYSSES GREEN ESCAPES

☐ Cycling in France . .	$22.95 CAN $16.95 US	☐ Hiking in the . . . . . Northeastern U.S.	$19.95 CAN $13.95 US
☐ Cycling in Ontario .	$22.95 CAN $16.95 US	☐ Hiking in Québec . .	$19.95 CAN $13.95 US

Order Form

TITLE	QUANTITY	PRICE	TOTAL

Name ————————————	Sub-total
Address ————————————	
————————————	Postage & Handling $8.00*
————————————	Sub-total
Payment : ☐ Money Order ☐ Visa ☐ MasterCard	
Card Number ————————————	G.S.T. in Canada 7%
Expiry date ————————————	
Signature ————————————	TOTAL

**ULYSSES TRAVEL
PUBLICATIONS**
4176 St-Denis,
Montréal, Québec, H2W 2M5
(514) 843-9447 fax (514) 843-9448
www.ulysses.ca
*$15 for overseas orders

U.S. ORDERS:
GLOBE PEQUOT PRESS
P.O. Box 833,
6 Business Park Road,
Old Saybrook, CT 06475-0833
1-800-243-0495 fax 1-800-820-2329
www.globe-pequot.com